To Dad
Happy Birthday
love from Steve +
Mandy + + + 1992

The
Golden
Age of
Football

The Golden Age of Football

Peter Jeffs

BREEDON
BOOKS
SPORT

First published in Great Britain by
The Breedon Books Publishing Company Limited
44 Friar Gate, Derby DE1 1DA
1991

ISBN 0 907969 91 7

Printed and bound in Great Britain by The Bath Press Limited, Bath
and London.
Jacket printed by Arkle Print Ltd of Northampton.

Contents

Acknowledgements

I am grateful to the following people who were kind enough to either lend or make a gift to me of various items of material which were invaluable: Gary Chalk, Brian Cook, Mick Cooper, Gordon Jeffery, David and Christine Lenton and, most particularly, Richard Owen. I also wish to thank Joanne Wheeler for her help with the typing. I must give Anton Rippon the credit for the original idea for the book and for giving me the chance to undertake the project.

Photographic Acknowledgements

Photographs were supplied by Colorsport, Hulton Picture Library and Popperfoto.

Introduction

NOSTALIGIA is defined as a sentimental longing for past times and I make no apology for attempting to invoke such a response from the reader of this book. Not a longing for a return to the dingy and drab life of the late 1940s, nor to the circumspection and restriction, the scrimping, saving and queueing of the decade. Much in the attitudes and lifestyles of people during the period seems quite remote from ours today but, for all that, those austerity years, dominated by the legacies of the war, were indisputably the golden age of football.

As war ended, the nation's culture involved the cinema, radio, holidays and, as a largely male preserve, professional football. It is said that football mirrors life, or more particularly modern society, and in the 'golden age' the game was watched and played in a naive and innocent fashion, for its own sake, by a people determined to enjoy themselves, to let their hair down and to seek relief from the tensions and stresses of those recent times. Inevitably, the game was held in great esteem by a people who valued its vital role in their lives as the very best of pure open-air theatre.

I hasten to add that my own recollections of that time are second-hand and regrettably not based on any first-hand experience. I was not taken to my first League match until Boxing Day 1954 and even then I was disappointed by the late withdrawal of Stanley Matthews from the Blackpool team visiting Fratton Park, Portsmouth. My research and examination of the game's reporting in the previous years showed that I missed out on that heady football mix of massive crowds, great action and seemingly countless celebrated heroes. There were few references to atmosphere, fans or stars. Large crowds brought their own atmosphere week in, week out. Almost everyone was a fan and star names were two a penny.

From the time 25 years ago when football's professional arm was first twisted and then kidnapped as a vehicle for hooligans, advertisers, sponsors, television companies, autocrats, kit-suppliers *et al* it has been at their various mercies. As a result, football finds itself having to be told by the politicians to improve what is on offer to its main sponsor — the fan. Moreover, the game is presently involved in funding research into its own activities and into its role in British society. In the 'golden age' which I have related, there was never any doubt of the unique and central position that football held in the nation's affections and culture. We lovers of the game long, in vain I fear, for a return to such an age.

Peter Jeffs
Titchfield
Hampshire
June 1991

The Prelude

THE newspaper headline of 3 September 1939, 'All sport brought to a halt,' said it all. War was declared that day and had broken the hold which football had upon its devoted public, with its recurring matches and the football pools.

Yet that seven-year break from League football, as a result of World War Two, was the prelude to a golden era in the game's history. As the public embraced football on its return, the game heralded an unprecedented boom at the turnstiles. Before that, however, the world had to go to war once more and many young men had seen and played their last game of League football.

As Everton prepared to defend their title as Champions, the break, when it came, was abrupt if not totally unexpected. The portents of war were all too clear but football, like its counterparts in the entertainments industry, had neither specifically ignored them or made plans for its future.

As the war clouds gathered, the League programme was doggedly resumed on schedule on 26 August 1939. In the following week the evacuation of children into the countryside started, but even the Friday invasion of Poland did not prevent the Saturday matches going ahead. Within days, however, war had been declared and football had ground to a halt with the automatic ban on the assembly of crowds.

Players' contracts were suspended, with the clubs retaining their registrations. The players were free to join the Forces or go into industry. The majority chose the former, like thousands of others, as they tired of waiting for weeks to find out what was going to happen to the game and its players.

When the Football Association secured permission for friendly and competitive matches to be played on Saturdays and public holidays, provided there was no disturbance to National Service or the war effort generally, the game was able to carry on in a fashion. Wartime fare for any potential spectators was made up of regional competitions with a good sprinkling of guest players, often in 'scratch' teams.

It was an unreal situation, with the games played without the reward of trophies — in the early days at least — or bonuses. Many famous

Goalmouth action from a wartime South Regional League game between Arsenal and Charlton Athletic at Tottenham's White Hart Lane in November 1940. The crowd of 1,477 saw a 2-2 draw.

Arsenal and Charlton trainers and reserves on the bench for the game pictured above. A policemen, complete with steel helmet, is on hand, more to assist if the air-raid sirens sound rather than for general crowd control in those well-behaved times.

players appeared in unfamiliar colours as they guested for teams near where they were stationed or working. At Aldershot, for example, the local team consisted almost entirely of internationals like Cliff Britton, Stan Cullis and Joe Mercer, England's half-backs, and forwards Tommy Lawton and Jimmy Hagan.

The competitive edge was enhanced by a spread of representative games around the country and these were soon extended to take in 'international' fixtures. When a War Cup scheme was introduced, it was a great success and the finals returned to Wembley. Football had certainly proved its worth as an integral part of the social structure.

The game gained a good deal of respect for its morale-boosting qualities. It became crucial to the war effort as players, determined to get their games in, and the public, determined to get to watch them play, temporarily forgot their stresses and anxieties. Somehow football managed to retain its identity and structure with the continued public relish for the game both sustaining it and giving it justification.

Training and coaching took a back seat to service duties, both in and out of uniform, and the approach to the game was not always as serious as it might have been. Given the abnormal conditions under which football was staffed and played, this was inevitable. The opportunities for young players were plenty as senior, experienced players were unavailable, probably even serving abroad.

There was no disguising the fact, however, that the war had dealt football a body-blow. Inevitably, many experienced and potential players had been killed or injured. It was estimated that up to 80 leading players were killed in action and an untold number of careers ended by death, injury or just old age. For all that, some players were to straddle the war with ease and play on — such as the great Stanley Matthews, already a star when the sirens sounded, Tommy Lawton, Joe Mercer and many others. Lawton accumulated over 200 goals in the seven-year break, for Everton, Tranmere Rovers, Aldershot and Chelsea; so had Albert Stubbins for Newcastle United and Jock Dodds for Blackpool.

The war in Europe ended on 8 May 1945 and it was clear to the football authorities that they, and the clubs, needed time to regroup. League football resumed in August 1945, but it was on a transitional basis with the top two divisions divided north and south of the River Trent to save travelling. The Third Division was made into two regional groups and there was neither promotion nor relegation at the end of the season. Many players were still in the Forces, so guest players were still permitted.

The FA Cup was re-started that season but with each round on a two-legged home and away basis — decided on the aggregate of goals. The trophy was in the possession of Portsmouth Football Club for nearly seven years after they had been the last winners in 1939.

General Eisenhower, Supreme Commander of the US Expeditionary Forces in Britain, meets the Chelsea team before their wartime South Cup Final against Charlton at Wembley in April 1944.

RAF men from Wales sport leeks in their hats to support their country in a wartime international at Wembley in April 1940.

Birmingham's Jock Mulraney (centre) turns away after opening the scoring against Leicester City at a bomb-damaged St Andrew's on Christmas Day 1945. A crowd of 30,000 saw Birmingham win 6-2. They went on to lift the Football League South title in this last season before normal League football resumed.

The outbreak of war destined Portsmouth to look after the Cup for the long war years. At every home match it was proudly displayed on the table in the boardroom.

After the death of Hitler in April 1945, the exuberant celebratory post-war spirit was immediately evidenced by the series of cricket Victory Tests against an Australian Services team, games played in festival atmospheres before massive crowds. The fourth of those Tests at Lord's brought in 85,033 spectators, a record crowd for a three-day match. When football resumed, the grounds were packed and the clubs were immediately able to gain great financial advantage. Not so the players, who were restricted to a nominal £4 for each appearance.

Football, in its transitional form, reappeared in an age of shortages but, despite the social problems and calls for austerity, peace brought a sustained demand for pleasure as the country strove desperately to make up for the years of grief, tedium, frustration and slaughter. The national games — summer and winter — dance-halls, cinemas and holiday beaches were the main beneficiaries and the leisure industries were boosted by the millions of returning service personnel with back-pay and gratuities to spend.

Similarly, many in factories and industry had money to spend as earnings built up during the war with little time or opportunity to spend it. Football, at the heart of the traditional working-class culture,

*The Chelsea-Moscow Dynamo game at Stamford Bridge in 1945 was the first visit of a
Russian side to Britain.* Top:*Crowds swarm on to the roof after the gates were closed.*
Bottom: *Archangelski, the Moscow winger, gets through the Chelsea defence.*

was the obvious attraction for this spending power, particularly as
many commodities and luxury items were either rationed or in short
supply.

The outstanding feature of that 1945-6 season was a short, controversial
tour by Dinamo Moscow from Russia in November 1945. In the first
of their bizarre matches, 82,000 spectators packed inside Stamford Bridge
to see them draw 3-3 with Chelsea. In the second game they totally
outclassed a plucky Cardiff team, 10-1, before 45,000 fans.

The third and last match in England was a farce for 54,000 onlookers
as the game at White Hart Lane, Tottenham, against Arsenal

(Highbury was still suffering from bomb damage) was played in dense fog. Very little of the 4-3 win by the Dinamos could be discerned by the crowd. The matches had been played in bad spirit against teams littered with guest players and ended with the Dinamos being called home unexpectedly after a 2-2 draw in Scotland against Glasgow Rangers played in front of 90,000. Days before a scheduled fixture against an FA XI at Villa Park the guests departed without a word of explanation.

As spectators flooded back to the game, it was clear that football grounds were in a state of disrepair and in many instances not large enough to accommodate them all. It was, with hindsight, inevitable that the handling and control of the huge crowds would create problems for football clubs. What was then the worst disaster in the history of British football occurred at Burnden Park, Bolton, on 9 March 1946, when an estimated crowd of 85,000 turned up — the official attendance figure was 65,419 — and were reportedly slow to assemble.

It was a second-leg FA Cup tie against Stoke City, who fielded Stanley Matthews — and Bolton Wanderers were 2-0 up on the first leg. One corner of the terracing at Burnden Park became over-crowded, mainly because some 1,500 people got in by climbing over turnstiles. As a result, crush barriers collapsed, 400 were injured and 33 people died. All the casualties were located in the space of ten square-yards near a corner-flag. The police had been reluctant to release more men to repel the gate-crashers. More officers were available but they were guarding stockpiles of food — then on ration — in the Burnden Stand.

A Home Office enquiry repeated many previous findings — closer examination of grounds, licensing and the construction of smaller sections on the terraces.

Despite this tragic incident, the reinstated FA Cup competition went a long way to taking the game back to its pre-war level of attraction and beyond. In several games, attendance records were broken and at the replayed semi-final between Derby County and Birmingham City, a crowd of 80,407 packed Maine Road, Manchester. It is still the biggest midweek attendance to watch two Football League clubs outside Wembley.

If anything, the home and away matches heightened the interest in the competition. The Government insisted that Cup games were played until a definite decision was reached and as a consequence the longest official match ever played went to 203 minutes when Stockport County and Doncaster Rovers met in the Third Division North Cup on 30 March 1946. At 6.43pm, bad light forced a close with the aggregate at 4-4 and a replay was necessary. It was reported that spectators went home for tea and returned in time to see the players still battling away.

One of the highlights of the FA Cup competition was the two-legged Newcastle United-Barnsley tie. Newcastle won the first leg 4-2 in front of a 60,284 crowd at St James' Park where the gates were closed two hours before kick-off. A train crash, including serious injury to several Barnsley supporters on their way to the game, marred the day but in the second leg, a classic match was won by Barnsley, 3-0, to put them through on aggregate. Inside-forward Jimmy Baxter — later to be transferred to Preston North End — scored the third goal in the last minute.

When the Finalists, Charlton Athletic and Derby County, played out a thrilling match it was just the appetizer for the new 'real' season to come, a season that football and its eager public demanded. It was an epic Wembley Final, reckoned to be full of all the glorious free-flowing football of pre-war days.

Derby beat Charlton 4-1 after extra-time, thanks largely to their two supreme inside-forwards, Peter Doherty and Raich Carter. The two blended perfectly in a natural, instinctive combination that was to flourish in the coming years.

But the 1946 Cup Final belonged to big, burly Jack Stamps, Derby's centre-forward. One of the most consistent players and regular goalscorers Derby had ever boasted, Stamps scored twice during extra-time. His powerful physique enabled him to brush aside a rapidly tiring opposition, although that supreme ball-artist, Raich Carter, says: "Jack Stamps wasn't just a battering-ram type. He was a good footballer who could play a fine game at inside-forward."

Normal time had been marked by two goals in the space of 30 seconds, both involving Charlton wing-half Bert Turner. First he deflected a Dally Duncan drive past his own goalkeeper, Sam Bartram, then sent a long deflected shot past Derby 'keeper, Vic Woodley, for the equalizer. Peter Doherty later claimed an own-goal — "The ball deflected off my thigh, otherwise Vic Woodley would have got it." But football folklore wanted Bert Turner to be the first man to score for both sides in an FA Cup Final.

In the closing minutes, the ball burst after a hard shot by Stamps and, curiously, the ball also burst when the two teams met in a League match five days later. It also burst in the 1947 Final between Charlton and Burnley and perhaps says much about the quality of 'utility' footballs in those austere days.

In extra-time, Doherty and Carter played havoc with the Charlton defence and Stamps, with his two goals, and Doherty, one, gave Derby a runaway victory.

In the Leagues, Sheffield United and Birmingham City took the North and South titles respectively but honours that season were soon forgotten and discounted as the return of the 'real thing' occupied all minds.

The grip of the football pools on the public was perceived to increase in the immediate post-war period. Their influence had begun in the 1930s but, despite various attempts to curb its spread, nothing could prevent the craze from becoming part of the weekly working-class existence. It was often felt that the hold which the pools had on the British people was a significant factor in creating the huge additional interest in watching the game in that early post-war era.

At this time most clubs had a secretary-manager, with the possible addition of a coach, and the directors had a large say in team and

The first post-war FA Cup winners, Derby County, parade the trophy after beating Charlton 4-1 in extra-time at Wembley. Veteran skipper Jack Nicholas is carried aloft on shoulders of Jack Howe.

selection matters. The success of Herbert Chapman, first at Huddersfield Town and then at Arsenal, encouraged more and more club boards to put team affairs in the hands of an expert. The most notable appointment in early 1946 was that of Matt Busby at a Manchester United club which was on its knees. The Old Trafford ground was a blitzed wreck, the dressing-rooms were derelict. There were no facilities for training, no offices for staff and United were dependent on the Manchester City club for fulfilling home fixtures at Maine Road.

United were £15,000 in debt when Busby went back to Scotland to make one of his shrewdest purchases. The deal brought Jimmy Delaney from Glasgow Celtic for £4,000 and was the catalyst which sparked a revival in United's fortunes in Delaney's five-year stay.

When Busby took over, United were an undistinguished 16th in the First Division. By the end of the season they had climbed to fourth place. It was the start of an amazing record in the post-war years which will be described in the coming chapters.

It seemed that professional players had a greater realization of their market value as a result of their experiences in wartime football. They had supplemented their working or service pay by playing football in that period, but returned to full-time football to find their wages fixed at the pre-war level of £8 per week.

The Players' Union threatened to strike but, happily, this was averted when £9 was offered and reluctantly accepted. The feeling still prevailed, however, that players' rewards were such that the pre-war differential between their earnings and that of the average working man had largely disappeared.

These were, indeed, unenlightened times so far as player-director relationships went. The Derby players threatened to go on strike if their wives were not given better tickets for the 1946 Cup Final. Says Jack Stamps: "They were in uncovered seats. Raich Carter, Peter Doherty and Dally Duncan led a deputation and told the directors if these weren't improved there would be no game. And we meant it, I can tell you." Better tickets were forthcoming and, of course, the game went ahead.

As that 1945-6 transitional season progressed, the Government became concerned about the effect of the mid-week afternoon matches on industrial production caused by the mass absenteeism. A ban on such matches followed, but this only served to make the Saturday afternoon excursions that much more attractive.

Football had reappeared at a time when the country's self-confidence and optimism were approaching a peak and football reflected this vitality. Despite a bitterly fought General Election that year, and a dawning realization that even peacetime had its problems, people were inspired by the hope of a new Britain. They thought that no internal difficulties existed that could not be overcome with sufficient resolution.

The period has an image of hardship and high endeavour but was an age of great achievement in the field of social justice — homes for all, the National Health Service and universal secondary education. The country dreamed of the banishment of the dole queues of the 1930s and was determined that greater social equality would bring the good things of life within everyone's reach.

Football was clearly about to face the sternest test in its history and for those clubs whom circumstances had left unprepared, it was to be anathema. It was already obvious that the general standard of play had suffered. The seven years had taken their toll of the pre-war establishment and there was not an ample reservoir of youth upon which the game could draw liberally, for conscription to military service and employment under the Essential Works Order had first to be answered. The majority of the clubs had to temporize, as yet uncertain of their needs.

If there was some doubt about the immediate future of those who played football, there could be no doubt about those who watched the game. Attendances had been growing year by year and there was clearly a healthy appetite for first-class soccer and every reason to think that, if the clubs could serve up the correct dish, they would be amply repaid in the shape of increased gate receipts.

All sports had attracted large attendances in that first year after the war ended, as the population fulfilled its need for relaxation. Football fitted the bill for the most part and was immediately watched by a quite staggering number of people. Somehow it seemed, more than anything else, to signal the complete return to normal for the working man and everybody wanted to pursue their dream — that of seeing 'their team' in action again.

The game in Britain is still a crowd-puller today, despite all its well-publicized and often apparently insoluble difficulties. Indeed, it is without parallel in any other form of activity or entertainment, but it will never again know such a golden age at the turnstiles when, in the space of six years, 236 million people — a figure equivalent to the entire population of America or Russia — watched League football. People attracted by, above all, star performers with names which have since become legendary. Lawton, Doherty, Carter, Mannion, Shackleton, Mortensen, Matthews *et al*, the list is endless.

The 1946 season, the offspring of that fateful 1939 season seven years earlier, was to open with little to show for the years that passed between. For all that, there were high hopes and so much to look forward to as that eagerly awaited first day drew near. A day awaited by a population, including four and a half million men and women recently demobilized from the Armed Forces, who were resolved to make up for their lost years.

The Great Day

THE morning of Saturday, 31 August 1946 dawned cloudy and overcast and it was soon clear that there would be no warm August sun to welcome the new football season in its traditional manner. The forecast was for rain and, in the event, many in the tightly-packed crowds on the terraces were rewarded with a drenching as rainstorms swept the country by the mid-afternoon.

The previous weeks had been marked by gale-force winds and torrential rain, with a spate of flooded rivers and fallen trees. As a result, the corn crop was a disaster with 25 per cent destroyed by the weather. Two thousand German prisoners of war were put on standby to work to save the cereal harvest.

Elsewhere, the news on the big day, outside sport, was centred on the 217th day of the Nuremberg Trials and that same afternoon the major Nazi leaders — Goering, Hess and Ribbentrop — were permitted to make their final impassioned pleas to the War Crimes Tribunal. Coincidentally, it was announced in Britain that there were still 388,000 German prisoners of war here and there was pressure for some settled policy of repatriation to be implemented.

In other sports news, the England cricket team sailed from Southampton for Australia that afternoon — the 20th team to visit Australia in the Ashes series.

Sydney Wooderson made his last appearance in big-time athletics and failed in his attempt on the two-mile record at Motspur Park, London. It was a sad conclusion to a great career as he finished limping with a slight Achilles tendon injury. Star sprinter MacDonald Bailey was a late non-starter in the 100-yard final with muscle trouble. Jockey Gordon Richards had a successful afternoon at Goodwood with three winners in heavy going.

More importantly, that Saturday was the day when, for almost a million people, all roads led to Football League grounds after seven years of 'makeshift' football with nothing at stake except the survival of the game. The opening of a new football season had never, before or since, been more keenly anticipated.

Those days when matches started at any old time and teams made up their numbers by borrowing from their opponents, or even from the crowd, were over. The game had to get down to properly organized and disciplined football. For seven long years, football people had waited for this moment — since 2 September 1939 in fact, when the last full Football League programme was played. Now there was to be a return to the ways they knew.

To promotion and relegation, to the full implications of continued failure, to sudden death in the FA Cup, to the Home International Championship proper, both amateur and professional. All the while the Continental challenge was growing and had to be met, although it is doubtful whether that crossed anyone's mind as tens of thousands hurried along the streets towards the grounds.

Capacity crowds were expected and would cause some clubs anxious moments. The tragedy at Bolton had brought light to bear on a dangerous state of affairs, with so many grounds in disrepair. For seven years the clubs had obviously been unable to maintain their establishments in a perfect state of repair because of the absence of labour and material.

The police authorities had fixed limits for all grounds and clubs were under instructions to close the gates when the required attendance figure was reached. In today's climate the limits appear high, but that afternoon the clubs were plainly unhappy. At Bristol City there was an outcry when the police fixed a limit of 30,000 at their Ashton Gate ground, which had a record of 43,335.

It was only three months previously that Charlton Athletic were losing the Cup Final and the League South Championship with such tragic swiftness. In that short waiting period, other sport had flourished. Petra of France had beaten Brown of Australia at Wimbledon in the Men's Singles Final, and Sam Snead of the USA had won the Open Golf Championship at St Andrew's. The first Henley Regatta after the war had opened in all its old glory and the AAA Championships saw Sydney Wooderson, Britain's world champion miler, win the three miles and break the British record.

Cricket, too, was to look on this period as its 'second golden age' with audiences growing to reach their maximum the following year in the glorious summer of 1947. On August Bank Holiday Monday 1946, some 160,000 spectators watched the nine first-class cricket matches and the England-India Test series was hugely supported by crowds thrilling to the exploits of Cyril Washbrook, Joe Hardstaff and Denis Compton making runs and Bill Voce, Alec Bedser and Doug Wright taking wickets. Yorkshire were still the major power in county cricket, winning the Championship that summer, just as they had done in 1939.

Cinema audiences reached an all-time high in 1946, as all aspects of the entertainment industry cashed in. The Marx Brothers returned in a new film *A Night in Casablanca*, screened to big audiences; to universal acclaim, Bob Hope won an Oscar.

In those summer months, whilst football's administrators worked furiously to prepare to meet the call of the nation, the country was pleased to welcome the relaxation of petrol rationing with a 50 per cent increase in the basic ration ensuring that the motorist could look forward to an average monthly mileage of 270 miles.

In a time of shortages, bread rationing had to be introduced in July and within weeks there was concern for adolescents apparently showing signs of undernourishment as a consequence. There was some compensation with the appearance of the first bananas for five years.

The week before the season opened, an England XI met a Scotland XI at Maine Road, Manchester, in aid of the Bolton Disaster Fund and the match was put to use as a trial for the coming internationals. In the 2-2 draw, Stanley Matthews, on the wing, was reported to be in an 'entertaining mood and uncontrollable'. Matthews was to be one of the players who straddled the war with success.

When clubs opened their gates shortly after noon, huge crowds made their way on to the terraces that last Saturday afternoon in August. Many wore their demob suits and macintoshes with a brown trilby hat; others, still in uniform, awaited demob. They paid 1s 3d (6p) each for admission to the terraces. It was a price that the Labour Chancellor of the Exchequer had insisted upon but, despite that, it was reported that many clubs charged 1s 6d for some parts of their grounds. Home crowds were boosted by away supporters keen to travel by train and coach for a day-out to towns not visited for many years.

To increase the illusion that life was starting up from where it had left off, the fixtures matched those which had been arranged for that aborted 1939-40 season.

The dispute with the Players' Union had still not really been settled to their satisfaction, despite a rise in their wages to £10 per week for established players and £6 for newly-signed professionals, granted out of the March 1946 Budget. The players, unlike now, were expected to keep up appearances and typically they would arrive for the games that day in their double-breasted pin-striped suits, covered by long raincoats with loose flapping belts.

To greet the new season, Hull City had moved to their new ground at Boothferry Park, whilst New Brighton had signed up a new set of players and restored their ground. It was announced that Clapton Orient would in future be known as Leyton Orient and Birmingham as Birmingham City. Newport County were set to play in the Second Division for the first time after a wait of seven years after their promotion.

Many of the teams appearing that day bore little resemblance to those which had represented their clubs for the first three games of

Stanley Matthews, pictured here in his Stoke City days just before the war. Matthews was one of the players whose career straddled the conflict.

the doomed 1939-40 season. Inevitably, many players, both the great and the ordinary, did not reappear — being either killed or overtaken by age. Supporters grieved to learn of the loss of the likes of Liverpool full-back Tommy Cooper, who died whilst out as a Military Police despatch rider; Blackburn Rovers' inside-forward Albert Clark, who was a D-Day casualty; Bolton Wanderers captain Harry Goslin, killed in action in Italy; the Luton Town goalkeeper, Coen, shot down over Germany.

Some players were still not available for selection — either retained in the Forces or tied up in essential industries. Clubs were forced to give League chances to players, who before the war would not have warranted a second glance. Some in the game were of the opinion that the return to the promotion and relegation system had been unduly hurried and that this should have been postponed until all clubs could compete on equal terms with equal resources.

The football pundits waited with eager anticipation to watch their favourites — amongst them Derby County, who had built a fluent team the previous season around inside-forwards Raich Carter and Peter Doherty; the youthful Wolverhampton Wanderers, with Wright, Cullis and Alderton forming one of the strongest half-back lines in the country and Jesse Pye, newly acquired from Notts County at inside-forward. Arsenal, too, were fancied with the return of Bryn Jones, originally signed in 1938 for a record £14,000, but the club whose name travelled round the world and dominated football throughout the 1930s had some great names missing.

The football correspondent of *The Times*, in his column on that Saturday morning, pleaded for a return to the attacking centre-half — 'the game cries out for such a man' was his cry from the heart.

As far as the day's fixtures were concerned, the biggest crowd was at Stamford Bridge where over 61,000 were crammed inside to see Chelsea beat their visitors, Bolton Wanderers, 4-3 but not before Bolton had hit the bar three times. The gates were closed well before kick-off with thousands shut out and that scene was repeated at many venues. In all, 950,000 spectators watched the 43 matches — showing an amazing average of 22,000 fans per match. There were five attendances over 50,000 in the First Division and in the Third Division South only two clubs showed gates of under 10,000. Even in reserve fixtures, attendances approaching 10,000 were noted that day.

Continuous downpours of rain during the afternoon brought some farcical conditions. In Wales, the Newport County-Southampton game was postponed at lunch-time after torrential overnight and morning rain flooded the pitch. The local fire-brigade was called upon to help, but they failed to get the ground ready in time for the kick-off. Thousands waited outside the turnstiles in vain and the cancellation robbed Newport of an expected 20,000 gate for their long-awaited

Bryn Jones, seen here challenging Everton's Torry Gillick in the last season before the war, when he signed for Arsenal for a record £14,000.

Second Division home debut after their promotion seven years previously.

In the First Division, names which were to become legendary in the coming years appeared in the goalscoring lists to give notice of their likely influence. Before 60,000 at Villa Park, Wilf Mannion scored the only goal in Middlesbrough's win; Lawton for Chelsea and Lofthouse for Bolton each scored twice in their fixture; Stan Mortensen scored the first of Blackpool's three goals at Huddersfield; Tom Finney scored one of Preston's goals in their home 3-2 win over Leeds; and Peter Doherty grabbed one for Derby at Sunderland.

Whilst Everton, defending the League Championship they won in 1938-9, were providing the day's one big surprise by losing at home to Brentford before 55,000, the Wolves went on a goal-spree in heavy rain in the second-half against Arsenal. After a goalless first half, Wolves rattled in six before a 50,000 Molineux crowd with new signing Jesse Pye scoring a hat-trick and Dennis Westcott two goals. It was an early, humiliating defeat for the Arsenal, from which they were to take many weeks of that coming season to recover.

Giving early pointers to their prominence that season were Manchester United and Liverpool. The former were many people's tip as the likely team of the year and they beat Grimsby Town with goals from Mitten and Rowley before 40,000 at Manchester City's Maine Road stadium.

Liverpool were to be the surprise packet that season and they, too, had a successful opening with a single-goal victory before 30,000 at Sheffield United, played against a backcloth of thunder and lightening.

In the Second Division, a crowd of 39,000 were at The Den to see Millwall concede four to a rampant Newcastle United with Roy Bentley, Jackie Milburn and Albert Stubbins amongst the scorers. This, too, was a sign of stirring deeds to come from the Magpies in the coming seasons.

That Millwall crowd was eclipsed by the White Hart Lane attendance of 57,000, who saw Tottenham Hotspur lose at home to Birmingham City, after their goalkeeper, Ted Ditchburn, had been beaten by a soft shot from 35 yards for the Midlanders' winner from Mulraney. The highest scorers were found in the Second Division where Bury hit seven against Fulham.

The best gate in the Third Division was at Hull for the opening of their new ground, but there were no goals for the 25,000 crowd who witnessed that historic opening fixture against Lincoln City.

The season had opened with the players having reluctantly accepted a new maximum wage of £10 per week but it was an uneasy truce and the undercurrent of dissent was to surface again shortly. This, and problems from the English winter, were waiting to be solved.

In the meantime, however, there was no doubt that for the football supporter it was a day of great excitement, a carnival sort of afternoon with, above all, a pervading general feeling of goodwill. Nothing was more important than that the game was back and that at last things were returning to normal.

A Warm
Welcome Back

THE 1946-7 season was to be unique in many ways. The terrible winter of 1947 was lying in wait and was to be the worst of the century, at a time when food and fuel were still restricted. The winter was to strike late and the resultant freeze-up led to a massive scramble to clear the backlog of Football League fixtures. As a consequence, the season became the longest in League history, lasting from 31 August to the following 14 June.

As the season unfolded, however, the crowds continued to flood into the grounds, plainly greedy for football and eager to forget the war. They were not particularly selective and when Chelsea played Charlton, for example, with both sides having made inauspicious starts, 61,566 people filed obediently through the turnstiles. Manchester United, Wolves and Blackpool were the early front-runners in the First Division. After a month Blackpool were back where they were when football was blacked out in September 1939 — at the top of the table. Immediately, Matthews, Mannion, Lawton and Shackleton were the Kings of Soccer. Pelé was just five years old.

After the seven years' absence the verdict from the punters was that the standard of play was satisfactory, but inevitably there was plenty of room for improvement, particularly in understanding.

This first full season was a difficult one for the clubs and their managers and it was to take them a couple of seasons to weigh up the assets and liabilities in their playing strength. The demand for players grew as the game found itself short of young and ambitious talent and illegal payments were clearly on the increase. Jimmy Seed, manager at Charlton Athletic, even went abroad looking for players and fixed upon South Africa as his hunting ground. The likes of Syd O'Linn, John Hewie (later to play for Scotland), Stuart Leary and Eddie Firmani were to make their mark in the First Division after arriving here as juniors from that country.

These were transfer-crazy days and players were on the move more than musical chairs competitors as the clubs had hitherto unheard-of-profits to spend. In mitigation for the colossal amounts expended on transfer fees, the clubs pleaded that, in any event, nearly half of the fees would have gone to the Government in income and profits tax.

Ordinary players looked for transfer-deals whereby they could make for themselves, albeit illegally, a nice tax-free piece of what they called security. Before the war it had only been the real stars who could cash in on the big rewards but as the season rolled on, transfer fees were to rocket out of all proportion with some quite ordinary players changing hands for over £20,000.

That same transfer system provided the post-war footballer with his best grounds for complaint. When he signed for a club, perhaps for a £25,000 fee, he received his £10 and no more. He was even prevented from making a contract to give the club his services for so many years and provide himself with some security.

There were frantic attempts to forge new combinations and in that first season, clubs often called on an army of players before finalizing their side. Arsenal had 31 men on first-team duty that season and Huddersfield Town 32. In the Second Division the trend was most pronounced with Newport County calling on 41 and most clubs topped 30. Beating them all, though, was Hull City in the Third North. The Tigers fielded 42 players.

In many quarters, in and out of the game, there was a growing feeling that the only people who were not profiting from the boom were the players themselves. The public and the Press had not forgotten how the players had kept the game alive and maintained morale during the war years and, when their profile increased in line with the game's prominence, their wages were compared with those in the entertainment industry.

There was a threat of a strike if the request of the Players' Union for compulsory arbitration in their wages dispute was not accepted. An advance ballot of the players had shown an overwhelming majority in favour of a strike. The clubs maintained they would carry on by fielding amateur talent.

Mindful of all this, the National Arbitration Tribunal of 1947 was convened to discuss footballers' wages and report later in the season. Two years later the Ministry of Labour set up a joint committee to report on their terms and conditions.

The complaint of most players was that not only was the lowlier player inadequately paid, but the star player was restricted to a maximum wage far from commensurate with his worth as an entertainer. Some of those stars, in an era of massive crowds, could easily be responsible for 20,000 of any attendance — which might top 60,000 altogether.

The players, then, were inadequately rewarded by a rich game made so by the entertainers who brought the crowds in through the turnstiles. Without them, they argued through their Players' Union, there would be no £45,000 or so at the season's end for the club to spend in the transfer market, before the tax collectors got their hands on the profits.

Midweek matches had been banned in the first post-war season so as not to interfere with production from factories, mills and shipyards. But for this new League season the ban was lifted.

The first few months of the season were significant for the poor showing by Arsenal and as the first third of the season closed, the Gunners could be found last but one in the First Division with only eight points and three wins from the 14 games.

George Allison had been manager at Highbury for 13 years but was largely a figurehead that season as his assistant, Tom Whittaker, took charge of the playing angle, as a prelude to his appointment to the top job at the end of the season. As a trainer, Whittaker had already won fame throughout the country as showbiz stars and stars from all sports took advantage of his skills, particularly as a masseur.

Arsenal's League position in those early days of the season was so desperate that only a slightly superior goal-average over Huddersfield kept them from the bottom place and humiliation for that great club.

In the short term, to put matters right, Allison and Whittaker signed two veterans who were apparently nearing the end of their playing career.

The signings raised many an eyebrow at the time but the pair proved to be just the tonic Highbury needed to lift the Gunners out of the doldrums and provide the springboard for the following season's Championship triumph. The two men, Ronnie Rooke, the 35-year-old Fulham centre-forward, and Joe Mercer, the craggy, bow-legged Everton left-half whose career appeared to have peaked during the war, were convinced that they were not 'over the hill' and Arsenal gave them the opportunity to prove themselves once more. Mercer's inspired leadership, irrepressible spirit and determination were priceless and Rooke, in tandem with Reg Lewis up front, began to rattle in the goals. In the event, he and Lewis were to share 49 goals between them that season.

It was reported that Mercer was thinking of retiring and was increasingly troubled by a damaged knee. For a nominal fee of £7,000 Mercer was persuaded by Whittaker to come to Highbury to rebuild his career and let Whittaker, the physiotherapist, rebuild his knee.

Rooke was unable to command a regular place in the Fulham first team but was seen correctly as the ruthless finisher Arsenal needed to snap up the chances made by the ball artists, Reg Lewis and Alex James. Arsenal lost only one of their next nine games, with Rooke scoring 11 goals in the period, and the Gunners were on the road to recovery and to becoming a football power again.

Rooke was the first product of a unique 'self-help' policy agreed by London clubs at an early-season meeting and the cosy arrangements saw several players criss-crossing the capital to meet the needs of various clubs. Rooke was the most significant, being exchanged by Fulham in return for inside-forward David Nelson and wing-half Cyril Grant from Arsenal. Goalkeeper Harry Medhurst was another, joining Chelsea from West Ham in exchange for forward Joe Payne.

There was no obligation at law upon the clubs to take players back on their return from the Forces and that led to a surplus of players and an enormous increase in wage bills. Some clubs placed their faith in such players who were seven years older in the hope that *anno domini* would not immediately catch up with them. Others were fortunate enough to have a sufficient supply of young men, who had progressed in their soccer education whilst in sheltered occupations, to balance their side.

The demand for young 'finished' players, however, was greater than the supply. Any form of youth policy was totally undermined by the conscription requirements. Normally a youth of 18 would graduate to take the place of the older men but in those days such youths were whisked away to the services to languish in army unit teams during their crucial development period.

Arsenal cited the example of a young full-back, a coal-miner playing in Yorkshire but working full-time at the coal-face in an essential industry. If he left the mines to travel to London to sign for Arsenal he would immediately be called up and that would put him out of top-class football for his conscription period.

Elsewhere in the capital, Chelsea's drawing-power was incredible and the crowds flocked to Stamford Bridge, often to laugh good-naturedly at their team. After the goal feast in their opening fixture, the Pensioners were involved in the highest scoring game the following week at Anfield before a near-50,000 crowd. Eleven goals were scored with Billy Liddell, Jones and Fagan each claiming two, as Liverpool won 7-4 .

Tommy Lawton was the main attraction for spectators at Chelsea. In an undistinguished side the only other saving graces were John Harris, the calm captain at centre-half, and inside-forwards Len Goulden and Tommy Walker who worked hard to make goals for Lawton. Chelsea hung around the middle of the table all season, although Lawton broke the club's scoring record with 26 goals.

In contrast, Liverpool were already making a strong challenge for the title and this was reinforced when, after only a fortnight of the season had elapsed, they paid a near-record fee to secure ginger-haired opportunist centre-forward Albert Stubbins from Newcastle United. Alongside him, Jack Balmer was a goalscoring bald-headed inside-forward who was one of the great minds of the game at the time, with a great loyalty to the Anfield cause. Strong Scottish left winger

Billy Liddell was the star of the sturdy, if not brilliant, side at Anfield.

At the back Cyril Sidlow, the Welsh international, was in goal, with support from Lawrie Hughes, reliable at centre-half, and Bob Paisley, industrious at half-back.

The Merseyside team were in the hands of a very shrewd manager in George Kay and unwisely were discounted by the experts in the early stages. Kay, who had skippered West Ham in the first Wembley FA Cup Final, had cut his managerial teeth at Southampton before joining Liverpool in 1936. He was a deep thinker and in 1946 he took Liverpool on a tour of North America, theorizing that sunshine and orange juice would be the best preparation for the First Division after the deprivations of war. The Liverpool players returned, each around half a stone heavier, so it is said, and, of course, went on to win the first peacetime League Championship.

Stoke City were showing up well early on with centre-forward Freddie Steele out in front as the League's leading scorer. The team from the Potteries was entirely home-grown with every one costing the club only a signing-on fee. It was probably the cheapest team ever to play in the First Division and the early news from the Victoria Ground was that a £25 purchase, George Mountford, was keeping the legendary Stanley Matthews out of the City team. Matthews had suffered from a pulled thigh muscle and in his absence Stoke had a very successful run, including a 5-2 defeat of Chelsea in front of 68,000 Stamford Bridge spectators.

When Matthews was fit again he was 'offered' a run in the Reserves but declined the invitation and this led to a long-running dispute with the Stoke manager, Bob McGrory, over his form and fitness. Matthews' growing disillusionment with the club was to lead to his departure to Blackpool in the summer.

A rare defeat for Stoke in the early weeks was incurred at Ayresome Park, Middlesbrough. After the police had ordered the gates to be closed, the 43,685 crowd saw a typically high-scoring first-half with six goals shared. The home side were the eventual winners, 5-4, with Micky Fenton scoring a hat-trick.

The gates were closed for Blackpool's first three successive home matches at the limit of 27,000 for Bloomfield Road. The Seasiders were showing up well with Stan Mortensen always prominent at centre-forward and Harry Johnston and Ron Suart strong as defenders. After winning their first seven home matches, Blackpool were First Division leaders but in the end their away form let them down and meant the title went elsewhere.

By the turn of the year, however, Wolves were strong favourites for the title, particularly on the strength of their high-scoring. The men from Molineux, particularly Dennis Westcott, left winger Jimmy Mullen and centre-forward Jesse Pye, were the leading scorers. Westcott

Charlton Athletic's 41-year-old centre-half John Oakes liked to get forward. Here he is charging the Chelsea goalkeeper Bill Robertson.

was a feared predatory inside-forward who hit peak form in early December 1946 when he scored four goals in a brilliant first-half at Anfield. The Wolves eventually ran out 5-1 winners against Liverpool and went to the top of the First Division. The Merseysiders were later to gain their revenge in the decisive return fixture however.

Wolves supporters had been weaned on success from the early 1930s onwards, when Major Frank Buckley was in charge. Under manager Ted Vizard it was to be Stan Cullis's last season as a player — as tough and dependable a centre-half and captain as he was later to become as their manager.

Wolves took part in a storming fight for the Championship and when they went to the top it was largely on the strength of Westcott's 24 goals, but the work of the then up-and-coming, and new international wing-half, Billy Wright was crucial alongside the dominant Cullis.

When Wolves visited London to play Arsenal in the Christmas holiday period their attraction as visitors could be gauged from the resultant clamour to see the game. With more than 60,000 people inside Highbury, another 20,000 would-be spectators were left outside when the gates closed 20 minutes before the start of the 1-1 draw. As buses unloaded spectators they quickly filled up again with those same supporters as they realized they would be unable to gain entry.

Even in those hooligan-free days it was reported that in a scramble to see the game, up to 10,000 people rushed one section of the ground and gained free entry through an open gate before the police could seal the entrance.

After their strong, late thrust the previous season, Manchester United were fancied, under Matt Busby who had taken over in October 1945, as a side who played football with flair and style. The backbone of the United side was made up of the fine players introduced that previous year — powerful centre-half Allenby Chilton and cultured full-back John Aston in defence with the inspired signing Jimmy Delaney, rangy Jack Rowley and skilful Stan Pearson in the forward line.

In that transitional season for United, playing away from Old Trafford at Maine Road for home matches, one of Busby's greatest and most significant achievements was the moving of both Johnny Carey and Aston from inside-forwards to fill the two problem full-back positions where they established themselves as the finest club pair in Britain.

In goal was Jack Crompton, nicknamed 'the man with the magnetic hands' after he had saved all three penalty kicks taken against him that season. The offenders were all England internationals — Don Welsh, Tommy Lawton and Jimmy Hagan.

The Second Division was not short of big crowds or star players, with the likes of Birmingham City, Fulham, Manchester City,

Wolves at the start of 1946-7. Back row (left to right): Ted Vizard (manager), Tom Galley, Angus McLean, Bert Williams, Billy Crook, Billy Wright, Jack Smith (trainer), Jack Howley (secretary). Front row: Johnny Hancocks, Jesse Pye, Dennis Westcott, Stan Cullis, Willie Forbes, Jimmy Mullen.

Stan Cullis, in his last season as a Wolves player, covering at Highbury in 1946. Young Billy Wright watches and waits.

Newcastle United, Swansea Town, Tottenham Hotspur and West Ham United attracting crowds in excess of 30,000, while Plymouth Argyle, Sheffield Wednesday and West Bromwich Albion drew over 20,000. It was the unlikely Barnsley, and their manager Angus Seed, who were sitting temporarily at the top of that Division as October 1946 came to an end, however, with George Robledo, later to move to Newcastle, as the leading scorer.

There was dissent in football, even then, and when Manchester City's Maurice Dunkley scored the only goal of their home game, the Coventry players protested strongly and play was held up for several minutes in the centre-circle as the referee's orders to restart were disobeyed. It appeared that only the intervention of big, imposing Frank Swift, the City goalkeeper and captain, succeeded in persuading the Coventry players to stay and play on.

In the event, the Second Division title was contested by Manchester City, Burnley and Birmingham City.

The problem of resources, both on and off the field, were magnified in the lower divisions. Bristol Rovers reassembled after the war without any money and with no more than a couple of players on their books. The manager, Bert Tann, collected his players to compete in the Third South from the parks and downs around Bristol. He announced his policy of fierce loyalty to the club and his players: "No buy, no sell. If we fail we go back to playing on the Bristol downs, where the club began."

Similarly, at New Brighton in the Third Division North, only Alf Ainsworth and Norman Richardson remained of the pre-war staff and a completely new side had to be put together. When their only goalkeeper, Alec Corbett, was injured towards the end of the season, manager Neil McBain (a centre-half in his playing days) was forced to turn out in goal at the age of almost 52. McBain still remains as the oldest man ever to play in the Football League.

Newport County were in the Second Division after being Third South champions in 1938-9, but were plainly ill-equipped to compete at that level with their ground derelict, the stands at Somerton Park dilapidated, no equipment for the players and, inevitably, poor playing resources.

By the end of January 1947 the 'great freeze-up', the like of which sport in general has never known before or since, had begun. By the end of January, games were being played in arctic conditions of exceptional severity with bitter winds and grounds having to be cleared of snow from one end of the country to the other. Pitches were a mixture of ice, slush and salt with lines marked in red. From January to mid-March, temperatures were below freezing and over 140 games were postponed. Outside football, about two millon men and women were thrown out of work by the freeze and in homes and shops electricity was cut off for five hours daily.

In the first week of February, only three games could be played in the First Division and two weeks later the weather had really got a grip with 23 games in all postponed in the League. Those played were subject to treacherous conditions for players and spectators with games only going ahead after massive clearing-up operations. Some clubs had to draft in former prisoners of war to keep the pitches clear from snow.

Those games which got started were often punctuated by snow falls — freezing in the players' hair, caking the ball and obscuring the markings. When Portsmouth melted the snow and ice from their Fratton Park ground with a steam jet, they were rewarded with an 11,500 crowd for a reserve-team fixture played in waterlogged conditions.

The problems were compounded by a severe fuel crisis and this led to a Government order for restriction of newsprint. Most national football reporting was curtailed and supporters were deprived of their Saturday night 'pink un' as a consequence.

With floodlighting still a dream and midweek games forbidden by the Government to ensure uninterrupted industrial production and movement of coal, there was an alarming backlog of fixtures and the season had to be extended so that it became the longest in history.

As far as the FA Cup was concerned that season, the third-round tie between the capital's giants, Chelsea and Arsenal, was decided only after three titanic matches. The first 1-1 draw at Stamford Bridge was watched by over 70,000, the 1-1 replay at Highbury by 53,000 and the decider at neutral White Hart Lane by 59,000, where two 'blinders' from Tommy Lawton put Chelsea through, although not before Arsenal had missed a penalty.

Lawton's two special goals, one from his head in typical fashion, the other a left-foot 'screamer' from ten yards, were best remembered from that tie, but Arsenal goalkeeper George Swindin made his name with several thrilling saves in the trio of matches.

Chelsea were involved in another momentous struggle in the next round, against Derby County. After a 2-2 draw at home, when Raich Carter snatched the equalizer for Derby in the last minute, they succumbed at the Baseball Ground to a goal from Jack Stamps. The feature of these ties was the determined play of Carter, who, at his scheming best, was reckoned to be the most talented player on the icy pitches.

Second Division Newcastle United looked strong contenders for the trophy, thanks to the prodigious goalscoring of Roy Bentley, Charlie Wayman and Jackie Milburn. United netted six in the third round, at home to Crystal Palace, and another three in the next round, against

Southampton. The latter game was played before a St James' Park crowd of 55,878. Newcastle had paid Bradford £13,000 for Len Shackleton earlier in the season and the first scoring feat of the former coalmining Bevin Boy was six goals against Newport County.

High-riding Liverpool reached the semi-final for the first time for 33 years when Stubbins scored a hat-trick in the defeat of Birmingham City at Anfield. And at Bramall Lane, before 46,911 fans, Newcastle edged through against Sheffield United. At Turf Moor, Middlesbrough — star man Wilf Mannion and all — were knocked out in a replay through a disputed extra-time goal by Burnley's Welsh international Billy Morris. It ended 'Boro's bid to reach their first semi-final. Charlton triumphed 2-1 at home to Preston, despite playing for all but the first half hour with ten men. All three of the goals came from the many defensive slips on the ice-bound ground at The Valley.

The Burnley-Middlesbrough replayed tie reflected the fraught situation created by the arctic spell. The ground had to be treated with salt and brine right up to the kick-off. The game was in great doubt at noon but that did not stop over 40,000 would-be spectators restlessly waiting outside Turf Moor for a decision to be made. Just an hour before the scheduled kick-off time, the pitch was declared fit but, at the request of the police, the game was delayed for 40 minutes to allow the crowd to get in.

When the Cup semi-finals were played at the end of March 1947, Burnley and Liverpool were goalless after extra-time at Ewood Park, Blackburn, thanks largely to glaring misses by the Merseysiders' Stubbins and Liddell. The match was a dangerous affair for the 53,000 crowd, too tightly packed, and the ambulancemen carried a stream of stretcher cases around the touch-lines throughout the match. Second Division Burnley edged through to Wembley in the replay by a single goal from Ray Harrison before 72,000 at Maine Road.

In the other semi-final there was a stunning, totally surprising victory for Charlton by four clear goals over Newcastle, with Don Welsh scoring twice. Frank Brennan, the normally reliable United centre-half, was blamed for both.

Charlton goalkeeper Sam Bartram played most of the match with a hot poultice on his stomach — applied by the trainer to combat food poisoning. Bartram finished with plenty of blisters but was heading for his fourth successive Cup Final at Wembley. He had played in the 1944 Final of the Football League South Cup for Charlton, and for Millwall as a guest player again in the Final of the same competition a year later. And he had been in goal against Derby County in 1946.

Burnley had a fine side that season, made up largely of good clubmen with remarkable understanding. Although rated as a defensive team, Burnley got to Wembley as underdogs from the Second Division,

*Chris Duffy of Charlton (far right) flings his hands in the air as his drive finds the corner
of Burnley's net for the only goal of the 1947 FA Cup Final.*

unfancied and unheralded. For all that they were in second place
and set for promotion to Division One when the Final was played.

Charlton, in danger of relegation from the First Division, sought
to win the Cup for the first time but only five of their team from
the previous years' Final had survived — Bartram, Jack Shreeve, Bert
Johnson, Don Welsh and Chris Duffy.

The Final did not live up to the previous year's feast of football
but Charlton did not complain as they brought the Cup to The Valley
for the first time, by a single-goal victory. Six minutes from the end
of extra-time, left winger Chris Duffy won the game with one of the
best and most memorable shots seen in a Cup Final.

On the day of the Final at the end of April 1947, a full League
programme was played and at the end of the afternoon only two points
separated Wolves, Manchester United and Stoke at the top of the First
Division.

Wolves were top after a thrilling 6-4 win over Chelsea, to take their
total goals to 90 in their 37 games so far. Stoke had won at Blackburn,

notable for a rare goal from Stanley Matthews, and Manchester United had a single-goal victory at Portsmouth, thanks to Jimmy Delaney.

In the Second Division, Manchester City were well out in front, having only lost three matches in 35. Cardiff and Queen's Park Rangers were setting a hot pace in the Third South. Doncaster Rovers were ten points clear at the top of the Northern Section and had won a staggering 17 of their 19 away games at this stage.

Shortly after the FA Cup Final came what was described as the 'Match of the Century' at Hampden Park, Glasgow, between Great Britain and the Rest of Europe. It was held to celebrate the return of the four British Football Associations to FIFA.

*Charlton skipper
Don Welsh receives
the FA Cup from the
Duke of Gloucester
after the 1947 Final.*

Almost 134,000 people lined the classic Hampden slopes and they were rewarded with a great display by the Great Britain team, who won comfortably 6-1. Mannion and Lawton both scored twice against a 'scratch' European side captained by Johnny Carey, the Republic of Ireland international.

The game made the reputation of Greenock Morton's Billy Steel, who attracted the attention of several English clubs with his fine display which included a goal from 20 yards out. Although on the small side, Steel was exceedingly clever and Derby County paid a British record transfer fee of £15,500 for him, eclipsing the old record, set in 1938 by Arsenal for Bryn Jones, by £1,500. Steel was bought by

Derby to fill the gap left at inside-forward by the earlier sale of Peter Doherty to Huddersfield Town.

As the seemingly endless season drew to a close, Wolves, Manchester United, Stoke and Liverpool were neck and neck for the title. Wolves had spent most of the weeks since Christmas at the top and were 11 points ahead at one time. They were still favourites to secure their first League title and present skipper Stan Cullis with a trophy in his last season, despite having their rhythm disturbed by not playing for five weeks.

On the last day of May, Wolves had only to beat Liverpool at home, in blazing sunshine, in what was the final fixture of the season for both clubs. They lost 2-1 before 55,000, with Jack Balmer the star of Liverpool's dramatic victory.

Liverpool had an agonizing two-week wait until the last Saturday of a season which had lasted almost ten months. On that Saturday, 14 June 1947, the final and, indeed, sole First Division fixture between Sheffield United and Stoke City had to be played. A win at Sheffield would have enabled the Potters to overhaul Liverpool on goal-average and take the title for the first time in their history.

In the event, Sheffield United's success in winning by 2-1 before 30,000 at Bramall Lane gave the Championship to Liverpool and consigned Stoke to fourth position. They had come nearer than ever before, or since, to the coveted title.

It was generally felt that Liverpool had all-round strength rather than any players of remarkable ability. This judgement gave no credit to Stubbins, a great marksman at centre-forward, and the magnificent Billy Liddell at outside-left. Balmer was a vastly underrated player, held in high esteem by his contemporaries and of great skill and poise. He was the star of the vital win at Wolverhampton and Balmer and Stubbins scored 24 goals apiece. The half-backs, Phil Taylor, Lawrie Hughes and Bob Paisley, were a workmanlike blend but the team's stamina was considered suspect and, as if to prove this, they sank to 11th place the next season.

Manchester United finished as runners-up — a position they were to take three times in a row in the ensuing seasons.

As the season was about to close, Blackpool manager Joe Smith secured the transfer of 32-year-old Stanley Matthews for a fee of £11,500. The growing dispute with Stoke manager Bob McGrory was significant in the demand by Matthews for a move but it was commonly known that Matthews owned a hotel in Blackpool and had been living and training there as a consequence.

In retrospect that historic, colourful first season, so bedevilled by the weather, was notable for the number of goals scored, with the goalscorers grabbing all the headlines. The sophisticated defensive strategies were still to come in the future.

Liverpool, the 1946-7 Football League Champions. Back row (left to right): George Kay (manager), Jim Harley, Phil Taylor, Ray Lambert, Cyril Sidlow, Bob Paisley, Bill Jones, Billy Liddell, A.Shelley (trainer). Front row: Willie Fagan, Jack Balmer, W.H.M.McConnell (chairman), Albert Stubbins, Cyril Done.

Clarrie Jordan topped the lot with 41 goals for Doncaster Rovers. followed by the likes of Wally Ardron of Rotherham United with 38, Don Clark (Bristol City) and Dick Yates (Chester) 36 each. Four of the Wolves' forwards reached double figures — Dennis Westcott (37), Jesse Pye (20), Jimmy Mullen (12) and Johnny Hancocks (10). Charlie Wayman made his name with 30 goals for Newcastle United and following on behind were Freddie Steele (29 for Stoke City), Stan Mortensen (28 for Blackpool) and Jack Rowley (26 for Manchester United). George Lowrie of Coventry even managed to score five hat-tricks.

It was an extraordinary season for Doncaster Rovers, who, in winning the Third Division North title, set four League records. Their points total of 72 was the highest number of points ever won by a club in any division of the League; that toal included 37 points won away from home; and 18 of their 21 away games were won. They were simply irrepressible — winning 33 of their 42 games, losing only three and scoring 123 goals.

Cardiff were also equalling the Third Division South record by winning 30 of their 42 matches and scoring 93 goals in the process. In contrast, Leeds United had a wretched season in setting a different sort of record — losing 30 of their 42 matches in the First Division to be relegated with Brentford.

Before the season had ended, the findings of the National Arbitration Tribunal were announced and it was clear that the players had won a great victory and the clubs were bound by the decisions. The maximum wage was set at £12 per week with a minimum of £7 for players over 20 years of age (summer equivalents £10 and £5 respectively). For players, who had not earned vital bonuses for weeks as a result of postponed games that winter, it was a more than satisfying outcome to the dispute.

In the close season their lot was further improved by a raising of both talent money for League placings, and of the win and draw bonuses to £3 and £1.10s respectively).

The club balance sheets at the end of the season made interesting reading as they reflected a total aggregate attendance of 35.6 million. Many inevitably reported substantial gains, with all but six making an overall profit. Stoke City made £32,207. Burnley, in winning promotion to the First Division and going to Wembley, made £18,000 and Liverpool, in taking the title, made over £15,000.

Internationally, for England at least, it was a season of great success with six of the eight matches played being won and only one reverse, in Zurich to Switzerland by a solitary goal to nil.

The Home International tournament was revived at Windsor Park, Belfast, at the end of September 1946 and nearly 60,000 spectators crammed into the stadium. After the start had been delayed, England coasted to a 7-2 win. Wilf Mannion hit a superb hat-trick, with one goal each for the other forwards Tom Finney, Carter, Lawton and Bobby Langton. The match was Billy Wright's first cap on the way to his eventual century of appearances for his country.

The main talking point from that game was the loss of key players suffered that Saturday by the clubs. As a result, Derby County lost Carter and Doherty and duly lost two points in their home defeat by Blackpool.

Not only were seven goals scored in that first international but eight were also netted against the Netherlands and finally ten in Lisbon, in a sumptuous England display against the Portuguese on the summer tour. Mortensen and Lawton were irresistible in a new pairing which gave lightning thrust to the attack and they shared eight of the goals, the first time two Englishmen had scored four in an international. If Mannion and Carter were superb on the international stage in this period, Stanley Matthews was positively dazzling.

There was an illusion of soccer supremacy in Britain and this largely hung on the fact that neither England nor Scotland had ever been beaten at home by a foreign team. That illusion had been considerably strengthened by the handsome victory during the season by the Great Britain XI over the Rest of Europe.

The shattering of that illusion was in the future but for now, despite the great names abroad in the land and the multitude of goals, it was recognized that the game's resources in the form of new young players, were still thin and stretched. Such an authority as the late Ivan Sharpe was moved to write: "More and more players, that's the need today."

The first post-war season, despite its crises, disputes and arbitration, had attracted a record number of spectators but this record was to be left behind in the next campaign, which, after the unprecedented weather — enforced extension, was only 70 days away.

It's 'Lucky Old Arsenal'

F OR the players and spectators of League football their rest and break had been short indeed. No more than two months had elapsed since the end of the 1946-7 season, a campaign remembered as one of excitement and drama, particularly in its drawn-out last weeks, and also of crisis, of dispute and arbitration. It has shown the consequences, still with us today, of a congested fixture programme and the dangers of the game being hedged about by external controls and over-administration. As the football correspondent of *The Times* put it so succinctly, on the opening day of the season: "We must, in fact, take care that the frame does not become too large for the picture itself".

After that most dreadful harsh winter, the summer of 1947 had been nothing short of glorious and with it came a record level of demand for seaside holidays. Workers took advantage of their paid holidays for the first time and the main recipients were the Butlin's Camps, to where half a million flocked for a 'Hi-de-hi'-style break. Dance-halls were at their peak with over 450 in Britain and three million tickets being sold each week.

Cricket audiences had reached their maximum, despite England being outclassed and outgunned throughout the winter tour of Australia. The loss of the Ashes by an enormous margin was soon forgotten in a sun-drenched summer which contained the extraordinary run-getting feats of Denis Compton and Bill Edrich, a close fight for the County Championship with Middlesex taking the title and a visit from the South Africans. Compton thrilled the crowds with 3,816 runs for an average of 90, which included 18 centuries, the most ever recorded in one season. The South Africans were easily beaten in the five-Test series.

The games of the XIV Olympiad — the Olympic Games, but renamed the 'austerity games' — were held in London, August 1948 and watched by what was then the largest aggregate Olympic crowd on record. On a temporary running track at Wembley Stadium, the likes of athletes Emil Zatopek and Fanny Blankers-Koen were thrilling the crowds. Whilst Great Britain were collecting a total of three gold medals, Mrs Blankers-Koen was taking home four for herself.

In the close season there was a flood of applications for admission to the Football League — 27 in all for the four places available. In the event there was not even an election and the four retiring clubs — Mansfield, Norwich, Halifax and Southport were promptly readmitted at the League's insistence. Out of all this grew an increasing disenchantment with the League by the non-League clubs and a demand for an expansion of the League.

As the new football season opened, the Labour Government was wrapped up in a sterling crisis which led to a reappraisal of economic policy and cuts which were to affect the general standard of living. The first consequence of that, in August 1947, was a cut in imports which led to butter and meat rationing. There was clearly to be a reduction in the average daily intake of calories per head and the newspapers were full of alarmist talk of resultant malnutrition. As a cheap alternative, whalemeat was introduced from South Africa but the British public did not take to it at all.

In the coming months, as the football season unfolded, Prince Charles was born, Mahatma Gandhi, man of peace, was assassinated and, to wild acclaim, American entertainer Danny Kaye made his first visit to Britain. As some consolation for the food rationing, petrol was to become more freely available.

In the short close-season many clubs had been busy team-building but the feeling was that Lancashire, with nine teams in the First Division, might dominate the Championship if only by sheer weight of numbers. Despite their 11th-hour title win the previous season, Liverpool were surprisingly discounted by the pundits who felt Manchester United were well-equipped for the title. Wolverhampton Wanderers were without Cullis, but were fancied after setting the pace for most of the previous season. The early-season interest would also centre on how Stoke City would fare without the great Stanley Matthews — and Blackpool would do with that gentleman now in their ranks. Derby, with new signing Billy Steel as a foil to Raich Carter, and Arsenal, with new faces Archie Macaulay and Don Roper, were also exciting interest.

Over one million people watched the opening games in blazing sunshine and the biggest crowd was at Maine Road, where Manchester City, after their promotion to the First Division, had acquired Eddie McMorran, the Irish international, and Roy Clarke to strengthen their forward line. Clarke had the distinction of playing in three different Divisions in consecutive games. He had appeared in Third Division South champions Cardiff City's penultimate game of the previous season, then been transferred to Maine Road in time to appear in the last Second Division game there. Now he was in the First.

A crowd of 67,800 saw City win their opening fixture against Wolves 4-3. But there was controversy when, with Wolves already leading

2-1, their pocket-sized winger, Johnny Hancocks, (5ft 3½in in his football boots) put all his 9st 3lb into a shot at goal. It caught City 'keeper Frank Swift on the wrong foot and toppled all 14st 5lb of him backwards into the net. As Swift fell he punched out the shot with his big hands and, despite the Wolves' protest, the 'goal' was not allowed. City celebrated the let-off with an equalizer from McMorran and then went on to win with goals from George Smith — he had suffered a gunshot wound to a hand during the war — and Clarke.

In the Second Division, a 48,000 crowd — many of whom had queued for three hours outside Ninian Park — saw Cardiff City's debut in the higher grade and it was George Wardle, an Englishman, and Doug Blair, a Scot, who formed their new left wing and paved the way for the 3-0 opening win over also newly-promoted Doncaster Rovers.

Newcastle United's immense crowd potential was highlighted again by their attendance of 52,642 to watch the 6-1 demolition of Plymouth Argyle. The late Jackie Milburn used to recall the amazing crowd scenes at St James' Park in those days and remembered how he and the other players 'often had to join queues around the ground in an attempt to reach the players' entrance and when we tried to break through the queue we were told to get to the back!'

Newcastle's average attendance eventually climbed to 56,299 that season and at the start of the campaign there were 15,000 applications for a mere 1,500 season tickets. Later in the season a hastily-arranged friendly match against Liverpool attracted 44,480 to St James' Park, although there was the added attraction of Albert Stubbins' return to Tyneside.

There was an unusual incident on that opening Saturday at Upton Park, where Millwall were the visitors to West Ham. Millwall players were spotted by the referee passing around a wet sponge during the game. The Millwall trainer was summoned and reprimanded and the smuggled sponge was duly confiscated.

In the early-season midweek matches, 43,067 saw Burnley's first home match in the First Division after 17 years' absence but visitors Derby County took the honours with Raich Carter and Jack Stamps scoring in the 2-0 victory.

A shirt-sleeved crowd of 60,000 at Charlton's Valley — the biggest midweek attendance in London for many years — saw a rejuvenated Arsenal beat the FA Cup holders 4-2. Mighty Wolves ran riot and riddled the Grimsby defence eight times after the visitors had taken the lead in a few seconds. Quicksilver centre-forward Jesse Pye claimed three goals in the rout before 45,000 fans at Molineux.

It was interesting to note that in the Spurs team which slammed Sheffield Wednesday 5-1 in the Second Division were ten players secured without a transfer fee. The only bought player was winger Ernie Jones, transferred from Swansea Town for £6,000 earlier in the year. A new name at Tottenham, creating an early impression, was little Johnny Jordan, an ex-Grays amateur who cost only the £10 signing-on-fee and who, after ten games, was their top scorer with seven goals. Curiously, he did not sustain his early promise.

Arsenal had agreed that the services of Denis and Leslie Compton be retained by Middlesex until the County Cricket Championship had been decided, but that did not stop the Gunners winning their first five matches of the season.

Arsenal were inspired by their brilliant wing-halves, Joe Mercer and the hard-tackling Scot, Archie Macaulay, from Glasgow Rangers. They complemented the forward line of Roper, Logie, Rooke, Lewis and McPherson. In defence, capable goalkeeper George Swindin was in his best form and the full-back partnership of the fast Laurie Scott and close-tackling Walley Barnes was a formidable defence once centre-half Leslie Compton had been released from cricket.

Typical of the new Arsenal spirit was an early 2-1 victory against Bolton Wanderers at Highbury when they were reduced to nine men after Reg Lewis and centre-half Alf Fields were injured. Skipper Mercer took over at centre-half to keep Bolton at bay and earn Arsenal one of the outstanding victories of the season. Ian McPherson, a 25-year-old Scot, earned rave notices on the Arsenal left wing after being converted to the position on his move from Notts County.

Denis Compton, at 29 years of age, declined a cricket trip to the West Indies and made himself available for Arsenal as a contender for McPherson's left-wing spot. After his first game, inevitably his 'dodgy' knee was playing up and he complained of being stiff and sore. At 12st 10lb, Compton was clearly overweight but the club and its supporters loved his unbridled enthusiasm as he went after the ball with what was described as 'atomic energy', like a rugby forward.

By mid-October, the Gunners had taken 24 points out of a possible 26, scoring 25 goals against six conceded, including a remarkable run of six consecutive games without conceding a goal. For all that, Arsenal were accused of being negative in their tactics and the tag 'Lucky Arsenal' was regularly applied to their efforts. The truth was that they were defensive with great counter-attacking by long, sweeping attacking movements.

Arsenal's fixture at Stamford Bridge against Chelsea created utter chaos in the capital. The game ended in a goalless draw but it was the scenes beforehand which created the headlines.

The gates were shut three-quarters of an hour before kick-off and police with radio-cars had to break up the jam-packed crowds, who had spent up to five hours outside only to find themselves shut out. Mounted police were also employed to clear the gates and the approaches to the ground. Ticket-holders had to show them for scrutiny three times before they got past ground officials. Only 67,277 got in before the gates were shut, although the ground record is 82,905. Police and the Chelsea club were determined to err on the side of safety, so tens of thousands were turned away. Reserved tickets sold out well in advance and many fell into the hands of the touts who were doing brisk business selling five-shilling seats for 45 shillings. It was significant, however, that thousands of would-be spectators refused to deal with the touts and queued for homeward buses within five minutes of arriving at the ground.

The Gunners' undefeated sequence continued right up to the end of November when, in their 18th game, they were finally beaten, 1-0 by Derby County at the Baseball Ground, thanks to a goal from little outside-right Reg Harrison.

At Blackpool all eyes were on Stanley Matthews as the Seasiders sat in second place, but it was the whole-hearted play of England centre-forward Stan Mortensen which was prominent in their rise. Blackpool's season was really Mortensen's season with the dynamic player at the very height of his powers. He gave freely of his immense energy and irrepressible spirit. His secret lay in his remarkable acceleration and 'nose' for an opening.

When Blackpool were at home to Wolves in a key match before 29,500 supporters it was reported that Mortensen had collapsed unconscious in the players' tunnel at half-time. It was put down to the strain of a fierce first half, many buffetings and lack of sleep which was too much, even for his lion-hearted physique. It was reported that Mortensen lived above a shop in a busy Blackpool thoroughfare — the only accommodation he could find — and he found his sleep fitful and uneasy. Apparently teammates carried him to the dressing-room and even when the game restarted, he was only just coming round. Eventually, despite his trainer's protestations, he shook his fuzzy head and stumbled out on to the field to 'make' a goal.

In those boom times, as we have already seen, the clubs had experienced a remarkable surge in their income and when Entertainment Tax was abolished they found themselves even better off. In particular the migration of Scottish players across the border continued unabated and the transfer market was a free-for-all amounting to something akin to a black market with little of the FA regulations observed. A then world record fee for a goalkeeper was created when Newcastle, still in the Second Division, paid £7,000 to Preston North End for Jack Fairbrother.

The transfer merry-go-round gained even greater impetus and extended to benefit the non-League clubs when it was reported that the quickest dual transfer in soccer history was arranged in the referee's room at Margate FC. Charlton manager Jimmy Seed signed two Dartford players, Cullum and Alexander, within six minutes of their leaving the field and handed over a cheque for £6,000 to the Dartford manager. Never before had a non-League club received such money for a transfer — beating the £1,250 paid to Dartford by West Ham for Fred Dell before the war. The feeling in the Press was that all this emphasized that football was approaching the fantasy of the £20,000 transfer. Incidentally, Riley Cullum made only 32 League appearances before disapppearing from the first-class scene four years later, and Alexander did not manage even one appearance in the top flight.

The newspapers were full of Tommy Lawton's disenchantment with life at Chelsea and the saga of his transfer demand had created continual speculation with the London club refusing some sizeable offers. While he was out of favour, Lawton's drawing-power was evidenced by the crowd of 23,000 one Saturday at Highbury to see him play for Chelsea Reserves. In the end his eventual move came as a major surprise.

Notts County had become a struggling Third Division South outfit but in A.W.Stollery they had a very enterprising manager. Not only did he fly to Vancouver to sign inside-forward Fred Wittover, but he also had the effrontery to approach Chelsea about Tommy Lawton, still an England regular, but demanding to leave Stamford Bridge. Somehow Lawton was persuaded to move to Meadow Lane at a fee of £17,500. On his first appearance the gates were shut before the kick-off of a first-round FA Cup tie against West Sussex amateurs, Horsham. With Lawton leading the line and making goals for Jackie Sewell, County ran riot before big crowds every week, commencing with nine goals against Horsham. Within weeks the all-time Meadow Lane ground record was shattered as over 46,000 spectators were attracted on Boxing Day to see Lawton hit the goal trail again against Swansea.

By his move to Notts County, Lawton became the first Third Division player since the war to represent England when he played in the 2-0 win over Scotland at Hampden Park in April 1948.

As Christmas approached, the Football Association, 'in an attempt to cut down foul play', issued what the Press termed 'the most startling document' which named 87 professional footballers who had been cautioned so far that season and the nature of the offences. It had been normal for suspensions to be published but previously, in an age without red or yellow cards, the record of the cautions had been jealously guarded at Lancaster Gate. It was noticeable that only one player, George Lowrie of Coventry and Wales, had incurred as many as three separate cautions but the Press and the clubs reserved judgement on whether the public exposure of their sins would have any effect on the players' behaviour.

In the same week Freddie Steele, the 30-year-old Stoke and former England centre-forward, made his comeback after breaking his leg three months earlier. Little had gone right for Stoke in his absence and when he scored the winning goal it was hailed as a great and welcome return. Greater even than in 1939 when, his goal-morale gone, a psychiatrist spent weeks probing Steele's mind, driving out fears and hypnotizing him back to confidence.

It was a soccer Christmas for 1,354,000 ever-faithful fans and Boxing Day 1947 brought the biggest crushes. Over 53,000 were at Liverpool to see Arsenal win and go three points clear at the top, leaving the Merseysiders in the bottom half of the table. The biggest attraction of the festive season was at Villa Park, where the gates were closed with 65,000 inside, and the Westcott-Hancock combination secured the points for Wolves.

Thousands were turned away from the Lancashire derby match between second-placed Preston and third-placed Burnley and 40,000 saw the North End come out on top.

There was great interest in the news that Blackpool's Stanley Matthews had an injection in his right thigh, five minutes before turning out to entertain 47,000 of his old fans at Stoke. He had bruised the thigh and was a doubtful starter but the club doctor had suggested a 'shot' so as to not disappoint the holiday crowd and Matthews played for the 90 minutes without feeling a thing. The Press were of one mind — 'It was a sample of the medical and scientific shape of things to come in professional sport'.

As the New Year 1948 arrived, Arsenal were sitting six points clear at the top of the First Division with Burnley, Preston and Manchester United, all from Lancashire, in pursuit. In the Second Division, Birmingham City were in a similar position to the Gunners with Newcastle United and newly-promoted Cardiff City behind them.

Birmingham were attracting 30,000-plus attendances but the Newcastle 'gates' continued to be astonishing and a crowd of 61,361 for the New Year's Day home fixture against fourth-placed West Bromwich Albion was typical. This game was spoilt after 25 minutes by an injury to Albion goalkeeper Norman Heath which ensured a 3-1 win for Newcastle with a brace of goals from Milburn. Albion's discomfort had curiously coincided with a substitute goalkeeper plan submitted by their directors to the FA that same week.

Even in a era of large crowds, the attendance of 81,962 at Maine Road for the Manchester United fixture against Arsenal in mid-January shocked the football world. It was, in fact, only 943 less than the League record established at Stamford Bridge in 1935. A 1-1 draw was the result of this clash of the giants but the gate receipts of £9,000-plus were staggering even for the period.

United had maintained a great offensive throughout the game but in the last few minutes, Arsenal's Reg Lewis got through and placed the ball wide of the goalkeeper only to see it roll through the mud,

Arsenal goalkeeper George Swindin is about to be beaten by a header from Manchester United's Jimmy Delaney as he meets a centre from Charlie Mitten. But the ball flew harmlessly over the bar. The game at Maine Road — Old Trafford was out of commission due to wartime bomb damage — ended in a 1-1 draw before a crowd of 81,962.

hit the inside of one post and then spin away and hit the other before being cleared to deny the Londoners a winner.

The leading scorers in the League were found at Carlisle United in the Third Division North and it was all down to the inspiration of the youngest player-manager in English football, the 24-year-old Ivan (known as Ivor) Broadis, who had single-handedly made the outpost football-minded to such an extent that he had trebled gates up to an average of 17,000.

Broadis was a brilliant dribbler and an inspirational figure whose wartime duties as a flying officer in the RAF had taken him north after he had originally signed as an amateur for Tottenham. In later seasons, Broadis moved into the higher division to gain international recognition but in 1948 he was working miracles at Brunton Park.

When the third round of the FA Cup arrived, Arsenal were favourites for the trophy after only one reverse in their previous 19 games, but that did not impress Second Division Bradford, who created a sensation by winning by a single goal, cracked in by winger Billy Elliott after 36 minutes. The 47,738 crowd was the smallest at Highbury all season and the concensus of opinion was that the fear of closed gates was keeping spectators away.

Close on 1,050,000 fans packed the terraces for the third-round ties and some of them witnessed the craziest day in the history of the

76-year-old competition as Arsenal, Bolton, Burnley, Huddersfield, Sheffield United and Sunderland all went out.

Southern League Colchester United, who had never before played a First Division club, knocked out Huddersfield Town by a single goal masterminded by player-manager Ted Fenton, the former West Ham player. Apart from the glamorous Corinthians, earlier in the century, it was the first time a club outside the League had toppled a First Division club.

The Aston Villa-Manchester United tie in that round was one of the most remarkable matches in the competition's history. In a feast of goals, Villa were 5-1 down at half-time to a rampant United side. They pulled back to 5-4, only for United to score a sixth at the death to win an amazing 6-4 away victory. That grey winter's afternoon at Villa Park had seen brilliant forward play from a United side at their peak and superb all-out attacking from both sides.

In the next round Colchester knocked out Bradford, Arsenal's conquerers, and reached the last 16. It was the furthest a non-League club had gone since 1911 when Darlington, then a North-Eastern League club, reached those dizzy heights.

A record Goodison Park crowd of 74,721 saw Manchester United, still unable to play at Old Trafford, beat Liverpool 3-0 and the all-Second Division clash between Tottenham and West Brom attracted 71,853.

Apart from the size of the crowds, what was still astonishing was the players' rewards. When a crowd of over 70,000 paid to watch a Cup tie the receipts were close on £9,000; of that the players received the normal wages, plus a £4 bonus for winning. In the fifth round the bonus rose to £6, and from then on spiralled to a dizzy £20 per head in the Final.

The never-say-die spirit that carried the little Essex side from Colchester into the fifth round of the Cup was scuttled by the magic of Stanley Matthews at Blackpool. Colchester took a lucky cork, a rabbit's foot and a secret 'M-Plan' to stop Matthews. Within three minutes it was in tatters as the great man darted through to give Munro a goal and then McIntosh a second minutes later. Five goals went past the non-Leaguers — all the scorers had the letter 'M' — Munro, McIntosh and Mortensen. The Press joked that manager Fenton's 'M-Plan' had worked in reverse.

The Cup holders, Charlton, went out to Manchester United and Sam Bartram reserved what was judged to be his greatest performance for the tie at Huddersfield. On a pouring wet day and a bog of a pitch, Bartram made save after save. In the 2-0 win for United, the second came minutes from time when Bartram, covered from head to toe in mud, only had the strength left to stand up. His red hair apparently turned black from mud, Bartram was carried off the pitch by spectators at the finish.

Spurs were challenging for promotion to the First Division and through to the sixth round of the Cup after a five-goal thrashing of Leicester. After scoring twice in the previous round, centre-forward Len Duquemin, from the Channel Islands, scored a hat-trick and earned rave notices for his cool finishing and seizure of half-chances.

The last eight in the Cup were Blackpool, Preston, Manchester United (the favourites), Derby County, Queen's Park Rangers (last of the Third Division clubs and reaching this stage for the first time since 1923), Southampton, Spurs and Fulham. United were apparently unstoppable — as they reached the semi-finals for the first time in 22 years.

The semi-finals, in which Blackpool met Second Division Spurs at Villa Park and Manchester United took on Derby County at Hillsborough, brought a tremendous demand for tickets. More than 150,000 fans queued through the night at the two grounds as the prospect of an all-Lancashire Final appeared likely. As it transpired the ties were decided by two 'Stans'.

Tottenham seemed to have won their semi-final, leading 1-0 with four minutes left when Stan Mortensen ran on to a Matthews pass to equalize for Blackpool. In extra-time Mortensen scored two more goals to put Blackpool through to their first-ever Cup Final, to play Manchester United, the first First Division club they had encountered in the Cup that season.

At Hillsborough, Sheffield, it was Stan Pearson who was the hero with the hat-trick against Derby that put United through 3-1. The Rams continually looked threatening through the Steel-Carter partnership but, despite Steel putting up a great-hearted performance, they could not find the punch in front of goal. United's three goals were all largely against the run of play, but on reflection United had got to Wembley by as uphill a road as could possibly be imagined. They had been drawn, in turn, against six First Division clubs, the first instance of this happening. They had to beat Aston Villa 6-4, Liverpool 3-0, Charlton 2-0, Preston 4-1 and Derby 3-1 to reach Wembley.

Despite Arsenal's prominence in the League, United were generally considered as the best footballing side in the country with a fine blend which cost next to nothing. They were one of the very few sides in the competition's history to start as favourites for the trophy and never to waver in popular estimation.

United had a powerful insistence on attack through Mitten with the wicked left-foot shot, Delaney with his never-say-die approach, and Rowley with his shooting and heading power. To this could be added Pearson as the restless midfield forager and Morris, that fine ball-player.

Blackpool were described as the most 'lop-sided' team in the League with all their apparent strength on the right starting with the incomparable Matthews-Mortensen wing, backwards to the impeccable Harry Johnston and highly-rated Eddie Shimwell in defence. It was true to say that the left-flank of the team was completely over-shadowed — the likes of Dick and Rickett in attack and Kelly and Crosland in defence paled by comparison.

It was judged at the time to be the most classical Final ever to be played at Wembley. Blackpool performed well enough to have beaten four out of five teams, but met a Manchester United side at their peak. At the 69th minute Blackpool were leading 2-1, but three goals in a dramatic 16 minutes in the second half won the Cup for United.

United had twice been behind but kept on playing superlative football under the direction and inspiration of Johnny Carey. The two centre-forwards were the stars — Mortensen, maintaining his record of scoring in every round, and Rowley with two memorable goals. The two teams set a new standard for their insistence on attacking football that afternoon and provided one of the most thrilling climaxes ever to a Final.

Whilst the Final was being played there was the usual full programme of League football and attendances slumped as a consequence from the usual one million or so to less than 700,000. The blame was put squarely on the Cup Final radio broadcasts and no more so than at the Manchester City ground, where only 20,782 turned up for the game with Arsenal — more than 30,000 below normal.

After taking a point at Huddersfield three weeks earlier, Arsenal were League Champions for the sixth time in their history and in Tom Whittaker's first year as manager. At the season's end they had topped the table from the start, had called on only 18 players in the League and conceded fewer goals (30) than any other First Division club had done since the change in the offside law in 1925.

April saw ground attendance records set at Roker Park, Sunderland; Hillsborough, Sheffield; and Dean Court, Bournemouth as promotion and relegation struggles drew the crowds.

Nearly 10,000 people were locked outside Bournemouth's ground whilst a record 25,733 saw Fred Durrant of Queen's Park Rangers score the goal that ensured their promotion from the Third Division South. Those outside were able to keep in touch thanks to a running commentary by megaphone by the Bournemouth secretary.

At Sunderland, 65,000 saw their favourites beat Cup Finalists Blackpool to assure themselves of First Division football in 1948-9. Only a handful saw the winning goal by Dicky Davis in a goalmouth scramble — the ball being kicked clear a split-second after it crossed

Eddie Shimwell, Blackpool's right-back, scores from the penalty-spot against Manchester United in the 1948 FA Cup Final.

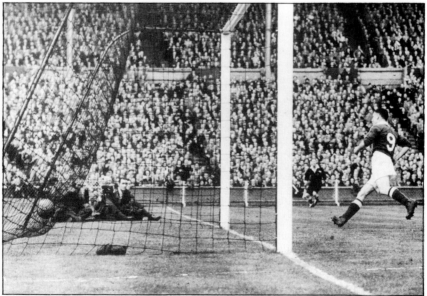

Jack Rowley (9) scores the first of his goals to set Manchester United on the road to victory at Wembley.

the line. To everyone's amusement it seemed like every member of the Sunderland team was chasing Stanley Matthews all over the field, when it was clear that he was the greatest threat to their place in the top division.

Hull City's enormous potential at their new Boothferry Park ground had not been realized under the stewardship of secretary-manager Major Frank Buckley, the former Wolves manager. The ground attendance record of 40,179 for the January 1948 FA Cup visit of Middlesbrough had been set but, despite the Major's experimentation with players — over 70 had been registered with the League in the previous season — the Tigers had failed to set the Third Division alight, despite a good start in the autumn.

Matters came to a head in March 1948 and the Hull board negotiated with Derby County for the release of Raich Carter for a 'small fee'. The 34-year-old was by no means finished as a player but it was the dual role of player-assistant manager which was on offer. Carter signed, little realizing that within a matter of days he would be taking full control following Major Buckley's resignation. When Carter made his debut, Hull raked in the first dividends on their investment from a home crowd of almost 33,000. Carter's methods, in contrast to those of his predecessor, were to bring record-breaking and astonishing success the next season.

For his part, Major Buckley moved quickly to Leeds United, another 'sleeping giant'. The Elland Road side, relegated the previous season, had been drawing average home gates of 33,000 for their Second Division fixtures.

When the season ended, on time, Arsenal had a seven-point lead over runners-up Manchester United. Clearly, the Gunners were the boom-team in that boom-year and showed why they were referred to as the 'Bank of England' team. Their home gate receipts had averaged £7,000 per game and grossed in excess of £150,000 for the season. They wound up their season with an eight-goal thrashing of Grimsby Town, who were relegated along with Blackburn Rovers.

Birmingham City took the Second Division championship with a new defensive record — only 24 goals conceded in the 42 matches. In 24 of those they did not concede one goal but, to counter that, the Blues scored only 55 goals all season. In fact the team from St Andrew's secured more points than they scored goals.

It had been a momentous season for Newcastle United, who accompanied Birmingham in promotion. Under new manager George Martin, United really captured the imagination and none more than Jackie Milburn who switched to centre-forward, a move enforced by the departure in early season of Charlie Wayman to Southampton, and established himself as one of the all-time greats.

United's promotion was secured in a tremendous finale and that

Johnny Carey, Manchester United's skipper, is carried shoulder-high by his victorious teammates.

after selling star forwards Roy Bentley to Chelsea, Len Shackleton to Sunderland and Tommy Pearson to Aberdeen. Shackleton's transfer to Wearside attracted a fee of £20,050 which was promptly spent at the season's close on George Lowrie, the prolific Coventry centre-forward. The home record was the key with 18 wins. Their end-of-season win over third-placed Sheffield Wednesday was crucial. Playing before 66,483 fanatical Geordies, United won a thriller 4-2 with wing-half Frank Houghton scoring the decisive fourth in the last minute. In doing so he collided with a post and was carried off with a broken arm.

After their runaway promotion in the previous season, Doncaster Rovers were relegated back to the Third along with Millwall, for whom the season had been marred by crowd disturbances which led to the Cold Blow Lane ground being closed for seven days.

Accompanying QPR to the Second Division were Lincoln City, but Norwich and Brighton had to apply for re-election to the Third Division South and Halifax and New Brighton to the Third Division North.

Norwich wound up by breaking their ground record by more than 4,000 when 37,847 went to Carrow Road for their last, vital fixture against Notts County. A Tommy Lawton 'special' secured a win for County and left Norwich at the very bottom.

Poor New Brighton had won only eight games, surprisingly three of them away from home. Only 38 goals were scored and two of these were by opponents, whilst 81 were given away. In comparison with the massive crowds watching First Division football, New Brighton attracted an average attendance of 5,229 to the Tower Ground, whilst an average 'gate' of 9,385 watched them away from home. At the end of the season they gave free-transfers to no less than 15 players.

Despite Ronnie Rooke of Arsenal finishing as top scorer in the First Division, with 33 goals, Stan Mortensen was clearly the most celebrated goalscorer of the season with a goal in every round of the Cup, one each for England against Scotland, Wales and the Scottish League, plus three against Sweden to add to his 31 in the League.

For England it was an altogether satisfying season, from the dazzling 5-2 defeat of Belgium in September 1947 in Brussels through to the comprehensive 4-0 win over Italy in Turin the following May.

Stanley Matthews was the architect and chief provider for the Brussels triumph and Lawton, Mortensen and Finney took the chances in that match and the subsequent victories over Wales, Scotland and Italy.

When Matthews was missing, Mortensen took centre-stage with a hat-trick in the 4-2 win over Sweden at Highbury in November 1947. His finest international goal was, however, reserved for the first meeting between Italy and England since the war, in sizzling heat before 75,000 in Turin. Four minutes after the kick-off, Matthews sent Mortensen away with a long pass. His Blackpool colleague went on a determined run at great speed before hitting a right-foot 'banana' shot into the top corner of the Italian goal from 15 yards.

There was still, therefore, every reason to think that British football had nothing to fear from Continental or South American opposition and nothing in 1948 had occurred to disturb this layer of complacency.

Needless to say, the season had been one of unparalleled prosperity thoughout the League. It had been a real boost for every club, without exception, and those clubs which did not go into the transfer market had built up a tremendous financial reserve. Rotherham United were typical — a profit of £9,612 enabled them to pay for their ground, wipe out their debts and leave money for ground improvements.

All this was the product of attendance figures which topped 40 million for the first time — a rise on the previous season of 4.65 million, with roughly £4 million taken at the turnstiles. An average of 21,785 per League match was recorded and the Second Division, with the likes of Newcastle, Sheffield Wednesday and Tottenham as crowd-pullers, accounted for almost 31 per cent of the total.

These crowds were not rewarded with goals, however, and the defensive game had become so pronounced that the number of goals scored differed little from what it was before the change in the offside law was made over 20 years earlier. Clearly, with their supply of young players effectively cut, the clubs were compelled to make the best use of the existing talent. The end of the season saw the end of many established players from pre-war days and no replacements of comparable quality were available.

In the very nature of football, it had always been an easier matter to prevent goals than to score them and the construction of solid defences became the priority. The evidence was the establishment of defensive records in each division of the Football League in the four seasons immediately after the war.

During the season the magic word 'television' had come upon the scene but, whereas the Football Association were in favour of televised football, the Football League were against it. The clubs agreed with the League's verdict and only internationals and Cup Finals were allowed. The BBC claimed that approximately one million people watched the 1948 Final on television but there were clearly nothing like that number of sets around.

It had been a season of even larger attendances, colossal transfer fees and dazzling dividends from the pools. If you had moved amongst the students of the game, however, the opinion would have been expressed that the standard of play had been lamentably below what it was before the war and that there was a dearth of really first-class players. If all this were true, then the faithful followers of the game who paid at the turnstiles were plainly unconcerned.

Reaching the
Peak

A S the 1948-9 season approached, it was clear that below the surface the unrest of the players, so noticeable since the war, continued and, indeed, occasionally surfaced. In August 1948 the main talking points surrounded the refusals of Wilf Mannion of Middlesbrough and Albert Stubbins of Liverpool to renew contracts with their clubs, and the persistent requests of Neil Franklin, England's centre-half, to leave Stoke City. These and other discontents were deadlocked and the hands of the clubs had been strengthened by an agreement between the Football Association and FIFA whereby avenues of escape to Eire and the Continent had been closed to unregistered players.

For the average player in the League, his remuneration between 1 August 1948 and 7 May 1949 was £8 per week. In the off season, extending from 8 May to 31 July, this was reduced to £7. A typical contract would contain such restrictions as 'all players must be in the house not later than 10.30pm', 'No player shall under any circumstances whatever own, use or travel in a motorcar' and 'Dancing is prohibited after Mondays'. The roots of slavery were to be seen in such documents, in those days of parsimony and exploitation.

In an age of Woodbine cigarettes and football pools for the working man, the players were indistinguishable, off the field, from spectators, with their ambitions not extending much beyond retiring from the game to run a small newsagents' or sweet shop.

In the 15 short weeks of the close season, the main news on the non-sporting front involved the start of the National Health Service, after a long, tortuous struggle by Aneurin Bevan, the Labour Minister of Health. When the scheme started employed people paid 4s 11d per week. Initially, the greatest pressure on the NHS was for the spectacles as demand exceeded supply.

After what had seemed an eternity, and after several false alarms over the previous months, bread rationing had finally been abandoned, to the nation's delight. Later in the season, sweets and chocolate were taken off rationing but within weeks the demand was so great that stocks ran out and rationing had to be reimposed.

It had been a momentous summer for cricket with the visit of the all-conquering Australians and the great Don Bradman on his last tour. Crowds flocked to see, not basically the Australian touring team, despite its powers, but Bradman. He did not disappoint them — with an average of 89-plus in the season, with 11 hundreds.

The first five-day Tests were played in England and the home country lost four of the five Tests with the other drawn under captain Norman Yardley. In the Oval Test England were humiliated by being bowled out for 52 but had the satisfaction of dismissing Bradman for nought in his last Test innings in this country.

Nevertheless it was a summer of runs all the way — Australia hitting 721 in one day at Southend versus Essex, and Harold Gimblett of Somerset registering the highest score made in England since 1939 with 310 against Sussex at Eastbourne. Before a record crowd of over 158,000 at Leeds in the Fourth Test match, a total of 1,723 runs were scored over the five days for the loss of only 31 wickets. Glamorgan, under the strong leadership of Wilf Wooller, were the County Champions for the first time, to everybody's surprise.

English football was in a cosy state and many of the great players were approaching veteran stage. As the new season's prospects were being discussed, it was clear that the Arsenal side which won their sixth Championship under Tom Whittaker was full of men who would shortly have to retire. Their situation was compared to Manchester United, who had played the best football in the country in the two League seasons since the war with a side, to all intents and purposes, reared locally. United had shown the way to breaking the absurd state of the transfer market by moving to producing their own players and building up their playing strength through the medium of junior sides.

There was great pre-season enthusiasm at Newcastle for their return to the First Division after 14 years. A crowd of over 30,000 watched a first team versus the reserves practice match.

In the weeks before the opening day there had been a surprising lack of activity in the matter of transfers with the main move being that of winger Bobby Langton to Preston North End from Blackburn Rovers, for over £20,000, to partner the incomparable Tom Finney on the other wing. For that reason Preston were among the favourites for the Championship along with Manchester United, everybody's choice, Derby County, Blackpool and Wolves.

Queen's Park Rangers were to carry their colours into the Second Division for the first time in their history but would face formidable opponents in the likes of Tottenham, West Brom, Sheffield Wednesday and Southampton.

The players would have to adapt to a rule change aimed at cutting out wilful obstruction, with a free-kick being the penalty for the widespread practice of 'holding off' and charging opponents when the ball was not within playing distance.

The season's opening day was marked by a shock home defeat for Manchester United as goals from Frank Broome and Reg Harrison sealed Derby's victory and gave notice of their threat. The top crowd of the day was 60,981 at Stamford Bridge where a single Roy Bentley goal for Chelsea beat Middlesbrough.

That crowd was eclipsed the following week at Highbury where 64,150 saw the visit of Manchester United. In the previous season it was just after Christmas before Arsenal met a home defeat, but now a single goal from Charlie Mitten brought a reverse in their second home outing. By the end of September 1948, another First Division ground record had been broken — Everton v Liverpool (78,299). Records were being smashed each week, a record 30,000 at Swansea, a record 14,000 at Torquay and a record 12,698 at Barrow for the visit of star attraction, Hull City.

All eyes were on the exploits of Raich Carter's Hull City in the Third Division North and when they won their first nine games, no team had ever performed that feat — 12,000 fans waited at Hull Station to greet the players on their return from Accrington. The previous record of eight games had been held by Everton, Sheffield United and the old Woolwich Arsenal. The tenth match saw the Tigers draw at Doncaster before a record Belle Vue crowd of 37,099. Two weeks later they eventually went down at home to Darlington, 2-1 before 43,801 at Boothferry Park.

Hull's record-breaking success had rested on only 12 players and Carter was determined to establish a stabilized team. "I am convinced that once a man has assumed a settled position he should be allowed to make a speciality of it. A minimum of switching and changing will produce the best results," he said.

Back in the First Division, Portsmouth had taken an early lead at the top in answer to their chairman's call for the League Championship to be won in their Jubilee year. Pompey's success was clearly down to wonderful team-work rather than individual brilliance. At this stage there were no obvious stars in a team which did not cost, all told, more than about £12,000. Highest-priced man in the team was inside-forward Bert Barlow, who was purchased from Wolves for £6,000 just before the war. The main goalscorer, Duggie Reid, cost £3,000 from Stockport County and the majority of the others, including future internationals Peter Harris, Len Phillips and Jimmy Dickinson cost only the mere £10 signing-on fee.

Derby County were unbeaten after 16 games and the inspirational work of 33-year-old Frank Broome, the former England and Aston Villa winger, in partnership with Billy Steel, was reminding the Baseball Ground fans of the vintage Carter and Doherty days. The 11 Derby players cost an average of £2,500 each, despite the heavy outlay on Steel.

Carter's successor at Derby, the young inside-forward Tommy Powell, a local lad signed for £10 during the war, was proving a great success with his scheming, and the understanding between Steel and Jack Stamps in their goalscoring moves was also instrumental in their successful season.

In an attempt to meet their players' demands, Derby had announced that all senior players may 'safeguard their future' by being given permission to take part-time jobs outside football. Senior Derby players had expressed their resentment at Steel's 'star' status in that he already had 'jobs' outside the game to bolster his income in these days of maximum wages.

One player already in such a position was Wilf Mannion who, to compensate for the loss of his £12 per week football wage, had taken a job with an Oldham building firm as an outside representative. When it was known that he also received expenses and a house, it began to look as though Mannion's great talents were lost to the game by his refusal to sign on again for Middlesbrough.

One club who had set their sights on signing Mannion was Oldham Athletic, from the lower reaches of the Third Division North, and to this end they launched a public fund. Collection boxes were passed around at their home games but after £2,000 had been raised in that way, to add to nearly £10,000 from their Shareholders' Association, the Lancashire club finally decided that the £20,000-plus required was beyond them. As the Mannion saga dragged on, it seemed as if every club in the League had been linked with him at some stage and it was with some relief that the football world learned, early in the New Year, that he had patched up his differences with Middlesbrough and re-signed.

The 16 October 1948 was a red letter day in the history of the League when the crowds numbered 1,171,732 in total — the highest ever recorded in a single day. That day brought a sell-out at Stamford Bridge where Chelsea, a magnetic crowd-pulling team but without any apparent prospect of honours, took on Blackpool. The magnet for the 78,000 fans inside and the estimated 25,000 shut out was the two brilliant Stanleys — Mortensen and Matthews — and they did not disappoint in the 3-3 draw. Shouting, disappointed fans besieged the secretary's office demanding their money back after not being able to get on to the terraces — many were allowed to sit on the dog track around the pitch.

A month later, Newcastle's visit to Highbury produced Arsenal's second home defeat and what the Press called 'the greatest shut-out in League history' when a supposed 30,000 were locked out. The 62,000 inside saw the Magpies deliver what the same newspaper called 'the decisive, if not final, chapter in the modern Arsenal saga'. With their edge and bite apparently gone, the Gunners' glamour and, indeed, their title hopes had receded. Many of their players were clearly in the 'twilight of their greatness' and it was ironic that Joe Mercer's first own-goal for 18 years decided the game.

When Denis Compton sailed for South Africa with the MCC party, Arsenal fans were resigned, mistakenly, to having seen their idol play his last game in big-time football. Compton was idolized at Highbury, more than any other player since Alex James or Ted Drake, but that season he had been a limping figure. Compton's recurring knee problems had finally reduced his speed and daintiness and all that was left was that irreplaceable enthusiasm. For all that, he still had one further part to play in the Gunners' story.

Derby County, Portsmouth and Newcastle United were by now in a thrilling race at the top of the First Division with Manchester United in close pursuit. When Derby were finally beaten in their 17th game before 64,061 at Newcastle, they thus failed to equal Arsenal's record, set the previous season, of an unbeaten run of 17 games to start a campaign. This win took Newcastle to the top at the half-way stage and they were the top attraction in the land with their personality-packed team.

Portsmouth's challenge had faltered, but their 4-1 home win over Arsenal, after a run of five games without a win, revived them, all the more so because they celebrated their Jubilee that same Saturday in November amid jubilant scenes. So keen were Pompey to show a distinguished audience what they could do on such an auspicious occasion, it would have taken an Arsenal team playing at their peak to have held them when, in fact, the Gunners all seemed to be playing with two left feet.

In the Second Division, Southampton were the team of the moment, with Fulham, West Brom and Tottenham close at hand, mainly on the back of the extraordinary goal-scoring talents of wee Charlie Wayman. He was a wizard, in his size 6½ boots, at sniffing out and taking the goal chances. He and Ted Bates (the only pre-war vintage player in their line-up) were proving to be a most capable partnership. The Saints' midfield play was outstanding with inside-left George Curtis and left-half Joe Mallett as the stars, backed up by the perfect stopper in centre-half Eric Webber.

At Craven Cottage, the Fulham challenge was also based on goalscoring talents — those of Arthur Rowley, brother of England and Manchester United's Jack, Bedford Jezzard, Arthur Stevens, and best of all at that time, Bob Thomas, a former Royal Navy champion sprinter. The Fulham side, total cost £15,000, had been astutely assembled by manager Frank Osborne.

There was disquiet among Tottenham supporters all season that disclosed assets of £160,000 were not being spent on new players to boost their bid for promotion. White Hart Lane was clearly the best

Notts County's star signing, Tommy Lawton, in action against Millwall's Walter McMillen.

ground in the country, with room for 60,000 under cover, and their massive crowds were watching a team which only included one man, Ernie Jones — £8,000 from Swansea in 1947 — who cost a fee. What those same supporters did not realize at the time was that the likes of Billy Nicholson, Ted Ditchburn and Eddie Baily were shortly to become household names, and that the club were on the brink of a great era.

A feature of the lower divisions was the goalscoring exploits of Notts County. Twice before Christmas they notched nine goals. In each of the defeats of Ipswich Town and Exeter City, Tommy Lawton bagged four and rising star Jackie Sewell also helped himself to four as poor little Exeter conceded six in one 12-minute spell. When Newport went two 'better' and conceded 11 after Christmas it meant 76 goals for the Meadow Lane club in their first 25 matches. Despite their prodigious scoring at home, the County's away record was mediocre and nothing like good enough to put them in the promotion frame.

New Year's Day was significant for Stanley Rous, the FA's secretary, who was knighted, and for Jock Dodds, whose two goals for his latest club, Lincoln City, at Tottenham took him to 400 wartime and peacetime goals. His nearest rival was Tommy Lawton with 357.

The packed terraces that season were full of humour and sheer good nature, typified by small unaccompanied youngsters being lifted bodily over the shoulders of their elders to enable them to reach the front for a better view. The on-field age of soccer chivalry was epitomized by a report from Anfield of a player who would even go to another's aid rather than score.

Some 40,000 Liverpool fans rose to salute Chelsea's Tommy Walker when their own Phil Taylor fell prostrate after a heading duel. Walker faced the choice of running on and scoring or stopping and helping — it was reported that he had no hesitation in choosing the latter.

The third round of the FA Cup included only one non-League club — Southern League Yeovil. Their exploits in the competition were to provide the biggest talking points of the whole season. Under player-manager Alec Stock, a great inspiration to his part-time players, Yeovil proceeded to knock out Bury, a good Second Division side, by 3-1 on their sloping pitch down in Somerset before 15,000 (Yeovil's population was only 19,500).

Arsenal were drawn at home to Spurs for their first-ever Cup meeting, although they had both been in the competition for 54 years. The Press built up the match as the 'Tie of the Century' but in the event so much publicity was given to the game that on the day, thousands stayed away for fear of a dangerously large attendance and another massive Highbury 'shut-out'. A relatively meagre 47,314 crowd led to a financial flop and an even greater anti-climax.

Arsenal's 3-0 win broke a run of four third-round defeats for the Gunners and the star of the show was inside-forward Jimmy Logie. Hanging well back 'Alex James style', he hypnotized the Spurs with his cultured play. The London Press reported that 'Logie played the role of Alex II to near perfection, proving an apt pupil of Professor Alex James, who had given him a Friday lecture'.

Of the other Cup favourites, Newcastle were surprisingly beaten at home by Second Division Bradford but Manchester United eased through their defence of the Cup with a home 6-0 crushing of Bournemouth.

In the next round Yeovil, too humble even for the Third Division, were drawn to entertain First Division Sunderland on their green, grassy slopes. The ground capacity was 17,000 but it was reported that there were 40,000 applicants for tickets. It was, as they say, 'a game that had everything'. An opening goal by the Yeovil player-manager Alec Stock; the nervy substitute part-time goalkeeper who gave away the equalizer; the ground mist that threatened to ruin the match; extra-time with hysterical excitement after Bryant had scored the winner a minute before the end of the first period.

There were no excuses from Sunderland and their star forwards, including Len Shackleton, were blotted out by first-time tackling. Yeovil, with only one full-time professional, were well worth their win and there was universal agreement that the eight-feet difference in the level of the ground between corner flags was no excuse for the North-East side.

The football world was intrigued by ex-Army captain Alec Stock, the former Queen's Park Rangers forward, around whom Yeovil Town had its being. An inspirational figure, but quiet-spoken and of medium height, Stock was clearly a supreme organizer whether it was involving office work, the laundry, accounting, talent spotting or tactics.

In the same round, the 'Cinderella' team of the League, Newport County, beaten 11-1 two weeks previously in the League, knocked out struggling First Division Huddersfield by 3-1 and away from home as well. The Welsh supporters were delirious and when the Newport party returned home that night they were met at the railway station by a 6,000 crowd and a police guard. The latter failed to stop goalscorers Eddie Carr and Bobb Harper being swept away and carried over the Newport Bridge by the masses before being released after a mile and a half.

On the same day, a freakish goal by Derby's Billy Steel knocked out Arsenal as their goalkeeper, George Swindin, struck his head on a post in trying to save the long-range winner.

A crowd of 82,000 at Maine Road saw 4-1 favourites Manchester United draw 1-1 with Second Division Bradford. The replay went the same way but in the third game, United handed out a five-goal thrashing which might have been 15, so heavily were Bradford overrun.

Yeovil were the next to be steam-rollered out of the FA Cup by United, 8-0, before 81,000 spectators at Maine Road. Centre-forward Jack Rowley had a field day with five goals, but Yeovil had the geat satisfaction of taking a half-share of the gate receipts of £7,141. This transpired to be more than the actual Cup winners received, for all the Football League clubs had to pay a percentage into the Cup pool.

Ten thousand Welshmen travelled to Fratton Park where Portsmouth required extra-time to beat Newport County, but not before the Welshmen had taken a 2-1 lead into the half-time break. After Len Phillips had equalized, the winning goal came five minutes from the end of extra-time from winger Jack Froggatt.

Not content with doubling Hull's gates and putting them within touching distance of the Second Division, Raich Carter, at the age of 35 one of the youngest managers in League football, had taken them into the sixth round of the FA Cup with an astonishing 2-0 win over Stoke City on the First Division club's own ground.

From the playing angle, Carter had by now moved out to the left wing where he was master-minding an outstanding away record such that after 13 trips Hull had still not been beaten. Now they were the last Third Division side left in the FA Cup. Whilst still registered as a player, Carter was not allowed more than £12 a week in wages, despite his great worth as a bright young manager.

The news from Second Division Leicester City was that one Don Revie, a 21-year-old Middlesbrough-born inside-forward who cost only £10, was one of football's most-barracked players, a man happiest playing his best football away from home. His cause with the fans was not helped by a missed penalty in the drawn fifth-round tie against Birmingham before 35,000 at Filbert Street. In the replay, Revie turned hero with the winning goal. At St Andrew's neither of the appointed linesmen made an appearance due to the late arrival of their letters of appointment. After an appeal, reminiscent of wartime football, two local referees stepped out of the crowd to fill the positions.

In the last eight in the Cup were Manchester United, Portsmouth and Derby County, three of the top four in the League but with Pompey by now three points ahead, plus Wolves, Brentford, West Brom, Leicester and Hull City.

Portsmouth and Derby County met in an epic match, before a record 51,385 crowd. With four minutes left and the score at 1-1, Ike Clarke, a 30-year-old former West Bromwich Albion centre-forward, shot the winner to seemingly put Pompey on course for a League and Cup double.

Hull's great run ended at Boothferry Park before another record crowd, this time up to 55,019. It was Stan Pearson of Manchester United who whipped in the only goal past the 28-year-old Hull goalkeeper, Billy Bly, who had played most of the match with a broken nose and concussion.

In the other quarter-finals, Brentford, the last London side, were put out by fellow Second Division strugglers Leicester City and Wolves triumphed over West Brom.

When Pompey were drawn against Leicester at Highbury, the semi-final produced a very real surprise, after the South Coast side had won four successive League games and were almost certain of the title. Pompey were complacent and ill-prepared for Leicester's breakaway game and were defeated 3-1 by a team inspired by Revie and playing well above themselves.

Leicester's brilliant performance on the day was typical of their road to Wembley, which was mostly tough-going in their role as rank outsiders. Three terrific struggles with Birmingham in the third round, then a comfortable win over Preston were followed by a fifth-round epic at Luton ending in a 5-5 draw. The replay was just as pulsating with Leicester going through 5-3. The sixth round saw them beat Brentford before they lowered Pompey's colours.

The other semi-final, involving Wolves and Manchester United at Hillsborough, was drawn after extra-time with the Midlanders disorganized by two crippling injuries to Pritchard and Kelly.

In the replay at Goodison Park, Wolves triumphed in a tense struggle and denied United the chance to become the first team of the century

Peter Harris in action for Portsmouth against Arsenal in Pompey's Golden Jubilee match.

to win the Cup two years running. The winner had the 72,500 fans arguing for weeks about its legality. Jesse Pye was apparently yards offside before making the opportunity for Sammy Smyth to score. For all that, it was no more than Wolves, and in particular Billy Wright, who played one of his greatest games, deserved. Their little winger, Johnny Hancocks, had been a great threat with two searing shots from 30 yards, both of which caused the crossbar to quiver violently. The Press enthused about 'that lad Billy Wright — the complete footballer who should be in the England team until his beard is white'.

The surprise of Leicester's appearance at Wembley as a struggling Second Division side of so little significance was evidenced by their only succeeding subsequently in avoiding relegation by a single point. Their hopes, if they had any, in the Final were dashed in advance by the 11th-hour loss of Don Revie, their most effective forward, due to a nose haemorrhage. To compensate, Leicester manager Johnny Duncan gambled by moving full-back Jim Harrison to centre-forward with Jack Lee, the regular leader, moving to inside-right to replace Revie.

Under Stan Cullis, in his first season as manager, the Wolves' plan centred on their fiery wingers, Jimmy Mullen on the left and short, spry Johnny Hancocks on the right, making the chances for goal-happy strikers Jessie Pye and Sammy Smyth. For their part, Leicester had to rely on the thrust and skills of winger Mal Griffiths and the bulldozing efforts of big inside-left Ken Chisholm.

In the event it was an uninspiring Final in which the flashpoint came a quarter of an hour after the interval with Wolves leading 2-1. After two goals from Pye had put Wolves well in front, Griffiths pulled one back after the restart and then Chisholm cruelly had an 'equalizer' controversially discounted for offside. It knocked all the heart out of the underdogs and from the free-kick, the red-haired Irishman Smyth beat three men in a mazy dribble to score the decisive third goal for the Wolves past the Leicester reserve goalkeeper, Bradley.

As far as the Press was concerned, Wolves' skipper Billy Wright — 'a human dynamo in defence and attack' — was the man of the match and by his performance alone carried the right to collect the Cup from Princess Elizabeth.

During the last quarter of the League season the race for the title had been led increasingly by Portsmouth, with Derby County, Manchester United and Newcastle United trailing behind. Pompey stormed to the title — from the day they collapsed in that fateful semi-final their football was irresistible. And never more so than a demolition of close rivals Newcastle on Tyneside by five clear goals — all headers.

The Championship was won by five clear points in Pompey's Jubilee season, to the great delight of the Club's president, Field-Marshal Montgomery, who received the trophy at Fratton Park, and manager Bob Jackson. The players had been continually exhorted by the famous soldier, either in person or by letter, and like his troops in an earlier campaign they did not dare resist. Pompey captain Reg Flewin remembered that at Christmas, Montgomery had written to him in characteristic phraseology that it would be a good idea 'to hit Chelsea for six' in the next home game. The team carried out his instructions to the letter.

Pompey's greatest attribute was their team spirit and Jack Froggatt's greatest memory was the comradeship — "We were always good friends, always stuck together". Built on the rock of an unpretentious half-back line — the fierce tackling Jimmy Scoular (once described as 'another Wilf Copping'), the experienced Reg Flewin, and the composed Jimmy Dickinson — Pompey were formidable in attack that season. Peter Harris was a fast-raiding winger and one of the discoveries of the season, Duggie Reid, had a fearsome shot. Big strong Jack Froggatt provided the left-wing thrust. The goals were shared out — Harris 17, Read 17, Froggatt and centre-forward Clarke 14. Even the creative and talented Len Phillips managed to score 11.

There was a tight struggle for the runners-up spot with Manchester United winning on goal-average to mean a third successive second place for United over a Derby side who had been a model of consistency in post-war football. The 13 goals in the same number of matches from Johnny Morris, including two hat-tricks, ensured the high placing for the Rams. Derby had broken the British transfer record

Cheerful Leicester City supporters at the 1949 FA Cup Final.

Wolves' Jesse Pye turns away after heading the first goal against Leicester at Wembley.

yet again when they signed Morris from Manchester United for £24,500 in March 1949.

Manchester United made the runners-up spot solely on the strength of a magnificent penalty save by goalkeeper Jack Crompton from Duggie Reid of Portsmouth in the final minutes of their last match, to ensure their vital 3-2 win. To add to United's pleasure, a petition by their supporters to the Ministry of Works for permission to rebuild the blitzed Old Trafford ground had been granted with a permit for 'the minimum necessary to bring the ground back into use'. As the season ended, United captain Johnny Carey was voted 'Footballer of the Year' by the Football Writers' Association.

At the end of the First Division table there was a desperate struggle against relegation between some of the most famous clubs in the land — Everton amongst them. They looked doomed early on but a succession of heavy defeats was arrested by the appointment of former player and England international Cliff Britton. Under his inspired management the defence, with the incomparable veteran Ted Sagar in goal and the artistic Tommy Jones at centre-half, stopped up the leaks. Everton provided evidence of the dearth of young players entering the game with eight players whose aggregate service actually exceeded 100 years.

The axe finally fell on Sheffield United and Preston North End. To the despair of the latter, the irreplaceable Tom Finney had been injured for a significant part of the season and the prospect of the star England forward playing in the Second Division led to a burst of transfer speculation. Finney's loyalty to North End was to be severely tested but in the end he was persuaded to stay.

In the Second Division the uncertainty of the game was never better exemplified than by Southampton. The Saints were set fair for promotion at Easter — with only six games left to play they were leading the division by eight points. In the course of beating Tottenham, one of their strongest challengers at the time, at White Hart Lane, Charlie Wayman, their centre-forward and leading scorer with 32 goals, pulled a muscle badly.

Wayman's absence for the remaining fixtures showed how much Southampton had relied on his marksmanship — a clear case of putting nearly all their eggs in one basket. In those last six games the Saints secured only two points and when they had completed their fixtures they were dependent on West Brom losing their last two matches. On the last day of the season the men from The Dell were pipped on the post by both Fulham, who popped out of the blue to pinch the table-topping spot, and West Brom.

For Fulham it was promotion for the first time since joining the Football League 41 years previously and a triumph for 52-year old Frank Osborne, of team spirit over the chequebook. Arthur Rowley, with 19 goals, was the bargain of the season and centre-half Jim Taylor was tipped, correctly as it transpired, for an England cap. Captain Pat Beasley, left-half and former Arsenal star, was a great inspiration and hero to the Craven Cottage fans who regularly numbered over 30,000 that term.

The star of the drive for promotion at The Hawthorns was Irish international Dave Walsh with 23 goals. Another to gain rave reviews was inside-forward Ray Barlow, later to move to the half-back line and be capped for England.

Still in the Second Division, Nottingham Forest were considered to be the unluckiest team of the year, losing almost 20 games by the odd goal but still being relegated to the Third Division along with Lincoln City. Swansea were outright winners of the Third Division South with a quite remarkable unbeaten home record with 20 of the 21 matches won and a 60-goal tally largely prompted from midfield by Welsh international captain Roy Paul.

As far as the manager of the season was concerned, there was only one candidate — Raich Carter, who in his first season in management had taken Hull City into the Second Division — pipping Rotherham for the Third North title; to the sixth round of the FA Cup; in the process more than doubling the gates at the new Boothferry Park; and given the Tigers an aura of glamour never previously or since identified with the Humberside club.

The season had been marked by a continuous volume of transfers funded by the record profits announced by many of the clubs and climaxed with the record £24,500 paid for inside-forward Johnny Morris by Derby County to Manchester United in March. The availability of Morris prompted an unseemly scramble for his signature with a reported 20 clubs in the hunt. The same amount was the combined fee paid by Newcastle United for the Chilean brothers, George and Ted Robledo, from Barnsley in the spring.

According to the Press reports this unparalleled transfer activity left the game 'seething with discontent' and there were strong suggestions, not for the first time, that there were widespread breaches of the rules. Equally, many clubs were disturbed at soaring transfer fees and there were demands from some quarters for limitations of some form. It seemed as though hardly a day of the season had passed without a significant transfer being announced at a fee above or approaching £10,000 and the lower division clubs were not exempt.

Inevitably, there was much talk as to how the players should draw a greater share in the game's profits. The alternatives centred around either increased wages, a share of transfer fees or increased talent money. The talent money, which, typically, could only be paid at the discretion of the clubs themselves, amounted to £550 per team for top place, i.e. £50 for each player, with £440 for second, £330 for third and £220 for fourth in the First and Second Divisions. When profits of the order of £20,000 plus were being recorded by the top clubs, the maximum payment of £550 seemed far from adequate. When 99,500 people paid £39,100 to see the England-Scotland international at Wembley, the share of the 22 players concerned was exactly £20 per man (£11 after tax) — just over one per cent of the total gate.

It came as no surprise when a new attendance record was set in that Diamond Jubilee season — the number of people who attended League matches alone reached the never surpassed total of 41,271,424. The respective average attendances in the First, Second, Third South and Third North Divisions were 38,000, 24,450, 15,240 and 10,400. Amongst the factors which contributed, aside from the game's universal appeal, were the improved transport links, the rising standard of living, the concentrations of population and the generally shorter working hours.

No less impressive was the popularity of the amateur game, evidenced by over 90,000 people paying over £20,000 to see Bromley beat Romford at Wembley in the FA Amateur Cup Final. Soon, clubs like Bishop Auckland and Pegasus would become almost household names, such was their fame outside the League.

Even in Wales, in the strongholds of Rugby Union, there was a definite swing-over to soccer. While Cardiff RFC were drawing crowds of 9,000, Second Division Cardiff City were having no trouble in attracting 36,000 and it was a similar story at Swansea.

It was a significant season as far as the England captaincy was concerned and Billy Wright, the new international star and clearly one of the 'players of the season', succeeded Frank Swift, who announced his retirement at the end of the season and often said that a goalkeeper was not the best person to captain a side.

Wright, at the age of 24, three years after his League debut and two years after his first cap, led England out for the first time at Belfast in early season where, with Matthews magnificent, a 6-2 win was highlighted by a Mortensen hat-trick. It was typical of the modern player at that time that Wright learned of his selection as captain whilst travelling on a bus and at that time he was still in 'digs' in Wolverhampton.

The moment had come that season for Tommy Lawton to be discarded as England's centre-forward when it was clear that many of the outstanding qualities that had won him renown and a sure place as leader of the attack since 1939 were rapidly dwindling, hastened by his playing in the Third Division. His successor, Jackie Milburn, became the first Newcastle player to play for England since Duggie Wright in 1939.

The season also saw the debut of Alf Ramsey, then of Southampton, at right-back at Highbury in a convincing 6-0 win over Switzerland, with West Bromwich Albion's Jack Haines — in his first and only international — scoring twice.

The April 1949 England-Scotland game at Wembley was remembered for a once-in-a-lifetime display by the tiny Morton goalkeeper Jimmy Cowan, who broke the spirit of the England forwards with his acrobatics. Scotland confounded the experts with their memorable 3-1 win and the only Anglo-Scot in the team, 5ft 3in tall Billy Steel, was the outfield star scoring the decisive second goal.

When the Football Association decided to undertake an ambitious tour at the end of the season, through Scandinavia, Holland and France, Walter Winterbottom, the England team manager, was anxious to introduce some younger players to replace some of his pre-war veterans. One such was Jimmy Dickinson of Portsmouth, another Johnny Morris of Derby, as reward for their outstanding seasons, with Bert Williams of Wolves replacing Swift in goal.

Reflecting on the season it was apparent that the football, in terms of sheer artistry and skill, had not returned to the pre-war level and had not yet recovered from the long interruption caused by seven years of war. Despite the lack of technical merit, however, there was no doubt that the game was faster with a greater concentration of thrills. It was a surprise to note that the goalscoring took a sharp downward trend — dropping to 2.84 goals per match.

No longer could wartime conditions be blamed for the lack of ideas and the lack of real coaching was put down as the main reason. The evidence was found in how far European football had progressed in the period, often under the guidance of exported English coaches. Sweden, the Olympic football champions, were displaying a scientific type of football — almost unknown in England — under coach George Raynor. In this country, management technique was almost entirely built upon assembling 12 or 13 technically good players and then giving them a free reign to express their ability on the pitch. Little thought was given to defensive play and the only tactical planning concerned the outwitting of the opposing defence and the scoring of goals.

The next season, however, was to see the advent of a new style — 'push and run' — introduced most successfully and attractively from a most unexpected source, to herald the rise of one of the country's great club sides — the source Arthur Rowe, the club Tottenham Hotspur.

Pompey Chimes Again

W ITH the rich harvest of the driest summer on record yet to be fully gathered in and the County Cricket Championship still to be decided, the players and spectators on the opening day of the 1949-50 season were greeted with bone-hard pitches, temperatures in the 80s, and the knowledge that the steady decline in goalscoring was giving cause for concern. *The Times* 'Association Football Correspondent' wondered whether the answer lay in bringing stimulus to attack by tinkering once more with the offside law or by a revolutionary upheaval of the field markings, 'so as to entice the defensive centre-half from his lair'.

The same correspondent concluded that the point had been reached where speed had outrun skill. 'Less speed, fresh tactical surprise in attack and a new outlook — there lies the solution. There is no real dearth of skill, but much of it is merely being misapplied.'

For all the cries of the purists, concerned with the emphasis on defence, football, as an integral part of the national way of life, had achieved a pinnacle during the previous season. With its big names and high excitement, it had clearly struck a chord at all levels of society and enjoyed unrivalled popularity as the winter game both for players and spectators. It now embodied the limited but essentially decent side of traditional masculine working-class culture.

In the summer game the Test series against New Zealand was inconclusive, with all four games drawn. Denis Compton and Len Hutton were amongst the runs in high-scoring games on hard sun-baked pitches. In the end, Yorkshire and Glamorgan tied for the County Championship with 192 points each — the first tie since 1889.

The hot weather had led to the reimposition of milk rationing in view of a consequent decline in production. In some compensation, the cheese ration had been increased from 1½ to 2oz per week.

The summer had seen the death of Will Hay, for years one of Britain's most popular comedians. The country had heard of the first and successful test flight of the new De Havilland Comet jet airliner. There was a sign of things to come when it was disclosed that colour television had been perfected in the USA after ten years' research.

Industrial troubles had come to the fore with the London Docks strike. A state of emergency had been declared in July 1949 with troops employed after 11,000 men and 121 ships were idle. Interestingly, at that time 263,000 were registered as unemployed, calculated as 1.3 per cent of the population.

In the coming season, a February 1950 General Election saw Labour returned to power with its majority cut to five seats. Within weeks of their return, the end of petrol rationing was finally announced.

In football circles, the main interest in the close season centred on the appointment of the Royal Commission on Betting which had raised once again the whole question of football pools. The Football Association had made it clear that they were opposed to all forms of betting on football. In the event the Commission, not surprisingly, recognized that the Pools had probably come to stay and emphasized that there was no evidence that the Pools had the slightest influence on the results of matches. As now, however, there were many in the game who took the view that the control of the vast sums of money involved — then estimated at £60 million annually — should be taken out of private hands and the surplus used for the benefit of football or sport in general.

As the new season opened, the highest expectations surrounded Wolves and Manchester United. Wolves were feared as a young and virile side, with the ubiquitous Billy Wright and one of the finest forward lines in the country. Every man was capable of a bagful of goals, with young centre-forward Dennis Wilshaw making a meteoric rise to stardom in the previous season.

Manchester United gained many admirers in the post-war years under Matt Busby, but the view was propounded that their older players might feel the strain in the new campaign. Portsmouth, the Champions, were still underrated, almost certainly by virtue of their unfashionable status and lack of star names.

Blackpool were fancied to recapture their 1947-8 glory, particularly as Matthews appeared to have recovered from the injury-ridden spells of the previous season and Mortensen was looking to rediscover his old fire. Blackpool's famous mascot, the duck with tangerine wings, reappeared on the opening day, after the original animal had been killed by a dog at the previous season's end. Newcastle United were a team with youth, strength and virility, with Milburn the new star and George Robledo adding further punch to the attack.

In the Second Division all eyes were on Tottenham Hotspur, Southampton, Sheffield Wednesday and Hull City. The Third Division had shown that it was no longer a home for lost souls. With the new-found money in the game, the less fashionable brethren had been able to attract distinguished players. That great tactician, Raich Carter, had transformed Hull City; Lawton had been with Notts County for over two years; and now Peter Doherty had gone from Huddersfield to Doncaster Rovers as player-manager; Freddie Steele from Stoke had taken up a similar appointment at Mansfield, and one Bill Shankly from Preston had taken up his first managerial appointment at Carlisle.

As early evidence of his flair for public relations, Shankly introduced a policy of broadcasting to the crowd at Brunton Park prior to a game, mainly to encourage their support and to discount rumours.

While Football League clubs were finding their level, the main focus in the first half of the season was centred on the home international matches. There was something extra at stake, for the winner and runner-up in the Championship would qualify for the competition proper of the Jules Rimet Cup — the World Cup — to be held in Brazil the following July.

A curiosity in the days before the big kick-off was the transfer request of Leon Leuty of Derby, England's number-two centre-half. What was curious was that Neil Franklin, the number one, was also seeking a move from Stoke City.

On the opening day, 1,140,000 people sweltered in the summer heat with the first-aid men working overtime. Portsmouth carried on where they had left off at the end of the previous season by hitting three at Newcastle for their first win. Before the day's biggest crowd of 50,000, at Highbury, Arsenal's Don Roper missed a penalty before Burnley's Billy Morris scored a surprise winning goal. Similarly, George Hardwick of Middlesbrough had a penalty saved by Everton's Ted Sagar to ensure an away win for the Toffeemen.

It was a highly significant day for Manchester United as 41,748 spectators greeted their return to Old Trafford after an eight-year absence. Charlie Mitten had the honour of scoring the first goal in their 3-0 win over neighbours Bolton Wanderers.

In the Third Division, player-manager Doherty marked his debut for Doncaster with a point-saving goal. The Rovers' players were trying out a new type of boot — canvas tops with studs and bars moulded on rubber soles, making it half the weight of an ordinary boot. Later in the season the Football Association asked the Boot Trades Research Association to design a lighter boot suited to the hard grounds to be encountered in Brazil.

The healthy old British shoulder-charge on goalkeepers in possession of the ball became the subject of much debate, largely over the inconsistent interpretation of the rule. The Press were calling for the charge to be scrapped and for us to follow the Continentals by posting the label 'with care — fragile' on all goalkeepers.

Typical of the situation was the Fulham-Chelsea game in early season when a goal was allowed after Gray, the Chelsea left winger, had charged Fulham 'keeper Kelly whilst the latter was in the air with both feet off the ground with the ball caught. The next second Kelly was felled by the aerial charge and the ball was in the net. Later in the game Rowley, the Fulham centre-forward, put his 14st

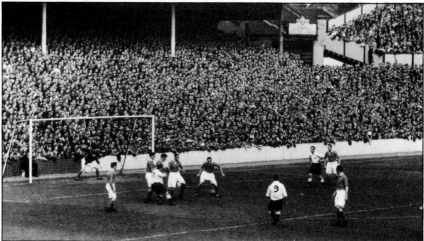

Tottenham's Len Duquemin fires a free-kick at the Bury defensive wall during Spurs' 3-1 win at White Hart Lane in September 1949, before 54,348 fans.

Seven months later, Spurs clinched the Second Division title with a 2-0 win over QPR at Loftus Road. Here Reg Allen, the QPR goalkeeper, is beaten by a shot from Duquemin but the ball went wide of the post.

into a perfect shoulder-charge on Medhurst, the Chelsea 'keeper, who was also in possession of the ball. Medhurst went down and the astounded Rowley was penalized to highlight the complete inconsistency.

Wolves confirmed their favourite status by making a storming start. After winning at Derby County, before a Baseball Ground record crowd of 37,652, the Wolves were finally beaten in their next match at Old Trafford, their 13th, in front of a crowd of 51,427. This left them three points ahead of Liverpool, the only unbeaten team in the League. Such was the attraction of the Wolves at that time that they also attracted a record 50,248 to Fratton Park, Portsmouth, shortly afterwards for a 1-1 draw.

The big four in the early months of the season were Wolves, Spurs, Notts County and Doncaster Rovers. As Spurs raced ahead at the top of the Second Division, several in their ranks were earning rave reviews and being tipped for international honours — such as Ted Ditchburn in goal, Alf Ramsey at full-back, Len Duquemin at centre-forward and even 28-year-old left winger Les Medley was not out of the reckoning.

After Spurs had put seven past Sheffield United, with right winger Sonny Walters grabbing three, and gone six points clear at the top of the table, the London Press were ecstatic and were asking: 'Is this the best-ever Spurs side?' Manager Arthur Rowe, who saw the 1921 Cup-winning team in action, felt however that only in goal, at left-back and centre-half were that 1949-50 side their equals.

Even full-back Alf Ramsey performed a party-piece at Grimsby when he scored a remarkable and rare goal by dribbling and feinting his way from the half-way line to the six-yard line before scoring.

Spurs had lain dormant and forgotten in the Second Division since the war but the arrival of Rowe as manager changed their history and laid the foundation of the great and smooth sides of the 1960s. Captain Ron Burgess was a shrewd reader of the game and the quick, interchangeing forward line of Walters, Bennett, Duquemin, Baily and Medley were primed on the factor of moving the ball quickly to an unmarked colleague. It was superb to watch and the side was never static.

Tucked in behind Spurs were newly-promoted Hull City, thanks mainly to the goals of their Danish international centre-forward Viggo Jensen and, of course, inspirational 36-year-old player-manager Raich Carter. It was felt that his extraordinary talents had ruined the international chances of QPR goalkeeper Reg Allen when, before the selectors, Carter had shot two stunning goals past Allen with instinctive left-foot volleys.

The Press report said it all: 'Carter may have silver hair but he played like an artist not a day over 26. He is not only good enough for England but would make the ideal captain. Carter commanded the Shepherds Bush match — he was the complete boss. Chewing gum for the entire 90 minutes he marched — in fact strutted — through the game.'

When Notts County went six points clear at the top of the Third Division South, it was largely due to the all-round talents and goals of Lawton and also his great captaincy. Such was his command of the team and the respect he had gained that Lawton, like Carter, was the subject of speculation over a possible recall to the England team and possible installation as captain.

Under Lawton's inspired leadership, and often before crowds of over 30,000 at Meadow Lane, County's forward line — former Derby man Broome, Sewell, Lawton, Evans and Johnston — had been welded into one of the most formidable attacking combinations in the League, under the managership of Eric Houghton.

The 'cold-war' over conditions in professional football continued with the publication, in October 1949, of the Players' Union suggestions to the Football Association and Football League on the sore points of the transfer system, the maximum wage, non-compulsory benefits and contracts which tied a man to one club indefinitely. Such was the Union's militant stance that a 'closed-shop' policy was adopted.

Typical of the clubs' dictatorial attitude to their players was the coincidental announcement by Derby County that 'all future transfer requests will be automatically refused, and if a player attempts to force the club's hand by not giving of his best, he will be dropped to the Reserves.' Players' Union chairman Jimmy Guthrie retorted: "In no other job is a man tied for life. If a footballer serves his club faithfully during the period of his contract he should have the right to ask for a change of club."

One of the many players looking to supplement their income at that time was Eddie Quigley, who had joined Sheffield Wednesday from Bury in October 1947. After Wednesday had refused to find him a job outside football and made it clear that they would not act as an employment agency for their players, unlike some clubs, Quigley was made available for transfer. The situation mirrored the frequency of part-time employment by even famous and highly-paid names. The outcome was, after the usual scramble, that Quigley was transferred to Preston North End for £26,000 to make him the new 'Golden Boy' of soccer.

In the same month of October, Leicester's Don Revie was available and, just when it seemed his transfer to Arsenal was imminent, it was announced he had joined Carter's Hull City for £19,000.

The South African FA were becoming concerned over the poaching of their star amateurs by English First Division clubs, of whom Charlton headed the list having picked up five for a total of £1,000, the price of their fares to England. The five were soon valued at £65,000, with two of them, inside-right Syd O'Linn and right-half Dudley Forbes, in the team which beat Newcastle United 6-3 at The Valley.

As Christmas approached, Liverpool went to the top of the First Division after registering 18 games in a row without defeat — the finest opening sequence in the top division for 50 years. They aimed for the achievement of Sheffield United, who in 1889-90 were unbeaten until the 23rd match. As before, Liverpool's record was built around their solid defence and the brilliant individualism of Liddell and Stubbins. Their colours were lowered in their 20th game by humble Huddersfield — 17th in the table — thanks to a winning goal a minute from time by tiny Irishman John McKenna.

Blackpool, Manchester United and Portsmouth were in challenging positions. The Champions, Pompey, were getting into the groove again and their match-winning qualities were still strongly in evidence — the thoughtful through-passing of Dickinson and Scoular; the complete domination of Flewin; and the superlative wing-play and goals of Harris and Froggatt. Harris had even stepped into the shoes of the greatest outside-right of the time, Stanley Matthews, for his international debut against the Republic of Ireland that autumn.

Somewhat overshadowed by the exploits of their North London rivals, Arsenal seemed to have found a goalscoring centre-forward, to fill the position vacated by Rooke, in young Peter Goring, newly converted from wing-half. The Gunners had also recruited winger Freddie Cox from Spurs but at the turn of the year, the 'top of the pops' at Highbury was 29-year-old Reg Lewis. After 12 years with Arsenal he had found his true position at inside-left and nine goals came in the same number of games.

Life, they say, begins at 40. No one in the Arsenal ranks was quite 40 but it was not to be long for some. For all that Arsenal were still difficult to beat, with the main obstacles being big Leslie Compton at centre-half and evergreen Joe Mercer alongside him. Nevertheless, the Gunners still remained the major crowd-pullers and evidence of that came when their biggest post-war crowd, 67,000, saw a titanic clash with Derby, won by a single goal from Logie.

Christmas holiday games were a tale of closed gates, shut-out crowds and all-time attendance records. Bang went the Football League record on Boxing Day as 1,226,039 surged through the turnstiles, exactly 58,652 more than the record set up on 16 October 1948. Within 24 hours that record was smashed as crowds totalled 1,253,572 and thousands were locked out at Villa Park, Highbury and Bramall Lane, Sheffield. Hundreds of fans broke into the Chesterfield ground at the Spion Kop End for the visit of Spurs and hordes of Wolves fans stood outside the Villa ground listening to running commentaries from over the walls by sympathetic ones inside.

Arsenal defend in numbers. Leslie Compton is beaten to a high ball by Derby County centre-forward Jack Stamps but there are still three Gunners' defenders on the goal-line. Arsenal won this game at Highbury in October 1950 by 3-1. A crowd of 64,750 watched.

There were still more attendance records broken — 19,104 at Northampton in the Third Division South for the visit of Nottingham Forest as the two teams jockeyed for position at the top, and 34,251 at Bristol Rovers' Eastville ground for the local derby with City, whose £10,000 signing from Newcastle, George Lowrie, scored the winner. City had apparently spent the previous week 'training' at a Somerset fruit farm where, equipped with sacks, they had helped out with the picking under manager Bob Wright.

In the same division, Watford were stranded in mid-table and in an effort to stimulate things the board of directors created some sort of record by buying five Leicester City reserves in one day. The following Saturday there were seven new players in the first team, but within a year five of the purchases had been released on free transfers.

The spectre of hooliganism was growing with reports from Plymouth of the referee being menaced as he left the field and their own goalkeeper, Bill Shortt, being laid out with a stone after Leeds United had been awarded a penalty. From Millwall there was obscene chanting and booing directed towards Lawton when Notts County were visitors. The Den's reputation was not enhanced when a hostile crowd of about 150 waited for the referee and linesmen outside the ground and greeted them with abuse and missiles after a contentious first-round FA Cup tie against Exeter. In the main, however, it had to be said that these were isolated incidents in the general feeling of *bonhomie* surrounding the game.

The amateur player in the League had all but disappeared but when Brentford caused a surprise by taking a point from Spurs, one of the main contributors was Dr Kevin O'Flanagan. A Corinthian type who held Irish caps at soccer and rugby, O'Flanagan also played golf, tennis, gaelic football and did the long-jump in his spare time. After O'Flanagan accidentally knocked-out Winter of Chelsea in an encounter, he promptly set to and rendered first-aid to prove what an asset a footballer-doctor was.

To stand a chance of being selected regularly for a League side, the time had come when the amateur had to become a full-time professional. The greater fitness and speed of the professional had now been clearly demonstrated — few amateurs could reach such standards.

As the third round of the FA Cup approached in January 1950 it included the name of Nuneaton Borough, the first Birmingham Combination side to reach that stage for 56 years. For the first time ever, one of the clubs, Chelsea, proposed to raise admission prices for their tie, against Brentford, and the Football Association upheld their decision.

In the event all three non-League clubs — Yeovil, Weymouth and Nuneaton — were knocked-out immediately and the big-time clubs had the jitters. Birmingham, Stoke, Huddersfield and Manchester City were among the casualties and at Plymouth, Cup holders Wolves were saved with a scrambled goal by Smyth a few minutes from the end. At Highbury, Arsenal scraped home against ten-man Sheffield Wednesday, thanks to a last-minute goal by Reg Lewis. Portsmouth were initially held at home by Third Division Norwich before winning the replay and, similarly, Preston drew with Watford from the same division and then surprisingly lost the replay. However, at Oldham before 41,000, Newcastle were rattling in seven, with Milburn scoring a hat-trick.

The next round ended the Wembley dreams of Newcastle, Middlesbrough and Sunderland from the North East and it looked like London's Cup year. Arsenal, Chelsea and Spurs romped into the fifth round but Manchester United were still the favourites. This was reinforced by a superb 3-1 replay win over Portsmouth at Fratton Park before nearly 50,000 and, coincidentally, United were also at the top of the First Division on goal-average from Liverpool.

The sixth round, however, brought United's demise when, before 70,362 at Chelsea's Stamford Bridge, goals from Campbell and Bentley knocked them out. With Arsenal, Chelsea, Liverpool and Everton in the semi-final, it was a London versus Liverpool affair. Modest Everton were the surprise team after knocking-out Spurs and fancied Derby.

The draw, however, paired the London and Liverpool teams separately to ensure the rivalry would be repeated in the Final.

This was the year when the slogan 'Lucky Arsenal' was heard in the land. In every match, from the third to the sixth round, the Gunners were drawn at home and they travelled only 13½ miles to reach the Final. In the fifth round they took a bold gamble by restoring Denis Compton to the outside-left position and he proved to be their 'lucky mascot' from then on. Despite the fact that he had put on weight and was said to be troubled by a knee injury, Compton, in his last season in football, finished in a blaze of glory, providing dash and enthusiasm right through to the final whistle at Wembley.

The semi-final against Chelsea at Tottenham found Arsenal down to two smash-and-grab goals in the first half by Roy Bentley. Then, with the whistle just about to sound for half-time, Freddie Cox, who had joined Arsenal from Spurs earlier in the season, took a corner which, helped by a gust of wind, twisted directly into the roof of the net. The equalizing goal for the Arsenal came from the Comptons' 'double act' 14 minutes from time. Denis took a corner on the left and signalled his brother Les to come up. Disobeying captain Mercer's orders, Leslie trotted upfield and arrived in time to head home.

The replay, again at Tottenham before 65,000, was won for Arsenal by Freddie Cox in extra-time with a low shot after a great run into the penalty area. The rabbit's foot in the pocket of the shorts of each Chelsea player had not brought any luck for the superstitious team.

Curiously, the semi-finals were held seven days apart and the following Saturday it was Liverpool's turn to win through against their Merseyside rivals before 72,000 at Maine Road, Manchester. Despite Liverpool's smooth, streamlined play, it took two freak goals to put them through. After Everton goalkeeper Burnett had punched clear, half-back Bob Paisley lobbed a high-spinning ball into the goalmouth and it swerved under the bar into the net. The second, by Billy Liddell, was a gift after Everton's Wainwright had passed the ball back into his own goalmouth.

Liverpool's strength, as previously, centred on their magnificent middle line — captain Phil Taylor, Bill Jones and Bob Paisley — but Liddell on the left and Baron on the right were the danger-men.

As now, there were strong complaints about the allocation of Wembley tickets for the Finalists. Liverpool had 100,000 chasing 8,000 three-shilling Cup Final tickets, so a draw was organized and applicants who lived 25 miles or more outside the city were barred.

The Final itself provided fewer thrills than expected from two such highly-rated teams. Liverpool were lying second and Arsenal seventh in the top division. Arsenal, although famed for their defence, had netted 72 League goals, recently scoring six against Stoke City, with another four against Newcastle.

There was nothing lucky about Arsenal's performance in their 2-0 win at Wembley. Not one team member showed any sign of nerves and their only special plan was that the wingers should play on the touch-line to open up the midfield for Lewis and Goring. The plan worked to perfection and Lewis rounded it off with two exquisitely taken goals. Liverpool's Liddell was a marked man and Arsenal's victory under the veteran Mercer was in no small measure due to their mastery over the star winger.

In the same month there were happenings which symbolized the fight which British footballers were making for their own freedom of action. A number of players were tempted to travel to South America, and Chile in particular, by the offer of massive signing-on fees and guaranteed contracts of the order of £3,500 per season.

Two Stoke City footballers shocked the British soccer world by closing their homes and flying off with their families to Bogota. One of them was England's centre-half Neil Franklin, the other was George Mountford, an outside-right or centre-forward. Very shortly they were followed by others — Charlie Mitten of Manchester United, Bobby Flavell of Hearts and Billy Higgins of Everton. Roy Paul of Swansea and Jack Hedley of Everton were reported to have gone to South America, but returned without signing.

Those who stayed in Colombia were quickly aware that war was the name of the game, when they saw the barbed wire around the pitches and armed sentries in the ground with rifles at the ready. Franklin's and Mitten's stays were short-lived and long-regretted.

Springtime in 1950 found Matt Busby's Manchester United level pegging with Liverpool at the top of the First Division but Blackpool, Portsmouth and Sunderland were chasing hard. As the season drew to a close, United faltered decisively and Liverpool appeared to find the pressure of going for a League and Cup double — last achieved 53 years earlier by Aston Villa — too much for them. At first, Sunderland slipped into a short-head lead at Easter as it became clear that the Championship battle was to be the hottest affair for years and anybody's race.

At a critical time in that race, the Scotland-England international was played and on the same day a full League programme was staged and clubs lost vital players. Blackpool lost Mortensen, Liverpool the services of match-winner Liddell and Manchester United, who were at home to Portsmouth in a crucial fixture, lost their defensive stalwart John Aston. That Saturday, at the end of April, saw Pompey win at Old Trafford while Sunderland were losing at home to bottom-placed Manchester City. Only one point separated the top four as Pompey went top for the first time.

The defeat for Sunderland was even more surprising as City had failed to win any of their last 18 away games. A feature of the game

Liverpool goalkeeper Cyril Sidlow and his fellow defenders get in a tangle during the 1950 FA Cup Final against Arsenal.

The Gunners' inside-left Reg Lewis puts Arsenal ahead at Wembley.

was two penalty saves by City's former German prisoner-of-war and paratrooper Bernhard (known as Bert) Trautmann from Sunderland's Stelling.

Almost a month earlier, Tottenham had clinched promotion to Division One with an unassailable 11-point lead and two games in hand. They were Champions by a street but their promotion companions were not to be decided until the last day of the season in a stirring three-cornered duel between the two Sheffield clubs, Wednesday and United, and Southampton.

White Hart Lane attendances topped 50,000 on 15 occasions as Spurs ended their 15-year exile in Division Two. In all, over 1.5 million fans came through the Tottenham turnstiles that season, a record for the club which will never be broken. Eighty-one goals were scored, 35 conceded and Arthur Rowe, who was in the Spurs side relegated 15 years previously, became a great hero in 1950, and a living legend one year later. In the end they won the title by nine points. Basically, Spurs played the game in triangles, always giving the man with the ball a passing option. Defenders became attackers, attackers became defenders. Ted Ditchburn had a major tactical part as well and his throws to Alf Ramsey to retain possession became an eye-catching feature. They were a magnificent team playing magnificent football.

There was an amusing incident at White Hart Lane on the afternoon of the presentation of the Second Division championship shield to Spurs. They were playing Grimsby in the last home match and the Mariners were holding a 2-1 lead when the shield, which had been propped against the side of the directors' box, toppled over with a resounding crash. It was viewed as a bad omen by some gloomy spectators in the vicinity and so it proved next season — but for the other members of the First Division.

In an interesting sideshow at that juncture, the schoolboy international between England and Scotland at Wembley was notable, not only for England's 8-2 victory but also for the hat-trick by 'man of the match', one Johnny Haynes, who it was reported 'strolled through the game with the nonchalance of an experienced campaigner, despite being the smallest player afield'. The report showed that he had signed amateur forms for Spurs.

The competition for the First Division title was close but so was that for the honour of accompanying Spurs from Division Two. Leeds United, Hull City and both Sheffield teams, were leading the pack but Southampton put themselves in the picture by beating both Sheffield clubs within a week. The key factor for the Saints was the return of Wayman, just as his absence the previous season had been critical. Then, as has been related, the Saints needed only eight points to ensure promotion but in fact only secured five. Sheffield United's chances of promotion were boosted by the return of key figure Jimmy

*Arsenal players parade the FA Cup through the streets on North London after their 2-0
victory over Liverpool.*

Hagan after an absence of 11 League games and in his first game
back he netted the winner against Spurs with only a minute left,
before 42,000 at Bramall Lane.

As a fitting finale the last Saturday, 6 May 1950, brought the most
dramatic season's end in football history. It was a day when managers,
directors and players alike grabbed their ready-reckoners — no pocket
calculators yet available — to work out the vital decimal points that
spelled promotion and relegation. That morning the top of the First
Division looked like this:

	Played	Goals	Pts
Portsmouth	41	69-37	51
Wolves	41	70-48	51
Manchester Utd	42	69-44	50
Sunderland	41	79-61	50

With Manchester United having completed their fixtures, the
Championship depended on the Portsmouth v Aston Villa, Wolves
v Birmingham and Sunderland v Chelsea fixtures. By virtue of their
superior goal-average, victory for Pompey would ensure the
Championship.

In the event, Portsmouth made sure with an emphatic 5-1 win,
whilst Wolves, hoping for a Portsmouth home defeat, slammed five

first-half goals past Birmingham and went on to win 6-1. Sunderland, too, made sure with a 4-1 win over Chelsea. The first 'goal-average' Champions for 26 years retained the title by 0.4 of a goal.

The proof of Pompey's quality was the fact that they were always at their best when the need was greatest. Seventeen points were secured from the last 11 games and their speed and culture were never sacrificed in the hunt for victory. In goal, Ernie Butler was agile without being acrobatic. Hindmarsh and Ferrier were reliable full-backs, but the half-back line was more than trustworthy — it was positively inspiring. This was reflected in the regular international honours bestowed on Scoular and Dickinson. All but ten of Pompey's 74 League goals were scored by four of the forwards and, between them, the speedy, sharp-shooting Harris and the powerful leggy Reid netted 32. Ike Clarke, the centre-forward, shot 17 and the boisterous, free-running Jack Froggatt claimed 15.

The team which won the two titles in successive years was forged, to a large degree, out of servicemen who first came to Portsmouth to help fight a war. The naval town also had supporters all over the country — other servicemen exiled from their native terraces, who spent their Saturday afternoons at Fratton Park and, when it came to flower, remembered the building of the team. It was for that reason that the Portsmouth side of 1948-50 was recalled, in later years, more vividly, and with more affection than any other Football League side.

Wolves had given them a terrific fight. Incessant attacking, backed by the driving Billy Wright, was their hallmark that season. Unlike Spurs, they were specialists of the long pass which was allied to the pace and penetration of the powerful Mullen and the diminutive, tricky Hancocks and the scoring of Pye.

Sunderland were the highest scorers, thanks largely to 29 goals from Dickie Davis, the joint top marksman in the division with Derby's Jack Stamps, and the creative work of inside-forwards Ivor Broadis and Len Shackleton.

The battle to accompany Spurs to the First Division was even tighter with a number of combinations between the three contestants. The placings below Spurs on that last morning were:

	Played	Goals	Pts
Sheffield Utd	42	68-49	52
Sheffield W	41	67-48	51
Southampton	41	61-46	50

With Sheffield United having completed their fixtures, the decisive games were Wednesday v Spurs and Southampton v West Ham. There was the possibility of two of the three being equal on points and goal-average, in which event a play-off would be necessary. If the

Portsmouth's players admire the Football League Championship trophy.

trio finished all-square, then this was not even catered for in the League book of rules.

After a goalless draw at Hillsborough, the 55,000 Wednesday fans waited behind to hear the result of the Saints-West Ham match at The Dell which had kicked off 15 minutes later. Southampton won a thrilling match 3-2, after being two goals behind at half-time, but it was not enough. Four more in the 'goals for' column would have been enough for the South Coast side or, alternatively, if they had even prevented the Hammers from scoring in that last match.

The final mathematics of goal-average saw Wednesday go up by 0.008 of a goal — the figures being Wednesday 1.395, United with 1.387 and Southampton trailing fourth with 1.333.

Three weeks earlier, Notts County and Doncaster Rovers had clinched promotion from the Third South and North sections, 46,000 County fans, the biggest crowd ever to see a Nottingham match, saw their side return to the Second Division. Lawton had put County on the football map and not only with his 33 League goals. Similar remarks applied to Peter Doherty at Doncaster with his 29 total.

The ready-reckoner calculations on the last day even extended to the re-election issue in the North section, when Halifax lost out by a mere 0.25 of a goal and Newport, in the South section, by 0.125.

There had been more than usual interest in the Home International Championship that season. After a shock defeat at Goodison Park against the Republic of Ireland in the Republic's first international appearance in this country, England went on to win the tournament with maximum points. The success was even more significant because the Championship doubled up as a World Cup qualifying competition, with the winners gaining one of the 16 places in the finals in Brazil. Both Wales (4-1) and Northern Ireland (9-2) were trounced and a narrow 1-0 victory over Scotland at Hampden Park secured the title.

The main interest centred around the England centre-forward spot, where Jesse Pye was a surprise initial choice, only to be succeeded by first Jackie Milburn and then Jack Rowley. The forward line was subject to experimentation with Len Shackleton, Stan Pearson, Stan Mortensen, Roy Bentley and the 'bad boy' of the previous season, Wilf Mannion, vying for the inside-forward spots. As if to hedge their bets, a twin centre-forward plan was evolved with any two of the aforementioned playing an interchanging game in which they took turns at being the spearhead of the attack, whilst the other roamed at will.

A variation on this was evolved at Chelsea — Roy Bentley was a roving centre-forward, moving out to the wings to pick up passes and leaving any other player to take up the open space left. Unfortunately, the other Chelsea players did not co-operate and while Bentley moved around, the other forwards merely sat tight. Elsewhere, the 'floating centre-forward' idea was being flirted with and Jack Rowley of Manchester United was another player to try it at club level.

When England met Italy at White Hart Lane in November, the highlight was a superb virtuoso performance by goalkeeper Bert Williams, who held the Italians at bay. After England's 2-0 win, inspired by Williams in the high spot of his career, the opposition named him 'Il Gattone' (The Cat) — a nickname which was to stick with him.

At the season's end, the England squad faced a continental tour in May, followed by their first participation in the World Cup in Brazil. They should have been accompanied to the finals by Scotland, as the original idea was that the Home Championship runners-up would also qualify. The Scots had made it clear, early in the season, that they would only go as Champions but the Hampden defeat, before the fanatical 138,000 crowd, pushed them into the runners-up spot and they had to live up to their promise and withdraw. The young Leeds United centre-half, John Charles, had become Wales' youngest-ever international at 18 years and 71 days and was clearly a star of the future.

It had been the most eventful and exciting season since the pre-war days, but it was also to be the last season in which total League attendances topped 40 million and in which 88 clubs featured, being divided equally between the four sections. Several outstanding managers had made their mark and the era of the showman or figure-head type of boss had gone. Arthur Rowe had changed the style of play at Tottenham so successfully, George Kay at Liverpool had developed Liverpool at considerably less cost than many of the other First Division sides, and Matt Busby had made Manchester United into one of the best teams in the country. Four player-managers, Raich Carter (Hull City), Freddie Steele (Mansfield Town), Peter Doherty (Doncaster) and Ronnie Rooke (Crystal Palace) had created a new *genre*.

As the twentieth century came up to its half-way mark, football had reached a watershed. The boom was a long way from over but the World Cup finals would provide the first truly competitive international test for the country which had given the game to the world. England were generally regarded as one of the favourites, but their ageing squad would learn to their cost of the progress of the world's footballing countries.

The Push & Run Revolution

BY the time the 1950-51 season opened, the post-mortems were over and all the excuses had been made and generally accepted. The pre-eminence of English football had been dimmed by her performances in the 1950 World Cup, staged in Brazil, and more particularly by the biggest shock that the English game had ever suffered. The story of the single-goal defeat by the USA and the early eliminiation from the finals has been told many times, but ultimately English football was to pay the price for its insularity.

Despite the disappointments in Rio, however, it was clear that the public enthusiasm for the domestic game was as great as ever. The majority were blind to the broader picture, to the global aspect, with no consideration for the part that English football should play amongst the nations. This complacency was drawn from the fact that, in 20 full international matches against Continental countries since 1946 (excluding the World Cup), England had won 15, drawn one and lost only four.

What was also clear was that England faced many nations who did not interpret the laws of the game in the same way as in the British Isles and that English football, whilst efficient enough, had become, on the whole, too sterotyped. As in previous seasons there were renewed cries for new imaginative ideas. It was still felt that for 20 years the game had sheltered behind the defensive centre-half and there was a longing for a return to the spirit of adventure and imaginative attack.

The Press were unimpressed by the state of the game and one journalist's cryptic comments were typical after the South American adventure: 'The game is currently being played by large numbers of young and not so young men who know little about the game, watched by very large numbers of others who know practically nothing about it. It is being administered in many instances by gentlemen whose attitude to a tough profession is unrealistic and directed in its performance by too many men who are nearly two wars behind its development.'

Just as the World Cup had opened in South America, a serious international crisis had developed on another continent following the invasion of South Korea by the forces of the North Korean communist regime. British troops and naval forces were sent to fight alongside the Americans, as part of a United Nations force, to stem the tide.

The summer months of 1950 had brought the end of soap rationing, more and more free spectacles from the opticians and, in the food line, a move towards a whiter and more acceptable loaf. The Princess Anne was born days before the start of the new football season and the early episodes of *The Archers* were being transmitted on the Light Programme of the BBC. The first scheduled helicopter passenger service in the world, between Liverpool and Cardiff, had been introduced to a curious public.

In cricket, four Tests were played in the home series against the West Indies with England losing by 3-1, largely after the English batsmen were mesmerised by those 'spin-twins' Sonny Ramadhin and Alf Valentine. Prospects were dim for the coming winter's Ashes series in Australia. In the County Championship, as the previous year, the title was shared, this time between Surrey and Lancashire.

By now, five years after the war had ended, a real change in public tastes and habits could be detected and the all-round austerity and drabness was disappearing. Such as cars, clothes, furniture, television sets and holidays featured prominently in people's thoughts and, at last, it was perceived that there were things other than soccer on which to spend money and time.

By now, as a result of the clamour by minor professional clubs for first-class status, the Football League had agreed to extend the Third Division from 44 to 48 clubs and to achieve this, each section was enlarged by two clubs. Colchester United and Gillingham in the South, Scunthorpe United and Shrewsbury Town in the North. Workington and Wigan were very close to election but Scunthorpe edged them out. Workington came in the following year, replacing New Brighton, but Wigan, as it transpired, had to wait another 30 years. Some consideration was given at the League management committee meeting to the forming of a Fourth Division, but it was felt that there were not enough clubs worthy of that League exalted status at that time.

The players approached the new season with a new sense of security, not only by virtue of an increase in basic wages granted by the latest Ministry of Labour tribunal, but by the inauguration of a provident fund which ensured that each player, on his retirement, received ten per cent of all the money he had earned during his playing days. At last the boom was benefiting the players and an ever greater number had the satisfaction of receiving the maximum wage.

That same tribunal had even come up with the suggestion that there should be a limit of £15,000 on transfer fees and that it should be split three ways — the transferring club, the player himself and a pool for the benefit of the game. In the event, unsurprisingly, the idea was turned down by the clubs.

As the season opened, a number of questions remained to be answered: Could Portsmouth equal the record of Arsenal and Huddersfield and become League Champions for the third successive time? Could Tottenham Hotspur maintain their style and prominence on their return to the top division? Had Manchester United and Arsenal reached their peaks? Could the rise of Notts County, led by Tommy Lawton, be maintained in the Second Division?

If any proof were needed of the game's continuing magnetism it came on the opening day of that 1950-51 season, when the fans set up a new all-time record for a Saturday football crowd — the aggregate of 1,189,401 being the best since 16 October 1948, when 1,167,446 attended that day's matches.

The biggest crowd of opening day 1950 — 64,978 — was at White Hart Lane to see Spurs play their first game in Division One for 15 years, but the visitors, Blackpool, sprung a shock with a 4-1 win. Even more surprising in that victory were the three goals from half-backs Harry Johnston (two) and Hugh Kelly. In Division Two, 41,000 welcomed Notts County but Coventry City spoiled their party. The day's opening goal, after 56 seconds, was an own-goal — Viggo Jensen, Hull City's Danish international, heading into his own net before 30,056 at Upton Park.

Fulham, with an outlay of close on £50,000, had been the biggest spenders in the close season, acquiring four internationals — goalkeeper Ian Black from Southampton, wing-halves Archie Macaulay from Arsenal and Eddie Lowe from Aston Villa, and inside-forward Bobby Brennan from Birmingham City. In their opening-day fixture they went down by a single goal at Old Trafford to a Manchester United side who were without Charlie Mitten — still in Bogota — but included goalkeeper Reg Allen, from Queen's Park Ranger's, and wing-half Eddie McIlvenny, captain of the USA team in that summer's World Cup.

By now the England and Stoke City defender Neil Franklin had returned from Bogota, admitting that his gamble had failed but having to face severe consequences. Not only were the Bogota authorities due to take action against him for breach of contract but also his former Stoke colleagues had made it clear that they did not want him back and the Football Association were preparing to punish him. It all amounted to a very sad state of affairs for the man rated by the Press as 'the greatest centre-half of his generation'.

In early season there were notable occasions for Port Vale, when their new £55,000 ground at Burslem was opened and greeted by 28,000

Blackpool centre-forward Stan Mortensen is thwarted by Spurs goalkeeper Ted Ditchburn at White Hart Lane on the opening day of the 1950-51 season. The game ended in a 4-1 defeat for Tottenham but they went on to lift their second successive title.

Spurs were now on target for a second successive title and, again, Channel Islander Len Duquemin was a key figure in their success. In this picture Duquemin challenges Bolton Wanderers goalkeeper Stan Hanson at White Hart Lane in August 1950. The ball eventually went in off Bolton left-half Don Howe and Spurs won 4-2.

Cardiff City inside-left Doug Blair scores his side's first goal against QPR at Loftus Road in September 1950, but Rangers went on to win 3-2.

fans, and at Gillingham when they celebrated their first ever victory in the League, at home to Millwall before 20,000.

In his first season in the First Division, Derby County's new centre-forward, Jack Lee, signed from Leicester City for £18,000, was a prominent goalscorer in the early weeks and earned an England cap in the first international of the season, against Northern Ireland. That international and that selection on a Saturday in October brought the discontent of the clubs over their being deprived of the services of their stars in the League to a head. Newcastle, in particular, took a poor view of their star man Jackie Milburn spending the afternoon as a reserve sitting on the bench. Milburn's feats had by then taken United to their temporary top spot in the League.

Chelsea were at the foot of the table in late October and included five defeats in a row in their record. That did not stop 65,992 watching their defeat by Spurs and on the same day 66,150 were at Highbury to see Arsenal beat Manchester United, so it was an aggregate of more than 132,000 at the two big London games that day with thousands locked out. When one considers that there were also League matches at Queen's Park Rangers (19,000), Leyton Orient (18,000), Millwall (35,000) and Watford (15,000), it illustrated the appeal of the game in the capital.

With all the money in the game, the transfer market continued unabated. Auctions surrounding players were prevalent with the bids of one club being pitted against those of another to the accompaniment of banner headlines firing the appetites of the fans but giving the game's critics powerful ammunition. Clubs were often asking the equivalent of a season's gate-money for one player — for a reserve player of a club near the foot of Division Two, it was reported that Chesterfield were being asked £12,000.

Sunderland were making most of the transfer headlines culminating in their record £30,000 purchase of Welsh centre-forward Trevor Ford from Aston Villa and their abortive pursuit of Neil Franklin. The persuasive Sunderland manager Bill Murray had already been responsible for the signing of Len Shackleton from Newcastle United, Ivor Broadis from his player-manager's job at Carlisle United and Willie Watson from Huddersfield Town. Broadis was reckoned to be the first manager to negotiate his own transfer.

As an example of money not ensuring success, Sunderland were subsequently a great disappointment and amazingly failed to score in a dozen of their 42 fixtures that season, including seven home games, and all with an inside-forward trio who cost close to £70,000.

One club who did plead poverty at this time were Second Division Brentford, whose manager Jackie Gibbons announced that unless a minimum of 26,000 fans rolled up every week they faced banruptcy. The average gate appeared to be a very healthy 19,000 but this was not apparently enough to make ends meet or purchase new players.

Eventually Gibbons was forced to put some of his best players up for sale. On offer he had a 22-year-old left-half with a 'Tommy Trinder chin' called Jimmy Hill. Hill had started as an amateur with Reading as an inside-left, but since moving to half-back at Griffin Park he had been a great success. Seventen-year-old Peter Broadbent had joined Brentford from Dover Town as a clever inside-forward and Ron Greenwood was a Lancashire-born centre-half who had started as an amateur at Chelsea whilst employed as a sign-writer. The outcome was that Hill went to Fulham, Broadbent to Wolves and Greenwood back to Chelsea.

Increasingly, a vital part of the game's equipment was coming under scrutiny and there was great interest in the use of a new type of ball at Southampton. The old-fashioned lace-up type was being blamed for gashed eyes and foreheads but the cause of the new ball, with a built-in bladder and patent valve, was not helped when it deflated after a few minutes at The Dell. Another was produced and it too deflated, to be replaced by the old type which proceeded to stay the course.

As Christmas approached, Middlesbrough, Arsenal, Tottenham and Newcastle were locked together at the top of the First. Middlesbrough were inspired by the creative Wilf Mannion, safely back in their fold, the goalscoring of Alex McCrae, the League's leading scorer up to the point, and the agility of Italian-born goalkeeper Rolando Ugolini.

Accident at The Valley where Arsenal's Jimmy Logie and Charlton's Jimmy Walls are treated after colliding during the First Division game on October 1950. A crowd of 64,000 saw Arsenal win 3-1.

Arsenal had made a good start with Peter Goring and Doug Lishman regularly amongst the goals. The Christmas fixtures were their undoing, however, when the Gunners not only failed to win a single point but also lost Lishman to a long-term injury. After Alec Forbes, Jimmy Logie and George Swindin all were subsequently hurt Arsenal were never the same force.

After a slow start the special Tottenham machine had slipped smoothly into gear and when they crushed first League Champions Portsmouth by five goals and then challenging Newcastle by seven, it meant eight wins in a row. The left-wing pair of Eddie Baily and Les Medley were a superb combination and were recognized as such by being recruited together by England that month.

The hammering of Tottenham seemed to signal both the passing of the Champions, as Pompey's title hat-trick dreams faded, and the rise of the brilliant, almost cocksure, revitalized Spurs. Portsmouth were left standing by the speed and craft of a well-balanced Spurs attack. Baily, the little Cockney nicknamed the 'Cheeky Chappie', was quite irrepressible that day and climaxed his display with a second-half hat-trick of stunning individual goals. Spurs moved into fourth place after that win as surprise contenders for the title.

As it transpired, it was a magnificent storming season for Spurs, many of whom had been home-grown coming through the Northfleet

Spectator's view of play. The goalkeeper watching play at the other end, around the Arsenal goal, is Wolves' Bert Williams.

nursery. The 'push and run' style formulated by the silver-haired Cockney, Arthur Rowe, was proving just as successful in the top division — in the words of the Press they were 'one team who can lead English football back to the top'. The secret of their success was explained by Rowe: "We play simply but accurately and quickly. If we have the ball we aim to keep it." The wisdom of Rowe's 60 years in professional football was concentrated in his maxim, "Don't kick the ball, pass it." Bill Nicholson, at wing-half, recalled that the whole idea was that 'whenever you made a pass you had to run to a new position'.

It seemed as if the capital was the place to be for quality football and there was no better example that season than the Arsenal-Blackpool encounter in December, when the two sides shared eight goals. For 57,000 spectators the game had everything — a vintage mercurial display from Mortensen, great artistry from the arch-wizard Matthews in his very best form and some great shooting from the home forwards. Matthews tormented the Arsenal defence with his bewildering runs and body-swerves, such that Lionel Smith at full-back was so dazed at one point that he threw up his arms in despair and had to be switched with Don Roper.

The Spurs-Arsenal match two days before Christmas — dubbed as the 'Match of the Year' — was anticipated with some trepidation by the authorities, particularly in relation to crowd control and as it looked likely that anything up to 30,000 fans of both sides might be disappointed. Both clubs wanted the match switched to Wembley under floodlights but the League just would not go along with such grandiose plans.

In the event, as had happened before, pre-match ballyhoo scared people away from the vital London derby and the attendance fell to 54,898 at White Hart Lane compared to the usual 70,000 plus. In a tense match Spurs pipped Arsenal by a single goal from Baily, scored with a tremendous left-foot drive. Untypical of the period and the contestants, but attributed to the tension, the match was scarred by arguments, squabbles and red-blooded tackling.

This was to be the season when Nottingham Forest first came to the fore in the post-war era and as the third round of the FA Cup approached they were to be found at the very top of the Third Division South, having lost only twice in 23 games and, more particularly, having scored 61 goals. Under the managership of Billy Walker, the former Aston Villa and England star, their tally had included nine against newcomers Gillingham, before a crowd of 20,000, and typically the veteran Wally Ardron and Tommy Capel were amongst the goals. Norwich City, too, were on the rise in the same division, for the first time since their Second Division championship success in 1934. The Canaries' success rode on the back of a 22-match unbeaten run with

Roy Hollis the main goalscorer and Norman Low the astute manager.

It seemed as if most Christmas games that season were played out in poor light and when some clubs began to promote the use of a white ball, the FA had to quickly give it their blessing and instruct referees to introduce it during a game if necessary. The fading light often made it impossible for spectators to follow the closing stages of matches and reporters were obliged to bring their match reports to a premature end.

In a domestic game with so many big names, the biggest and most expensive was that of Trevor Ford and there was an unseasonal rumpus at Fulham when the Sunderland management decided at the last minute that Ford could not be exposed to the rigours of a frozen ground. With the Fulham attendance up to 35,000 from its usual 25,000, in anticipation of his appearance, there were apparently some very angry fans when the highly expensive soccer property did not make an appearance. Remember, this was an era when an individual player could add thousands at the gate. There was no televised soccer to speak of and this was perhaps the one occasion in a season when many fans could see a star name. For all the game's popularity it was hardly over-exposed.

The third round of the FA Cup that season was a triumph for the Third Division. Out of the 20 ties, 15 'minnows' went back into the hat for the fourth round the following Monday. Taking pride of place were Bill Shankly's Carlisle United, who held the mighty Arsenal to a goalless draw at Highbury, despite having key-men Twentyman and Walters limping throughout. The replay was a tragedy for their goalkeeper Jimmy MacLaren. Before 21,215 at Brunton Park, MacLaren was apparently in tears at the end after making three errors which gave the Gunners an easy 4-1 victory.

First Division casualties in that round were Spurs, surprisingly knocked out by lowly Huddersfield at Leeds Road; high-riding Middlesbrough, beaten for the first time since September, by Leeds United from the Second Division; Portsmouth, knocked out at Luton; the fragile Everton eclipsed by Raich Carter's Hull City; and, outstandingly, Liverpool, the previous year's Cup Finalists, who were thoroughly beaten by Norwich City at Carrow Road.

All this came at a time when it was reported that the Football Association was toying with the idea of excluding the little clubs from the competition and creating a colourless substitute called the Intermediate Cup with the consolation of staging a poor man's Wembley Final amongst themselves.

In the fourth round the 72,408 crowd at Arsenal for the tie against Third Division South club Northampton Town was the biggest Highbury attendance since the war. The Gunners' 3-2 win was described by the *Daily Express* as 'the roughest, bitterest game I have

Blackpool's Jackie Mudie heads his side's first goal against Mansfield Town in the fifth-round FA Cup tie at Bloomfield Road in February 1951. The Seasiders won 2-0 before a crowd of 33,060.

seen since the war.' Northampton had gone to Highbury still groggy from a 'flu epidemic but their fierce tackling and physical appoach made the pitch look like a casualty-clearing station. Logie, Lewis, Roper and Mercer all suffered cuts which needed stiches but Lewis still managed to score twice to give Arsenal their narrow victory.

The 38,384 crowd at Derby was a Baseball Ground record as the Rams lost to Birmingham City. An all-ticket record crowd of 20,000 crowd at Exeter (at doubled prices) saw a 1-1 draw with Chelsea before the Grecians gently succumbed in the replay, 2-0 before 46,000 fans at Stamford Bridge.

Third Division Mansfield Town earned a replay with a goalless draw at Second Division Sheffield United and in the return game 34-year-old player-manager and centre-forward Freddie Steele was mobbed after the Stags' extra-time victory. It was the first time that the Mansfield club, founded 40 years previously, had reached the fifth round and the crowd of 20,374 beat their previous best of 18,863, set up in March 1948.

Newcastle United were having good fortune in the Cup and after beating Bury in the third round they were 2-1 down at home to Bolton Wanderers before edging through 3-2. In the fifth round the Magpies survived a Stoke onslaught before a Potteries crowd of 48,500 and went on to win 4-2, with George Robledo scoring twice.

In the same round, Arsenal's hopes of reaching the Final for the second year in succession were dashed when they were knocked out by the only goal at Old Trafford, before 55,058 who saw a drab game. An interesting sideline to this match was the ban, imposed by the Manchester Docks Authorities, on dockers from attending because they were needed to work that Saturday to clear backlogs caused by a strike. It was reported that thousands disobeyed the order and a move by the authorities to import Fleetwood dockers also failed as they insisted on going to Bloomfield Road to see Blackpool put out Mansfield.

The Manchester United-Arsenal tie, despite its pre-match bally-hoo, was significant for a gamble taken by Matt Busby in giving two teenagers their debuts in United's forward line. The two 18-year-olds, Cliff Birkett and Brian Birch, were a great trial for the experienced Arsenal defenders and caused enough confusion to lead to Stan Pearson's winning goal. At the final whistle, young Birkett collapsed in a dead faint and had to be carried off the field by two United defenders to be revived by smelling salts in the dressing-room. It evoked memories of the moment, 17 years earlier, when a mere slip of a Manchester lad called Frank Swift collapsed at Wembley in similar fashion.

The other big story in that fifth round came from the West Country, where Raich Carter's Hull City were put out at Eastville by a Bristol Rovers side assembled by Bert Tann for £350, the whole of which sum was paid for goalkeeper Hoyle from Exeter. Some 31,000 fans saw the Rovers snuff out the threats from the scheming Carter and the striking partners Jensen and Don Revie. Two goals from Watling and another from Lambden brought a comprehensive 3-0 win.

The sixth round gave the 'no buy no sell' Bristol Rovers an away tie against a Newcastle United side which had cost in the region of £57,750 to put together. Before 63,000, Rovers held star-studded United to a goalless draw but were not so lucky in the replay at Eastville. Rovers took the lead in the first half — for all of 37 seconds — but three copy-book goals in 13 minutes by Ernie Taylor, wing-half Charlie Crowe and Jackie Milburn took United into the semi-final.

The Bristol side's exploits in the Cup had fired the public's imagination but a magnificent gesture at the end was typical of those sporting times. Before the players had struggled their way through the crowd who invaded the pitch, the Bristol club's secretary had spoken over the loudspeakers: 'On behalf of the Bristol team and their supporters, we congratulate Newcastle, and wish them every luck in the semi-final.' This was followed by the playing of the Rovers' theme song *Good Night, Irene* in solemn slow time.

Newcastle had to meet Wolves, who had decisively put out Sunderland in the quarter-final, at Hillsborough; and Birmingham City, from the Second Division, had to play at Maine Road, Manchester, against Blackpool. The Midlanders had knocked out Manchester United in their quarter-final before 50,000 at St Andrew's in a hard match littered with infringements and won by a goal from forward Jimmy Higgins, scored 20 seconds after kick-off. The Press were of the opinion that United's defeat was caused largely by the switching of John Aston to centre-forward and the consequent weakening of their defence.

In the other quarter-final, Blackpool's single goal, a penalty from £28,000 new signing Allan Brown from East Fife, was enough to put them through at home against Fulham. In two months the burly ex-Fifeshire miner had made a meteoric rise to stardom. Brown had stayed out of football for half a season in a determined bid to leave East Fife. Now, within weeks, the inside-forward looked likely to make a Cup Final appearance and win a Scottish cap.

Both semi-finals were goalless, thanks to a brilliant display by Bert Williams in goal for Wolves against Newcastle and a hard-tackling performance by the Birmingham defence in keeping out Blackpool's star forwards. The Midlanders came so close to a Wembley appearance when, three minutes from the end, their £7,000 signing 26-year old Scottish right-winger Jackie Stewart saw his shot hit a post. Stewart was an abject figure at the end as he had missed an open goal earlier in the game, hitting the Blackpool 'keeper's legs from three yards.

In the replay at Huddersfield, in the midweek afternoon, Newcastle scored twice in 29 seconds, through Milburn and Bobby Mitchell, to beat Wolves, who had earlier taken the lead through Walker, and put themselves through to their eighth Final.

Blackpool had been to Wembley only once before, in 1948, but were there again after a dramatic 2-1 victory in their replay at Goodison Park. Stan Matthews, inevitably, was at the root of their victory, being everywhere and figuring prominently in both goals from Mortensen and winger Billy Perry. When Bill Smith scored for Birmingham it sparked a great fight but in the end the classical football of the First Division side won through.

The two clubs then had to wait seven weeks for the Final and this was considered to be too long. Blackpool manager Joe Smith and the Newcastle acting unpaid manager and director Stan Seymour launched a campaign to cut down the senseless wait. They commented: 'It is cruelty to the players. They get edgy and nervous. We want this to be the last time any player is exposed to this miserable spell of anticipation.' Smith was probably thinking back to 1948, when Blackpool failed against Manchester United. Players had run out of form and confidence, the club were split on team changes and it was felt that the long wait had beaten them out of the Cup.

As if to substantiate the argument, it was reported that Newcastle's Jackie Milburn was later a victim of 'Wembley Willies' when he was left out of a League game against Fulham. The explanation was that 'Milburn is a highly nervous player and has got nothing more than a bad attack of Wembley jitters'. The team also suffered, going eight games without a win after their semi-final triumph and played 11 games in all before the Final, winning only one. Clearly, nobody in the team was prepared to take an undue risk.

Newcastle had good fortune on their way to the Final but there was nothing fortunate about the two spectacular individual goals by Milburn which decided the Wembley match. To the despair of the neutrals, Blackpool adopted offside tactics which led to their surviving nine hair's-breadth decisions in the goalless first-half. They were undone five minutes after the restart as Milburn beat the trap with a long run from the half-way line. He outstripped the Blackpool defenders to tuck the ball past the advancing goalkeeper George Farm from 15 yards.

The second Milburn goal in the comfortable 2-0 win was one of the most spectacular ever seen at Wembley. Little Ernie Taylor set up the chance with a brilliant backheel and Milburn hit the ball immediately with great force with his left foot from 28 yards into the top corner of the net.

Blackpool were without inside-forward Allan Brown, who was suffering from a knee injury, and his guile and craft were missed. The only Blackpool forward to come out of the match with credit was Matthews, who put in a tremendous effort in his second attempt for a Cup winners' medal. The maestro was busily taking free-kicks, corners and throw-ins and, uniquely, had five shots at goal. His first goal since New Year's Day 1949 would not come, however.

The Newcastle side as a whole was probably their best-ever. In goal was big Jack Fairbrother, with his distinctive white gloves, and the full backs Bobby Cowell and Bobby Corbett were a hard-tackling pair. The side was driven on by right-half and skipper Joe Harvey and up front the tiny Ernie Taylor was the creator of chances for Chilean goal-ace George Robledo and Milburn. Tricky Bobby Mitchell was at outside-left and was a great crowd pleaser with his close dribbling.

The 1951 FA Amateur Cup Final compared very favourably with the professional version and was watched by 100,000 at Wembley, a record for the amateur game. Pegasus, the side made up of Varsity men from Oxford and Cambridge, beat Bishop Auckland 2-1, thanks largely to the coaching and 'push and run' principles passed on by Tottenham's Vic Buckingham. Pegasus were in only their third season.

Whilst the Cup was being won, three individuals were making the headlines for different reasons. Neil Franklin had ended his personal nightmare of isolation since his ill-fated Bogota trip and served his four-month long suspension imposed by the FA. The former England centre-half had moved to Hull City from Stoke for £22,500 and made his debut before nearly 39,000 at Boothferry Park, despite the Humberside club's disappointing Second Division mid-table position. Sadly, not even the acquisition of such stars as Revie, Franklin, Alf Ackerman and Syd Gerrie could revive the Tigers' fortunes that season or the next.

Jackie Sewell had made his name as an imaginative goalscoring partner for Tommy Lawton at Notts County, but Sheffield Wednesday, rooted at the bottom of the First Division, paid £34,000 for his services a few minutes before the March 1951 transfer deadline. This deal not only shattered the British record but made Sewell the first player to be literally worth his weight in gold. Wednesday had belatedly turned to Sewell after Jimmy Hagan had turned down a £33,000 move across the city of Sheffield from Bramall Lane to Hillsborough.

Hans Jeppson had led Sweden's attack in the World Cup in Rio and when he came to England for three months on business, Charlton manager Jimmy Seed moved quickly to sign him as an amateur. The Swede made his first appearance in January, with Charlton fourth to bottom in the First Division, but by March, after a run of eight games without defeat, they were half-way up the table. By the time Jeppson returned home he had scored nine goals in 11 appearances and nearly all the goals were worth two points. He had saved Charlton from possible relegation and as a result of his exploits received £18,000 for himself when he turned professional and signed for the Italian First Division club, Atalanta, in August 1951.

Stan Mortensen wheels away after scoring for Blackpool against Newcastle United in March 1951. The result of the First Division match was a 2-2 draw.

The sides met again in the FA Cup Final that year. Newcastle skipper Joe Harvey is shoulder-high with the Cup after the Magpies' 2-0 win at Wembley.

Two 18-year old centre-forwards who were destined for stardom made their debuts that spring. One, Tommy Taylor, a National Service soldier, collected his first League hat-trick in his second game for Barnsley; and down south, young Bobby Smith was collecting a broken collar-bone in an early game for Chelsea. Taylor to Manchester United and Smith to Spurs were, of course, their eventual destinations.

If Spurs were unquestionably the 'team of the year' as they seemed on course for the title, Preston North End were running them close as they swept through the Second Division. Back in 1891, Preston had earned the title 'Old Invincibles' by winning 13 League games in a row. By the end of March, the 1951 Preston team had gone one better by winning their 14th game, 3-2 at Leicester. That equalled the League record at the time and made promotion a formality, even though a 15th win could not be added.

It was a season in which Preston broke four club records: those consecutive victories; eight successive away wins; most points (57) gained; and most wins (26) in a season. North End, with 91 goals, were the highest scorers in the top two divisions. Manager Will Scott had done well to re-establish Preston, aided by match-winner Tom Finney and the shrewd if expensive purchase of the high-scoring Charlie Wayman from Southampton, and the emergence of a fine young wing-half in Tommy Docherty.

Another club who provided even more goals were Nottingham Forest, who registered 110 goals in winning the Third South title with six points in hand over runners-up Norwich City. Forest's return to the Second Division after an absence of only two years saw 60 League and Cup goals shared by only two players that season — Ardron (36) and Capel (24).

Rotherham United, in the Third North, were also amongst the high scorers with 103 League goals and none more so than Jack Shaw, who notched 44 in League and Cup. Rotherham at last secured the promotion prize after finishing runners-up three times in four seasons. Their 71-points total compared with Forest's 70 — the first time in the history of the League two clubs had reached 70 in the same season.

On the other side of the coin, Gillingham and Accrington Stanley in their respective sections both conceded 101 goals and yet still avoided the bottom places.

It was a momentous season for Mansfield in the Northern section as they collected the first set of runners-up medals in the history of the club. Inspired by player-manager Freddie Steele in their attack, they not only broke new ground by reaching the Fifth round of the FA Cup, as we have seen, but also were the only one of the 92 League clubs to be unbeaten at home. It was a close thing however — they were within four minutes of losing the record in their final match

Nottingham Forest goalkeeper George Walker is beaten by a shot from Southend United's right-half John French just before half-time in the game at Southend Stadium in April 1951. Southend won 3-2, netting the winner in the final seconds, but Forest still won promotion as champions of the Third Division South.

Norwich City made a gallant attempt to win promotion from the Third Division South. They beat Crystal Palace 5-0 at Selhurst Park in April 1951 with the help of a hat-trick from Roy Hollis, seen here scoring one of his goals. But it was Forest who went up, six points ahead of the Canaries.

against Southport. At 2-1 down the record was preserved when wing-half Johnny Lewis equalized from the penalty-spot.

Another notable last home match of the season was at Tranmere. Notable for the winning headed goal by centre-half Harold Bell — only his second post-war League goal in 214 games, a full complement of appearances since peacetime soccer resumed and more than any other player.

In the First Division as that last day of the season dawned, the matter of which two sides would plunge into the Second Division still had to be decided between Chelsea, big-spending Sheffield Wednesday and Everton.

At the end of the day, Chelsea pipped Wednesday by 0.044 on goal-average and were safe. All three clubs finished on 32 points, but Everton were 0.213 behind Wednesday to be forced into the bottom spot. Ironically, Wednesday had to meet Everton and had everybody's sympathy as they thrashed the Toffees 6-0. The 41,000 crowd at Hillsborough lingered on for another 15 minutes to await the result of the Chelsea-Bolton match which had kicked off later. Chelsea were leading 4-0 at that 75-minute mark and the Owls fans needed one

Derby goalkeeper Joe Sharman pushes the ball out from a Chelsea attack at the Baseball Ground in April 1951. The Rams' full-backs on the line are (left) Charlie Revell and England's Bert Mozley. Centre-half Ken Oliver is the other defender. Derby won 1-0.

goal from Bolton to save them. But the score remained unchanged at Stamford Bridge.

Chelsea had won three games in a row after seeming doomed to relegation but Everton's demise surprised nobody. The previous season the Toffees had finished fifth from bottom and this term had relied heavily on an ageing team who had slid rapidly to destruction on a lengthy succession of defeats. It seemed that Everton were continually being linked with players available for transfer, such as Broadis, Sewell and Bentley, without ever actually making the major purchases necessary.

As far as the big-name clubs were concerned, Manchester United finished four points behind Spurs, but in acquiring 56 points they had done enough to have won the title in some past seasons, even though they lost the services of those two great wingers Charlie Mitten and Jimmy Delaney for a long period. It had also been a season when United had undertaken the drastic experiment of shifting John Aston to centre-forward.

Wolves had failed to come up to expectations and it was difficult to reconcile their position in the lower half of the table with the number of fine players at the club. Pompey, Champions two years running, dropped to seventh, largely as a result of drawing as many as 15 games. The Fratton Park men reserved their best form for the season's end when they played 12 consecutive matches without defeat. The most interesting aspect of Pompey's season was the unusual conversion of the versatile Froggatt from outside-left to centre-half.

Only three months after the switch, Froggatt found himself capped for England in the position which was a problem for the national side that season. Allenby Chilton of Manchester United, Leslie Compton of Arsenal and Jim Taylor of Fulham were also tried in the position without establishing themselves.

There were other surprise England selections that season and if the choice of 38-year-old Compton raised eyebrows, so did that of his Arsenal defensive colleague, Lionel Smith, at full-back. Eddie Baily's fine partnership with Les Medley for Tottenham earned both of them caps and the Huddersfield schemer Harold Hassall was another new cap with his club partner Vic Metcalfe. When Yugoslavia became the first Continental side to avoid defeat in England in a full international there were two goals from newcomer Nat Lofthouse of Bolton.

In the opinion of the Press, Billy Wright was jaded and out-of-form for England that season and one critic was even moved to comment: 'This official idolatory of Wright is really extraordinary. The Wolves star has turned in a succession of drab and lifeless international displays. The selectors stick to Wright with the consistency of opium-eaters returning to their favourite lotus-land.'

One of those 'displays' was against Scotland at Wembley in April when their 3-2 win secured the Home International Championship for the Scots, thanks to a rumbustious display from Hibernian's Lawrie Reilly. The game was not only notable for the impact of debutant Hassell and the experienced Finney, but for a terrible injury suffered by Wilf Mannion. His head injury, after a collision with Scotland's Billy Liddell, which led to him being carried off with a suspected fracture of the skull, was described by colleague Mortensen as 'the most shocking injury I have seen on the field of play'.

Two end-of-season home victories over Argentina and then Portugal seemed to temporarily revive England's international spirits. Wright was eventually dropped, to be replaced by Nicholson of Spurs for the Portugal match which was part of the Festival of Britain celebrations. The programme also included the likes of European club sides Rapid Vienna, FC Austria, Anderlecht, Partizan and Red Star of Belgrade touring with matches against English and Scottish premier clubs.

The Austrians gave notice of their superiority in technique when in one of those Festival matches before 30,000 at White Hart Lane, FC Austria defeated League Champions, Spurs. The renowned centre-half, Ernst Ocwirk, showed he was not a stopper in the position by patrolling the whole field and then popped up to score the only goal after 18 minutes.

It was generally agreed that the standard of domestic football displayed that season had reached the pre-1939 standard but realistically, England's international reputation was still tobogganing downhill as news filtered through of the form and style of the Central European sides. The England selectors had shown a tendency that season to pick players based chiefly on their individual form with no regard to building up a squad with the purpose of matching up to Continental styles and methods.

Spurs had proved that top-class football pays dividends — in their case with the reward of a first League Championship since their formation in 1882. With an apparently simple formula, Arthur Rouse had taken a moderate Second Division team and transformed them into the best in the land.

Attendances that season topped 39 million but there was evidence that the honeymoon between football and its public was coming to an end when it was noted that this was one million down on the previous season and two million down on season 1948-9. And on top of that, the League was bigger by four clubs. For all that it meant that in five campaigns the first-class game had attracted some 197 million but now the first small hole in the dyke could be detected.

Busby's United
to the Fore

AS football took the stage again, the new 1951-2 season began with many problems of a political nature weighing down upon the game once more. In spite of an agreed increase in the maximum wage, from £12 to £14 per week, there was still general unrest amongst the players and, following pressure from the Players' Union, a revised form of contract was under review by a national arbitration board.

There was also the vexed question of televison and radio broadcasting of matches. A decision had been made by the League, at its annual general meeting in June, to ban live commentaries in the coming season in an effort to halt the decline in League attendances. The move had been proposed by Sunderland and it was ironic that the proposal came from the Wearsiders, who had attracted an average of 39,000 to their Roker Park ground in the previous season, with a similar figure attracted to their away fixtures. Pressure against the ban from several quarters grew as the season opened and the League, in a smart about-turn, lifted the ban with the provision that, as now, the destination must be kept secret up to the kick-off.

It was a sensitive issue and in the first month of the new season, the second-half of the Newcastle United-Spurs match could not be broadcast as planned because of a supposed 'leakage'. The BBC switched the 'secret' broadcast, at lunchtime, to the Second Division match between Queen's Park Rangers and Swansea which had been kept in reserve.

As far as television was concerned the main decision centred around the date of the Cup Final, which was moved one week later in May to climax the season and avoid clashing with the normal full programme of League fixtures.

In that summer of 1951, the star attraction for millions was the Festival of Britain — 'an official celebration of Britain's recovery from the War' — which had been inaugurated by King George VI and which ran for five months in London, on 27 acres of land by the River Thames. Before the coming season had been completed the country were mourning the death of the monarch and anticipating the Coronation of Elizabeth, his daughter.

The Korean War had escalated as UN Forces came into conflict with the Chinese, but the danger of a third world war was averted by the signing of an armistice with the Chinese. That war had a profound effect on life in Britain with the announcement that every young man would have to do two years' National Service in one or other of the Armed Forces. In addition, a massive re-armament programme was instituted and this inevitably led to a cut in the standard of living. Increased taxation was the price that had to be paid and Britain was faced with a new problem — rising prices, or as we know it today, inflation.

In politics the nation braced itself for another General Election and after a bitter campaign the Conservatives, led by Churchill, were returned to power in October with a majority of 17. This brought no change in the shortage of supplies, however, necessitating a continuation of the rationing of basic foods.

Ernest Bevin, that giant of the Labour movement, had died in April but already that summer his free NHS had been eroded by people having to pay part of the cost of dental treatment and spectacles and by the imposition of a one shilling prescription charge.

It had been an exciting Test Cricket series against the touring South Africans, with the 3-1 rubber victory being secured in the final decisive fifth match, won by England on the Saturday of football's opening. Alec Bedser took most of the wickets and Len Hutton made most runs. The latter was involved in the first-ever dismissal in Test cricket for 'obstructing the field'. After a lapse of 40 years, Warwickshire became County Champions for the second time.

The League annual meeting in June had re-elected Accrington Stanley, Crystal Palace and Watford, but New Brighton — the 'Wallasey Rakers' — passed out of the League and Workington, from the North-West, joined the Third Division North ranks in their place.

At the time that a FA Commission was considering Charlie Mitten's application for reinstatement to Manchester United after his Bogota adventure, Jackie Milburn's football future was also put in some doubt. He, like many in the game, had sought permission to take an outside job to supplement his income and had been met by a refusal from the Newcastle club. Milburn did not re-sign for some weeks and was even reported to have received an attractive offer from a Rugby League club to transfer his allegiance to the handling code.

As the coming season's prospects were discussed, the Spurs were clearly the glamour boys but as usual Manchester United, Newcastle, Blackpool and Wolves were expected to be in the vanguard and there was hope that Bolton Wanderers and Preston North End would draw nearer to the power of their former days in the First Division.

Everton's great name and Sheffield Wednesday's costly stars were welcomed by the smaller clubs in the Second Division. Wednesday were strong favourties to regain their premier status, particularly with expensive Jackie Sewell as a renowned goal-getter and wing-halves of the calibre of Eddie Gannon and Doug Witcomb. Coventry City were expecting to do well if Tommy Briggs began to 'pay off' the £20,000 expended on his signature the previous season.

In the Third Division, Grimsby Town were back in the Northern section and turned to one Bill Shankly. As a player he was a dynamo of a wing-half at Preston, and an inspiration at Carlisle in his first managership. It was no surprise when Shankly made several Scottish signings to improve Grimsby's prospects. It was interesting to note that Oldham Athletic had appointed George Hardwick, the former England skipper, as player-manager, and Vic Buckingham had taken over at Bradford, after impressing with his coaching of the successful amateurs, Pegasus.

For England it was to be a busy season and the Press were warning that the proud unbeaten record on these shores was in danger as visits from France and, more particularly, Austria, justly claiming to be unofficial champions of Europe, were anticipated.

When the gates opened on the 46 League grounds it was immediately plain that, despite the threepenny increase, Mr Public was going to thumb his nose at the football politics. A million fans poured like a tidal-wave through the turnstiles for the 'great kick-off' and on a day of surprises the general concensus was that they had got their 1s 6d worth.

Spurs, the champions, were beaten at Middlesbrough 2-1 before 45,000, but the real surprise came at Blackpool where Chelsea, the butt of so many music-hall jokes, beat the previous season's Cup Finalists, by the same score. The credit for the Chelsea bonus went to the new goalkeeper, Bill Robertson, and to the goalscorers Bobby Campbell and youngster Bobby Smith. Sitting out the action that day were two big names who had refused to re-sign for Chelsea — John Harris, their stopper, and Roy Bentley, their England star striker.

The Cup holders, Newcastle United, swarmed through Stoke's suspect defence in a six-goal deluge at St James' Park with Milburn helping himself to a hat-trick. A new centre-forward in the headlines was 22-year-old Cliff Holton, who had displaced Peter Goring at Arsenal, earning rave reviews on his debut and an equalizer against Huddersfield.

There was an unusual twist at Aston Villa when Con Martin, after a long run and international appearances at both centre-half and centre-forward, returned to his original goalkeeping role. In his first half-dozen games in the position Villa were unbeaten and had dropped only one point. Villa manager George Martin was delighted with his experiment. "Con is a grand goalkeeper," he said. " He makes it look as easy as eating strawberries."

The first Saturday in September was notable, not only for Tommy Lawton's 200th League goal, scored at Meadow Lane for Notts County, but also for the shedding by Tottenham of the glamour and aura of invincibility that had made them the greatest team in post-war football. It would be fairer to say it was ripped from them by Newcastle United as Spurs were routed 7-2 at St James' Park before 50,000 disbelieving fans.

By that score Tottenham had conceded seven goals for the first time ever in a League match. With the exception of an 8-0 defeat at Birmingham in October 1945, during the unsettled days of the transitional season, it was the highest ever 'goals against' total against the North Londoners. The absence of key men Clarke and Baily was important but 'man of the match' was the Chilean international George Robledo, who scored three goals. The main reason given by the London Press for the astonishing defeat was an 'off-day' for goalkeeper Ted Ditchburn. The strange feature about the nine-goal affair, apart from the goalless last 15 minutes, was that the previous six meetings between the two sides had yielded only six goals.

The early pacemakers were Bolton Wanderers as the goals flowed from Nat Lofthouse and Willie Moir and the defence was bolstered by new skipper Johnny Ball and the emergence of a bright young centre-half in Malcolm Barrass, soon to be capped by England as they still worked to solve their defensive problems. Bolton manager Bill Ridding worked with only 19 full-time professionals but looked like he might restore the glories of the era of Joe Smith, David Jack, Dick Pym and Ted Vizard.

Goals were as plentiful as strawberries in June in the run-up to Christmas that season and there was one in particular that set the terraces alight. It came from Stanley Matthews, for Blackpool at Sunderland, and was his first since New Year's Day 1949 at Villa Park — almost three years earlier.

Jack Rowley of Manchester United was much more prolific, scoring his third hat-trick of the season in the first week of September — the quickest trio of hat-tricks ever performed in the First Division. Rowley staked an irresistible claim for an England place as he celebrated his 200th post-war League appearance. George Robledo of Newcastle had temporarily taken over Milburn's goalscoring mantle and snapped four of United's seven against Burnley, normally noted at that time for their 'iron curtain' defence.

Andy Graver of Lincoln topped even that with his six in the 11-1 win over pilotless Crewe, a feat which established a new scoring record for the Imps. The 23-year-old had come to Lincoln at a bargain-basement price of £3,000 from Newcastle a few weeks earlier. In the same weekend, Wolves led the way in the top division with seven goals at Huddersfield with three for Jimmy Dunn and two for Jimmy

Mullen. A key factor was Billy Wright's mastery of Town's talented inside-forward Harold Hassall.

On the same autumn Saturday, Arsenal and Spurs were playing out a pulsating 1-1 draw before 68,164 and it was estimated that a bigger crowd was turned away from the locked gates than attended any of that day's Third North games. Many of the overflow made their way back to White Hart Lane from Highbury to watch the Spurs reserve side in action and keep up with the latest score from the regular loudspeaker announcements. What they missed was reportedly the 'first real classic of the season' which starred the great little, largely forgotten, genius of Jimmy Logie.

The Arsenal goal stemmed from what the same Press report called 'the maziest, craziest dribble of all time — a composite mixture of Alex James and Stanley Matthews at their most devilish' which forced the Spurs full-back Willis to end the 40-yard run by conceding a corner. Logie crossed from the flag-kick for a Lawton-like goal from the forehead of young Cliff Holton. This equalized an earlier Spurs goal from Peter Murphy, but it was Logie's vintage display that day which brought the gasps from the tighly-packed crowd. Arsenal had figured that Logie's ball-skill would have more freedom of movement if the little man was given longish spells out on the wing and so it proved.

Another artist to emerge at that time, taking advantage of Baily's injury-enforced absence from the Spurs line-up, was little Tommy Harmer, a 22-year old former printer's apprentice from Hackney, who resembled a jockey in his build. Arthur Rowe, his manager, was moved to admit, "His ball-play is fantastic — he can make the ball talk." But Rowe doubted his stamina on heavy grounds, and so it proved throughout Harmer's career.

The number of near-£20,000 moves was on the increase, following the bench-mark set by Sewell's £34,000 fee the previous season. The former Wolves Cup Final hero, Sammy Smyth, to Stoke City; the Newcastle inside-forward, Ivor Broadis, to Manchester City; and little Ernie Taylor, also from Newcastle, to Blackpool; they were amongst the several who moved at that level before Christmas.

In the Second Division, Sheffield Wednesday were hovering uneasily near the foot of the table after the first third of the season when manager Eric Taylor tried the massive 6ft 3inch tall, awkward-looking Derek Dooley at centre-forward. In his first match, against neighbours Barnsley, the raw youngster scored the two goals which brought a vital win and from then on Dooley's impact on Wednesday's season was nothing short of sensational. Promotion conscious Notts County were an early victim for the rampaging Dooley as he grabbed five of Wednesday's six. All five came in the second-half at Hillsborough — three in one hectic 11-minute spell.

It was their neighbours, Sheffield United, who made all the early

Liverpool's Jimmy Payne puts a shot out of reach of Chelsea goalkeeper Bill Robertson at Anfield just before Christmas 1951. There were 26,459 present to see a 2-2 draw.

running in that division, thanks mainly to the goalscoring of winger Alf Ringstead. When United beat Wednesday 7-3 in their 'derby' match, Ringstead scored three in a thrilling encounter played at terrific speed before over 50,000 fans at Bramall Lane. With the score at 2-2 and less than 25 minutes to play, six goals followed in that last period to leave the Press admitting that they became confused over the goalscorers. It might have been eight for United if Wednesday goalkeeper Dave McIntosh had not saved a penalty from Fred Furniss.

When United completed a double over Wednesday at Hillsborough, in a game which attracted the biggest crowd — 65,384 — since the Cup visit of Manchester City had established the ground record of 73,000 in February 1934, it seemed that they and not their neighbours must be promoted. Unfortunately, the Blades slumped dismally in the final weeks as they missed the inspiration of star inside-forward Jimmy Hagan.

As Christmas approached the goals were coming in even greater quantities. One Saturday produced the greatest welter of goals since the war — 182 in 46 games, averaging nearly four per game. Arsenal kept their unbeaten home record by walloping West Bromwich 6-3 with Doug Lishman scoring his third hat-trick of the season; Blackpool trounced Newcastle by the same score; Derby hit Fulham for five, including three in 12 minutes; but the top scorers were Bury in the Second Division with their eight against Southampton. Only one game that day, at Sunderland, finished goalless as the whole programme gave value for money.

The Press, who weeks before had been doom-laden in their

expectation of the visit of the much-vaunted Austrians to Wembley for what was being termed the 'Match of the Century', hailed the invigorating quality of our game which had suddenly emerged: "Just when we had about reached the despairing depths in the search for football that would measure up to the standard we have held in the mind for many a year — Glory be! We found it! Here was the kind of football we have been cajoling for, begging for, bullying for — rumbustious tackling, man-to-man movement of the ball . . ."

Before the passing of the Clean Air Act in 1956, London had more than its fair share of foggy days. Known as pea-soupers, that mixture of smoke and fog called smog, they gave football in the industrial cities an eerie look on occasions. The last Saturday in November produced such an occasion and Arsenal and Wolves did their best at Highbury and Molineux respectively to brighten the scene.

Wolves tripped out for the second half against Charlton in changed bright yellow shirts, whilst Arsenal had a 'sight-board', painted a fluorescent yellow-green colour, behind each goal. It certainly helped Arsenal's Doug Lishman to find the way to goal against Bolton, for he notched his fourth hat-trick of the season. No one had managed the feat in Division One since Freddie Steele hit five for Stoke City in 1936-7.

Floodlights might have pierced the gloom that day and that season the calls for their use with a white ball became insistent. Southampton were the first club to take the plunge, hastily rearranging their reserve fixture against Spurs at The Dell to ensure the distinction. For the record, Tottenham's Tony Marchi, later to become a regular first-team wing-half, but playing that night at centre-forward, became the first player to score a goal in a floodlit competitive match in Great Britain.

As the Government inquiry into the conditions and wages of the players dragged on, the League clubs were suggesting a £20 per week maximum wage. The Players' Union were in no mood to accept any ceiling payment and through their militant chairman, Jimmy Guthrie, were aiming hard for a minimum wage for all players with no limit for the elite. As Guthrie put it: "For too long we have been the Cinderella men of the entertainment industry. We will protect the little man in the lower grades by making certain he is paid a reasonable wage. But when it comes to the stars we are not interested in any plan which pins them down to a wage far below their value at the turnstiles."

One of the prime movers behind the League club's offer was comedian Tommy Trinder, one of the four directors at Fulham, and at his club that week an 18-year-old inside forward Bob Robson — later known as Bobby — was making the news by keeping Wolves captain Billy Wright fully occupied at Craven Cottage in the 2-2 draw before 30,000.

When the Christmas fixtures were complete, the top three sides in the First and Second Divisions were on the same number of points. Arsenal, Manchester United and Portsmouth were locked on 32 points and Cardiff, Sheffield Wednesday and Birmingham were on 30. Wednesday had been whisked to the top of the table by Dooley's 24 goals in 12 games, almost proving that one man can make a team. More than that, Wednesday's attendances had rocketed as a consequence — from 35,000 plus in early season to a peak of 61,187 on Christmas Day.

One schoolmaster enjoying his Christmas holidays was 24-year-old George Robb, Finchley's England amateur international winger, who made his debut for Spurs at Charlton outside-left to give Medley a rest. Robb had reportedley not only declined offers to join a string of leading English clubs, but had turned down a name-your-own-terms invitation to join the leading Italian club, Padua. It was therefore no surprise when Robb made several appearances for Spurs in the coming seasons and even went on to appear for England in a full international whilst still an amateur. On that Christmas Day debut, Robb had made an immediate impact, scoring one goal and making two more.

Cardiff City were joint top of the Second Division and skipper Alf Sherwood was the toast of Ninian Park. After a cut over his eye which needed four stitches, full-back Sherwood returned, swathed in bandages, to score two goals as a one-eyed outside-right to beat Doncaster Rovers. Before that double, Sherwood had scored only a single goal in League football since the war, and that had been a penalty.

When the FA Cup came round again, the third round brought two major shocks with the defeats of high-riding Manchester United and the previous year's Finalists, Blackpool. United were surprisingly beaten at home by Second Division Hull City, who were masterminded by Raich Carter. The Seasiders made their early exit at West Ham. Immediately two FA Cup giants of the period had been eliminated.

The most despondent team in Britain at this time was clearly Chester, who had lost 11-2 at Oldham after twice leading in the first-half of their Third Division North encounter. Eric Gemmell, the Oldham centre-forward, was a part-timer and travelling salesman, but his seven goals in the match was the best individual performance in the League since Joe Payne hit the headlines with his ten for Luton Town in 1936.

All this was embarassing for Chelsea, who had been given the Cup scare of a lifetime by Chester a week earlier. The Sealand Road club had taken a two-goal lead by half-time at Stamford Bridge, through

Coffin and Greenwood, but the Pensioners scrambled a draw with late goals from Gray and Armstrong. In the replay it was not until extra-time that Chelsea squeezed through before 20,500 at Chester with young centre-forward Bobby Smith scoring the winner in the 3-2 victory.

The advent of more scientific attacking play and the plethora of goals had suggested that more were being shared amongst the line of forwards in most teams, despite the evidence to the contrary from Messrs Dooley and Gemmell. In that week four League hat-tricks fell to inside-fowards — Arthur Rowley of Leicester, Jeff Taylor of Fulham, Peter Murphy of Birmingham — on his debut after a £15,000 transfer from Spurs — and Ken Tucker of West Ham. Rowley's goals brought him up to the 50-mark since joining the Filbert Street team 18 months previously. Taylor's three had come in a 6-0 win over Middlesbrough to lift Fulham off the bottom. The match, played in front of 30,000 fans, had been described beforehand by manager Bill Dodgin as 'the most critical match in our history', so desperate was he to pull out of the danger zone. A key factor for Fulham was the form of Charlie Mitten, the former Manchester United winger, recruited after his 'Bogota Sentence' had been served.

It was also a momentous week for Reading in the Third Division South as they notched up their 13th successive win, over a Gillingham team who had, in turn, lost ten in a row.

In the Cup, the fourth round was notable for Newcastle's 3-0 win at Tottenham before 69,000, thanks to two goals from George Robledo. The deciding factor was not only the muddy conditions, which did not suit Spurs, but the mastery of tricky winger Bobby Mitchell over Spurs right-back, Alf Ramsey. One shock was at Second Division Birmingham where Third Division Leyton Orient, under the guidance of manager Alec Stock, triumphed by a single goal following upon their similar conquest of Everton in the previous round. The other shock was at First Division Middlesbrough where Peter Doherty led Doncaster Rovers to an amazing 4-1 win.

The diffident 34-year-old Stock was thrilled when the fifth-round draw paired the little East London side with the mighty Gunners. "I prayed that the draw would give us Arsenal. They are the ultimate in English football. Their coming here makes me happier than anything in football ever has," he said. In the unhappy event, a record 30,000 crowd at Brisbane Road — paying record receipts of £5,691 — saw their illustrious opponents score three goals to win with embarassing ease, with Lishman scoring twice.

While Cup favourites Newcastle were going through at the expense of Second Division Swansea, Blackburn Rovers, from the same division, were beating West Bromwich Albion by a single penalty goal by Bill Eckersley three minutes from time. The Ewood Park crowd was 50,000,

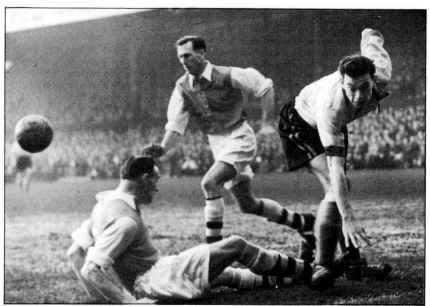

Arsenal beat Norwich City 5-0 in the third round of the FA Cup in January 1952. Lionel Smith, the Gunners' left-back, falls after tackling a Norwich forward. Skipper Joe Mercer is the other Arsenal player.

Arsenal score their first goal after 20 minutes when Jimmy Logie runs on to a back-pass and slides the ball past goalkeeper Ken Nethercott.

to revive memories of the 'good old days' of such attendances at the famous club, so quiet in post-war years.

The sixth round paired Newcastle and Portsmouth at Fratton Park and the titanic struggle, played out at a fierce pace but with great skill, was generally reckoned to be one of the classic matches of the period. Indeed, Alan Hoby of the *Daily Express* headlined his report: 'The greatest game I have ever seen,' and was emphatic that Newcastle's Jackie Milburn 'turned in one of the best centre-forward displays of all time'. United won 4-2 with a hat-trick from Milburn and both sets of fans thrilled to his third goal — a 25-yard cross-shot with his left foot. His duel with Froggatt, both with extraordinary pace, was crucial, with the Newcastle leader a narrow victor.

The late Geoffrey Green of *The Times* was moved to rate the match as one of the best three club matches he had seen in 30 years of reporting the game and that incredible shot from Milburn — coming with 15 minutes left and the score at 2-2 — vitually settled the match. The scenes after the match, which reminded many observers of the spirit of the pre-war golden age, were memorable, as hundreds of rival supporters linked arms outside the ground to sing the 'Blaydon Races', the Geordie anthem.

Arsenal's passage to the semi-final was less dramatic before a record 28,000 at Luton when two goals from Freddie Cox ensured a comfortable 3-2 victory. In the semi-final they were drawn against a Chelsea side who had come through an intense and hard-fought quarter-final tie at Bramall Lane against Second Division Sheffield United by a single goal, scored by the game's outstanding player, Roy Bentley.

Blackburn Rovers had to meet Newcastle in the other semi-final and it was an amateur, Bill Holmes, who ensured their place by the 3-1 win over Lancashire neighbours Burnley. In a typical derby match, Holmes scored the second and made the third for Glover, but the Press were unconvinced about Rovers' chances of going to Wembley, as a surprise packet, when they were paired with the Magpies.

A violent snowstorm in London on Boat-Race Saturday caused the Arsenal-Chelsea tie to be postponed at Tottenham but on the same day, the Newcastle-Blackburn tie was goalless at Hillsborough. The replay, at Leeds, was heading for another draw after Robledo, for Newcastle, and Quigley, for Rovers, had scored. But with four minutes remaining the Magpies were awarded a penalty after Campbell had handled on the goal-line. Mitchell beat Rovers goalkeeper, Reg Elvy, with a calm left-foot shot to put Newcastle in the Final again. Mitchell, who had never previously taken a penalty, had to take the kick after Milburn, the normal penalty-taker, had declined. "Not me, my legs are too shaky," was his response.

When it was played the following week at White Hart Lane, the

In the sixth round, Arsenal won 3-2 at Luton after the Hatters had scored first. Here goalkeeper Bernard Streten collects Don Roper's cross to Doug Lishman. Over 28,433 fans packed Kenilworth Road.

all-London clash was drawn 1-1, but on the following Monday at the same venue Arsenal won through easily by 3-0 with two typically violent, almost freakish, goals coming from Freddie Cox, the Gunners' battering ram of an outside-right. So the most slandered team in the country were back at Wembley for the second time in three years and were in with a good chance of a League and Cup double that year.

Whether it was based on pure envy or sound reasoning, the Press — and millions outside Highbury — found Arsenal's almost continuous success hard to understand. The Gunners were variously accused of being negative, stereotyped, ruthless and of relying almost entirely on a defensive plan almost 20 years old. What was clear was that, in that season, as always, you either loved them or loathed them, but you could not ignore that aura of invincibility which stemmed from their inflexible will-to-win. The Arsenal fans would have pointed to the power of their fiery, controversial red-haired wing-half Alex Forbes, to the precocious talent of the young Welsh centre-half Ray Daniel and to the youthful vigour of Cliff Holton at centre-forward. Not to mention the invaluable experience of men like 38-year-old captain Joe Mercer, the craftsman Logie and the goalscoring Cox.

By contrast, Newcastle were given every credit for their swift, scientific and brilliant attack which had already destroyed the might of Tottenham and Portsmouth on their own grounds. Milburn and Robledo scored over 60 goals between them that season, as the spearheads with great support from Walker on the right wing and the super-dribbler Mitchell on the left.

The Magpies now included seven of the men who had gained winners' medals the year before — the newcomers being Ronnie Simpson in goal, Alf McMichael at left-back, Ted Robledo (George's brother) at left-half and Billy Foulkes at inside-right. Foulkes had a remarkable rise to the top that season. Early in the campaign he had moved from Chester to Tyneside, had made his debut for Wales and scored with his first real shot, and then finished the season with a Cup winner's medal.

As the Final approached, a positive horde of afflictions beset Arsenal. Days before the Wembley game, Lishman, Ray Daniel, and Logie were injured and admitted to hospital. In the event the last two played with unhealed injuries, Daniel had to turn out with an injured arm heavily bandaged and Logie was only half-fit with a thigh injury.

In the Final, Arsenal were on top for the first 15 minutes but their famous luck deserted them completely in the 19th minute. Full-back Wally Barnes tore the ligaments in his right knee as he rapidly changed direction on the rich Wembley turf and after a valiant attempt to stay on, the Welshman was helped off to leave Arsenal with ten men and over an hour to play. Don Roper was switched to full-back and ten-men Arsenal proceeded to put on the most gallant rearguard action, even managing to hit the Newcastle cross-bar through a Lishman header.

It was a stuttering, stumbling performance by United and most untypical. And with only seven minutes remaining of a gruelling but sterile match, there was still no score. The ten men looked like holding out for a replay when, in their only penetrative attack, Mitchell floated the ball across the Arsenal goalmouth to Robledo, who raced in from the inside-right position to head the ball gently down and into the net off the near goal-post.

The hollow victory for the Magpies, with all the glory going to the magnificent losers, made them the first team this century to take the Cup in successive years, but it was only captain Joe Harvey who played to form and Milburn was seldom his usual spectacular self. Winston Churchill, at his first-ever Final, presented the Cup to the Newcastle captain, who appeared to be genuinely sorry that it was won in such a fashion.

Manchester United had made an early exit from the Cup that year but, despite a loss of rhythm before Christmas, had been strong and well-balanced throughout the campaign. The side was substantially that which had won the Cup in 1948, but there were two new wide-men. Roger Byrne on the left-wing and John Berry on the right — the latter signed from Birmingham for £25,000.

When United showed signs of staleness Matt Busby made some astute

Newcastle skipper Joe Harvey in familar pose, carried aloft with the FA Cup.

positional changes, moving left-back Byrne to outside-left, although later returning to full-back he was to become an England regular; Carey to right-half; Aston from left-back to centre-forward. Byrne was a revelation, scoring seven goals in the last vital six matches.

Their nearest challengers were Arsenal, in search of the League and Cup double, and after winning through to Wembley the Gunners stood level on points with United, with two games left. Hard-hit by injuries, the Arsenal team for the penultimate fixture at West Bromwich included six reserves and they lost 3-1. It meant that the Highbury side had to beat Manchester United 7-0 at Old Trafford the week before the Final, the last Saturday of the League season, to win the title but in the event they were well beaten by a morale-shattering 6-1. Typically, Jack Rowley scored a hat-trick and Stan Pearson a double to make a combined total of 52 goals for the pair for the season out of United's 95.

So Manchester United had won their first League Championship in 41 years, after taking the runners-up spot four times in five post-war seasons. At last Busby and the entertaining, well-combined efforts of Johnny Carey and company had received full reward and no-one begrudged them their popular success. The foundation rested in Carey, the studious exemplary captain, the tall Allenby Chilton at centre-half, and little Henry Cockburn, who always seemed a match for bigger and stronger opponents.

Spurs took the runners-up spot on goal-average from Arsenal but had not hit their Championship push-and-run form of the previous season. Man for man, it was virtually the same side but Les Bennett had emerged as a fine centre-forward to contest the berth with Len Duquemin. Although the White Hart Lane side showed great consistency, they were considered extremely fortunate to secure second place with the aid of two hotly-disputed goals which brought two late-season 1-0 home wins over Preston and Huddersfield.

The latter brought a protest to the League by Huddersfield against the result being allowed to stand. Their case was that the winning goal, in injury-time, was scored after Baily for Spurs, when taking a corner-kick, had played the ball twice before it was touched by another player. Newspaper reports and Baily himself subsequently supported their view that the ball struck the referee and was then centred by Baily, from whose cross Duquemin scored the winner for Spurs. The League allowed the result to stand after the referee, in response to their enquiry, indicated that he did not agree that Baily had played the ball twice. The point would not, as it transpired, have saved Huddersfield from eventual relegation, but it added to their end-of-season despair.

Fulham finished bottom and, despite star forwards Bedford Jezzard and Charlie Mitten, were a source of irritation throughout, to the dismay of their fans and team boss Bill Dodgin.

Portsmouth finished fourth but generally failed to stay the pace. Their half-back line of Scoular, Froggatt and Dickinson was clearly the best in the country and all three were engaged in the Scotland-England international at Hampden Park that season. Bolton Wanderers were also in the talent money, thanks mainly to their glorious early-season burst. Their strength was in attack with the internationals Willie Moir, the gifted Harold Hassall, and the expensive Bobby Langton to aid the muscular power of Nat Lofthouse. Liverpool were draw specialists which did not enhance their chances. Eleven of their 21 home games were drawn and at one stage they had not won at Anfield for four months.

The 'shuttlecock' side of the era was Sheffield Wednesday. Promotion to the First Division had been gained in 1949-50 and, although they were relegated the next season, now the Owls bounced back up again. Theirs was a dynamic run to promotion but it was not secured until the penultimate match, before 36,000 fans at Highfield Road. Derek Dooley scored in the first two minutes and the last two minutes as Wednesday won 2-0. By the end of the season Dooley had brought his personal goals total to 47, and Wednesday's total to exactly 100. The raw-boned 'Roy of the Rovers' folk hero beat the post-war scoring record of Rotherham's Jack Shaw by one goal and by his extraordinary feats transformed Wednesday's season and propelled them back into the big-time.

As the Cup Final was being played, Cardiff City were defeating Leeds United 3-1 in front of a capacity 55,000 crowd at Ninian Park to pip Birmingham City for the second promotion place. Cardiff had to win to secure their return to the First Division after an absence of 23 momentous years, which had seen the Bluebirds sink to such depths in the 1930s that they had to apply for re-election to the Third Division South. The meticulous grey-haired Cyril Spiers, a former Aston Villa, Spurs and Wolves goalkeeper, was in his second spell as manager at the Welsh club, but it was an Englishman, Wilf Grant, who was the most popular man in the Principality that Saturday. Previously an outside-right with Manchester City and Southampton, Grant scored twice that day from centre-forward and was carried from the field in exuberant scenes.

Blackburn Rovers had a more than eventful season in the Second after a wretched start which found them at the bottom in the week before Christmas. A magnificent revival brought a club record with seven successive victories and a final run-in of 14 victories in 18 matches. In this period Rovers lacked the services of goal-a-match Eddie Quigley but defenders Bill Eckersley, graduating to England recognition, Willie Kelly and goalkeeper Reg Elvy were in fine form and Wharton, Crossan and Nightingale star forwards. As Cup semi-finalists, Blackburn had come so close in the replay with Newcastle to springing a major surprise.

It was to be Second Division football the following season for promoted Plymouth Argyle and Lincoln City, at the top of the Southern and Northern Sections respectively. Argyle were led by the mountainous bearded figure of 'Jumbo' Ken Chisholm and the goals from him and Maurice Tadman were vital, as was the goalkeeping of Welsh international Bill Shortt. It was a triumph for Lincolnshire in the latter section with Bill Shankly's Grimsby Town finishing runners-up in a season in which they had a sequence of 11 successive League wins — still a club record. Top scorer was Billy Cairns for the Mariners with 31 goals and already a veteran when he joined in 1946 after being a pre-war Newcastle star.

In the Third Division South, Walsall and Exeter City had to apply for re-election and in the North, Workington and Darlington were the unfortunate pair.

It had been the Welsh national team's 75th anniversary season and not only did Wales win Rugby's Triple Crown, but Cardiff City also won promotion to the First Division. More than that, Wales beat the combined might of England, Scotland and Northern Ireland, in the form of a 'Rest of the United Kingdom', at Cardiff in the celebration fixture and also went on to share the Home International Championship. Indeed, the Welsh knew that they should have beaten England at Ninian Park — victory would have ensured the title — rather than allowing an outplayed English team to escape with a 1-1 draw.

The Welsh star was Swansea inside-forward Ivor Allchurch, whose scintillating international displays, and in particular a winning goal scored at Hampden Park against the Scots, drew unsuccessful bids from a pack of First Division clubs, which reportedly reached £40,000 from Newcastle United.

For England, Billy Wright was restored as right-half and captain and his later 'Footballer of the Year' accolade confirmed that his form and confidence had been regained. The opening international of the season, when England scrambled a 2-2 draw against France, the poor relations of European football, was a bad omen for the stiff test against the Austrians, regarded as the finest side in Europe. This important match, as a yardstick for England's international standing, was gleefully hailed by the popular national papers as yet another 'Match of the Century'. Most significantly, the Austrians had beaten Scotland both home and away in recent months.

The game were a fascinating clash of styles with Austria, relying on their cultured, almost leisurely, but measured build-up, and England on speed, first-time passing and maximum efforts. The tacticians were intrigued by the play of the very talented Ernst Ocwirk, who, with a number-five on his back, played in a free role behind the forwards, setting up moves and taking every chance to use his powerful shooting. A scratch England team, ravaged by injuries to the likes of Finney, Mortensen, Nicholson and Lionel Smith, all suffered in the previous Saturday's League programme, again salvaged a 2-2 draw as a result of a late coolly-taken penalty by Alf Ramsey. Surprise first caps had to be awarded to young winger Arthur Milton of Arsenal, after only 11 first-team games, and the 28-year old inside-forward Ivor Broadis from Manchester City.

So England had kept her proud, if somewhat bruised, unbeaten home record and the return fixture in Vienna to be played six months later was eagerly awaited by those who could work up an enthusiasm for the national cause, Club most definitely came before country at this time and a measure of apathy abounded towards the tottering England team. The average fan could not work up an enthusiasm for his country and England's soccer slide was largely due to the lack of interest and passion shown by the fans. Most supporters were not attracted to an international unless members of their own team were playing and the England team suffered from what could only be called an 'identification crisis'. They were supported by no more than a cheerful modest patriotism rather than the fervour reserved for the

Wolves and England star Billy Wright, voted Footballer of the Year in 1952.

club sides. The growth of a more fanatical, even violent, English nationalism in football lay some years ahead.

The clubs themselves were expressing the views, usually in private, but not too difficult to discern, that there were too many internationals matches , that they were badly spaced, and that they had a disturbing effect on their players. Certainly there was little co-operation with the Football Association and even less appreciation of the prestige and all-round advantages for the game to be secured by the national team's successes.

The return against Austria in Vienna, played two weeks after the season had ended, and regarded as the unofficial championship of Europe, earned Nat Lofthouse the nickname 'The Lion of Vienna'. The game went into the last quarter with England hanging on to a 2-2 draw again before it was settled by a typical brave Lofthouse break. Dashing through from the half-way line he never flinched as the goalkeeper collided with him but coolly slid home his shot. It was an historic victory and a triumph for English grit and spirit which finally overcame the science and technical ability of the Austrians.

No one doubted that the Europeans had the more skilful ball-players who seemed to possess a deeper knowledge of the game but for the moment our status as a first-class football-playing country was intact and our methods had met the challenges. The message from one national newspaper, before the victory over Austria, had come true: 'The Austrians do not like being hustled. An England team fighting like tigers for the whole 90 minutes can beat them.'

The 1951-2 season had been marked by goals and more goals. The most pleasing feature was the spate of individual marksmen with as many as 27 players totalling 25 or more goals in Cup and League, and ten of them reached the 30 mark. The remarkable Dooley headed the list, inevitably, followed by prolific Third Division marksman Ronnie Blackman, with 39 for Reading, and Andy Graver, who netted 37 for Lincoln. Jack Lewis, the Reading right-half, scored 15 goals to create a record for a player other than a recognized forward. Even full-back Alf Ramsey at Tottenham managed six goals.

Apart from Dooley, the greatest goalscoring impact was made by West Bromwich's Ronnie Allen who, in his first season in the top flight, managed 32 League goals. It was as recently as the previous September that the 22-year-old Allen was transformed into a successful spearhead, after a £15,000 move from Port Vale.

In that season attendances began to exhibit a steady, but still gradual, decline and were shown to be down overall by 1.5 per cent. The figures showed that this was due to reduced gates in the First Division, whereas in the Second Division and Third North the attendances increased slightly. Live broadcasting of a big game again demonstrated its effect on attendances when in early April people stayed home beside their sets for the Scotland-England match and the corresponding full League programme suffered as a consequence. Derby County and Manchester City, as an example, were each 10,000 down and the Wolves almost 20,000 down on their previous home attendances. Despite the moving of the Cup Final away from a League Saturday, a further lesson had been learned by the authorities in the vexed question of live broadcasting.

The slump was clearly alarming the Football Association and the game was now perceived as losing in the entertainments race numerically and financially, despite the huge amount of money that appeared to change hands every week. The feeling was that the fans were becoming so sated with the game that only the very best sides would satisfy them in the future. Even now less popular clubs were 'feeling the pinch' and deficits, even up to £100 per week, were being reported in some quarters.

Floodlights were about to give the game a new and exciting dimension and, as if to demonstrate their appeal, Arsenal and Glasgow Rangers had played a friendly in mid-winter before a curious and excited 60,000 plus crowd at Highbury. Clearly, old notions were about to be challenged and new ideas promulgated and accepted as the football theorists introduced new tactics and training methods to the game in those early 1950s.

The players' surge in militancy had not only increased their self-esteem but had also improved their rewards such that, even if they were not in 'the big league' in the entertainment world, at least it could be said that the maximum wage put them at the top of the manual wages pyramid. As the Players' Union made its small gains, edging up the maximum wage and stressing the provident and sickness benefits, so the ground was being laid for the moves towards the scrapping of the maximum wage and freedom of contract to follow in later years.

Football was about to feel the impact of television and the post-industrial affluence. The regular televising of key games, to an increasing number of set-owners, was bound to have an effect on attendances in the future. The affluence was to herald a shift away from the restricted pre-occupations of earlier generations so that the game would no longer provide a focus for collective urban leisure. Already, even, the thousands of working men in caps and mufflers had been replaced by a more mature working-class culture.

The Matthews
(& Mortensen) Finale

W E have lived easily with inflation in this country for many years, but in 1952 the rise in the minimum entrance fee to football matches, from 1s 6d to 1s 9d, aroused much comment, much of it adverse. The game had become a more expensive commodity for the second successive year, mainly as a result of the clubs' anticipation of the imposition of a higher rate of Entertainment Tax by the Government. Football to the Englishman was still not a luxury, more an essential. This was also perhaps true on a far wider horizon when it was realized that over 80 nations were now in membership with the Federation Internationale de Football Association (FIFA).

As we have seen, overall attendances dropped in the previous season despite the game's vast expanse and apparent wealth. In spite of the deep roots that football still had in the people, it was about to face stern examinations, both on and off the field of play, and time was no longer on the game's side.

The summer of 1952 had been a close season in which there was relief from the staggering transfer fees and little movement of players. Instead there had been an unprecedented upheaval on the managerial side. It was a remarkable fact that 16 Football League clubs would begin the season under new managers and of the five clubs which finished at the foot of the First Division, only Bill Dodgin of Fulham kept his job. Other managers to move included Bob Jackson of Portsmouth and Joe Smith of West Brom, who moved to Hull City and Reading respectively for higher salaries. This was yet more evidence that the successful Third Division clubs could compete with the best in the land, despite all the hardship that was gradually being experienced in the lower reaches of the League.

At the League's annual meeting in June, a proposal by Spurs for four-up four-down had been defeated and a tentative proposal to allow League and Cup games to be televised was quickly put down. With the prompt re-election of the four teams forced to apply, it was much a case of 'as you were'.

In the summer game, Len Hutton had been appointed as the first professional cricketer to captain England and the three victories ensured that the four-match series against India was won as a young fast bowler called Freddie Trueman burst upon the international scene. Surrey, under the fine leadership of Stuart Surridge, were outright champions for the first time since 1914, with great bowling contributions from Laker, Lock and Bedser.

As the nation looked forward to the reign of Queen Elizabeth II, a million new television sets were purchased in the run-up to the Coronation. The first television broadcast for schools was made that summer as the BBC completed the building of five high-power stations. These made it possible for 80 per cent of the population to receive television programmes. As a result Britain was shown to have the highest coverage in the world — compared with only 50 per cent in the USA. It was estimated that there were now four million viewers — 11 per cent of the total potential audience. It was no wonder that the entertainments industry, and football in particular, was watching its growing appeal with much concern.

For the housewife there was the welcome news that the meat, bacon and tea rations had all increased, but the sugar ration was still 10ozs weekly and the cheese ration had even been reduced from 1.5ozs weekly to 1oz. Happily, the family allowance was increased during the summer months from 5s to 8s per week for each child after the first.

In London, the last of the trams had disappeared as the scheme, started in 1950, to replace them with buses was completed. The purchase of a motor-car was increasingly fulfilling people's widening material ambitions and figures showed that £90 million had been spent on new cars in 1951.

Almost as much money was being expended on the football pools at this time and the Churches' Commission on Gambling reported a £5 million increase in expenditure in 1951 over the previous year. It was, they said with great concern, attributable to the 'extensive propaganda undertaken during the year by the three biggest firms, which had sent unsolicited sets of coupons to persons who had not applied for them'. An early example of the results obtainable from 'direct mailing' exercises or the 'junk mail' syndrome.

In the week before the football season opened, the West Country experienced the worst thunderstorms and torrential rain it had ever known. The consequent flooding of 250 square miles in the Lynton/Lynmouth area of Devon led to 30 deaths and hundreds losing their homes with the incident being designated as a 'national disaster'.

As for the coming football season, any discussion of the prospects included the questions as to whether Newcastle United could go one better and win the FA Cup for the third successive time; whether it might be Tottenham's year now that their White Hart Lane pitch had been relaid so that their classic close-passing game should not be clogged up by mid-winter mud; whether the enigmatic Chelsea might be revived under the drive of their new manager Ted Drake, the former Arsenal and England centre-forward, so that the music-hall comedians might have to look elsewhere for their jokes; whether newly-promoted Sheffield Wednesday's long-striding rough diamond of a centre-forward, Derek Dooley, might terrorise First Division centre-halves with the support of clever inside-forwards like Sewell and Quixall; and whether the Championship would again be fought out between Manchester United and Arsenal.

The Second Division promised again to be a real dog-fight with Huddersfield Town, Blackburn Rovers, Birmingham City, Leicester City and Sheffield United expected to be involved. Huddersfield had shown an earnest for their future by their purchase of Jimmy Watson, an inside-forward from Motherwell, for £16,000 — one of the few large sums expended in pre-season. After 32 years of successive membership in the top flight, Huddersfield had a new manager in Andy Beattie. They had a new full-back, Ron Staniforth from Stockport, but their main strength was expected to be in strikers Jimmy Glazzard and Roy Shiner.

Birmingham had missed promotion the previous season by 0.14 of a goal and in four post-war seasons had not finished lower than fourth in the Second Division under manager Bob Brocklebank. Centre-forward Tommy Briggs was their main hope for goals, having been recruited in the previous season. In the Third Division, Norwich City were very strongly fancied for the Southern Section championship and they were waiting for South African centre-forward Alf Ackerman to repay some of the £9,500 expended on him from Hull City a year earlier. Coventry City were also favoured after their relegation from the Second and they had secured star players — centre-half Roy Kirk from Leeds and centre-forward Eddie Brown from Southampton.

In the international arena, Wales, as the joint Home champions, looked forward to the long overdue honour of facing England at Wembley in November and England themselves had to meet another challenge from Europe in the shape of a visit from the Belgians before Christmas. Still, it seemed, most managers, directors and officials, brought up in a game post-war which had enjoyed the undivided loyalties of the fans, saw little need to look abroad and a marked insularity had been generated. It had clearly become imperative that British football should involve itself more closely with the game abroad, particularly in Europe, to keep in the mainstream of change and progress. The change of heart could not easily be found in the coming seasons, however.

In some ways it was a crisis season for the big-time clubs. With Treasury restrictions on bank loans and overdrafts, the majority of clubs no longer had the money to buy up expensive stars. As a consequence the new season was to be significant for the rash of new names and faces which spread to every club in the land. The highly-tuned mechanisms of the scouting organizations had to be put to work at full pitch to enable the steady flow of a new generation of top-class players to emerge. The success slogan for the future had to be 'grow your own talent' if every major club was to bring their staff up to pre-war strength.

The biggest shock on the opening day was Tottenham's 4-3 home defeat by West Bromwich Albion, and the biggest impact was made by the young black-haired centre-forward Ronnie Allen. He not only scored two of the four but also forced Spurs centre-half Harry Clarke to put through his own goal.

Behind the West Bromwich victory was team-coach Jesse Carver, appointed in May. The one-time centre-half with Newcastle United and Blackburn Rovers had been coach of Juventus of Turin and had not only taken them to the national championship for the first time in 15 years but had also led them to the Final of the Champion of Champions series in Rio in 1950. In addition, Carver had been national coach in Holland to a team which lost only one game in three years.

Carver's new plan, which out-paced the highly mobile Spurs, was to produce a '100-minute team' — all his training schemes were designed to produce a team that lasted that ten minutes extra with a resultant increased efficiency. The early results showed that the managerless West Brom were no longer a Cinderella side tucked away in the Black Country.

In the Second Division, Leicester's ace striker Arthur Rowley scored four against his old club, Fulham, in their 6-1 win. Fulham's single goal came from goalkeeper Ian Black who had moved to centre-forward after suffering an arm injury.

Another notable feat early on was the headed goal scored by Aston Villa full-back, Peter Aldis, from all of 35 yards. It was not only Aldis's first goal in League football but supposedley created a distance record for a headed goal.

Inevitably, the centre of the greatest attraction was Derek Dooley and even more so when after three weeks and no goals he was left out of the team for one match. The reason, according to Sheffield Wednesday manager Eric Taylor: "To emphasise our protest against the rough treatment he was getting from defences and for the marked-man attention from referees." Wednesday's previous opponents, Liverpool, were upset by the implication from this gesture: "Dooley got no more than he gave. We didn't squeal and we cannot see why Wednesday should squeal." It all added to the controversy already surrounding the burly striker.

Trevor Ford, of similar style, was also disturbed by the attitude of referees who appeared determined to curb his natural aggression, particularly in the way of his persistent charging of goalkeepers. Lectures for Ford were often on the menu when the Sunderland striker was out to ruffle defenders.

On the day that Dooley hit his first goal of the season, Fulham's Bobby Robson was silencing his persistent barrackers at Craven Cottage by scoring twice in a 6-0 hammering of Notts County, which brought his tally to eight in as many matches in the Second Division.

The early season also saw Norwich City equal the away scoring record of the Third Division South when they scored four in each half at Shrewsbury. It matched Walsall's eight goals at Northampton in 1946-7 and was also achieved with only ten men in the second-half after wing-half Don Pickwick was injured.

Another high-scoring feat was achieved by Bolton's Nat Lofthouse when he netted six consecutive goals for the Football League to break the inter-League goal record. The League XI managed seven in all in a typically one-sided contest against the Irish League.

Blackpool, Wolves and Liverpool were the early autumn pace-setters in the First Division and it was a surprise to find that Stanley Matthews had notched four goals in the Seasiders' first nine matches. At the age of 37, Matthews had shed none of his peerless artistry but his new-found intensity was evidence that he was fighting for a return to the England side. Allan Brown, Blackpool's husky inside-forward, showed the £26,000 touch with his second hat-trick of the season in the 8-4 dubbing of Charlton, but it was Matthews who was the chief tactician behind Blackpool's early surge and he was clearly heading for a vintage 'Indian Summer' of a season.

Wolves had won six out of seven and their 6-2 hammering of the League Champions, Manchester United, before 38,000 fans was the highlight. Rowley had put United two up before a second-half avalanche engulfed them. Young Roy Swinbourne led the way with three goals to give him ten in 11 matches.

Liverpool were the 'bargain-basement' team of the First Division and as they moved to the top it was noted that every player in the side cost exactly the £10 signing-on fee. Taking all the credit was manager Don Welsh but as he put it: "It shows that clubs can be run without paying big prices for youngers. The Liverpool and Manchester areas are teeming with young talent. So why go searching the country?"

Still on Merseyside, but in the Second Division, Everton had made a slow start but when they put seven past Doncaster, the Irish winger Tommy Eglington claimed five. The staticians worked overtime to reveal that a five-goal feat by a winger had only been achieved three times previously in the League and coincidentally the last was also by a Doncaster man, Albert Tanner, in 1935,

Portsmouth goalkeeper Ernie Butler knocks down a shot from Jimmy Payne at Anfield in September 1952. Nearly 50,000 fans witnessed a 1-1 draw.

Manchester United joined their neighbours City at the bottom of the First in mid-October after they lost at home to Stoke City before a paltry 28,000 crowd. United had opened the season with the side which had won the Championship but before long manager Matt Busby, with an eye to the future and conscious that his great players were getting old, was breaking up the team. One by one a flood of brilliant youngsters were introduced — David Pegg, Billy Foulkes, Tommy Taylor, Duncan Edwards, Dennis Viollet, Jeff Whitefoot, Jackie Blanchflower and Eddie Lewis — to fortify the 'Old Brigade'.

It was during this season that the term 'Busby's Babes' began to be used and no wonder. Edwards was 15 years of age on his debut, Pegg was 17, Viollet 19 and Foulkes 20. Taylor was a 21-year old 'veteran' signed from Barnsley for £30,000 and he flourished immediately in Old Trafford's unique atmosphere. In the event inevitably it was a season of transition for United who were to finish eighth, their lowest position since the war.

One team feeling distinctly aggrieved were Charlton Athletic, who found themselves playing their home games that season in competition with Chelsea and Arsenal. With the club needing an average attendances of 26,400 to pay their way, manager Jimmy Seed and the chairman Stan Gliksten were stunned by a crowd of 11,800 for their end of November home fixture against Stoke. Against 39,161 customers at Arsenal and 34,1422 at Chelsea, the chairman was forced to admit, "I know that we were regarded as the Cinderella team — now it looks as though we are ranked as one of the ugly sisters."

Charlton were at the time holding a better League record at that point than their glamorous neighbours but looked in vain for a replanning of the First Division fixture list. Those missing thousands missed a hat-trick from the 19-year-old South African inside-forward Eddie Firmani, so successfully converted from full-back by Seed. Firmani, John Hewie, the talented full-back, and Stuart Leary, the cultured centre-forward, all recruited from South Africa by Seed three years earlier, were playing in the same team.

As Christmas approached, Sheffield United and Huddersfield were making all the running in the Second Division with Leicester in close pursuit. When United beat Leicester 7-2 before 32,000 at Bramall Lane there were two goals each for Alf Ringstead and Jimmy Hagan, but the week before, Leicester had inflicted the first away defeat on Huddersfield, 2-1 before a post-war record crowd of 39,000 at Filbert Street.

The very first giant-killers in the FA Cup that season were non-League Bath City and the man planning the first-round defeat of Third Division South Southend United was the former England and Arsenal skipper, Eddie Hapgood. A record 14,000 Bath crowd saw their team, after being reduced to ten men, score twice in the second half without reply. Also bridging the gap, this time between the Midland League and the Third Division South, were Peterborough United, under player-manager Jack Fairbrother, the former Newcastle goalkeeper. They put out Torquay United 2-1 before 12,000. No famous exploits for Yeovil, though, as they and their slope were conquered by Brighton.

Top of the Third Division South were Bristol Rovers and the spirit and determination, engendered throughout the Eastville club by manager Bert Tann, was never better exemplified than by the 7-0 home win over Brighton which was their best-ever League victory. Snow fell heavily throughout the game and half-a-dozen supporters were busy sweeping the lines clear the whole time to ensure the 12,000 crowd were not left disappointed by an abandonment. There were two goals each for George Petherbridge and Vic Roost as Rovers recorded their sixth successive League win. Christmas brought a club record for Rovers — 20 matches in League and Cup without defeat — as Queen's Park Rangers were defeated before a 30,892 crowd.

Early December fog-smog brought the worst Southern and Midlands football black-out for years and in the FA Cup second round, amateurs Walthamstow Avenue drew 1-1 with Watford in the only completed major game in London. At Finchley, two Crystal Palace players did not make the Cup kick-off due to the travelling conditions. A loudspeaker appeal for 'any Palace players here, please go to the dressing-room' brought a response from two youth players but in any event the fog ensured the tie only lasted 61 minutes when the amateurs were leading 3-1. Days later, Finchley repeated the score in the replay to go through to the third round.

Sheffield United in 1953. Back row (left to right): George Hutchinson, Harold Brook, Fred Furniss, Ted Burgin, Harry Latham, Graham Shaw, Joe Shaw, Jackson (trainer). Front row: Alf Ringstead, Jimmy Hagan, Len Browning, Sam McNab, Derek Hawksworth.

One interesting name to emerge in the FA Cup was Brian Close, the young Yorkshire cricketer, who had scored three of Bradford City's goals in their two outings. Close had settled into the Bradford forward-line after failing to make the grade at Leeds United and Arsenal. However, his whole-hearted approach soon made him a casualty — a damaged cartilage for the Yorkshire and England all-rounder made the cricket fans complain that cricket and football just did not mix.

Walthamstow Avenue made all the headlines after the Cup third round as the first amateur side to reach the fourth round since the immortal Corinthians 24 years earlier. Stockport were their victims before 10,000 and their reward was a 'David and Goliath' tie at Old Trafford. The Third Division shock troops were led by Gateshead, who knocked out Liverpool at home in front of 15,193. Scunthorpe held Sunderland at Roker Park to shock a 56,000 crowd and Tranmere similarly drew 1-1 with Tottenham in their home tie. The First Division sides finally triumphed in the replays — Sunderland by 2-1, Spurs by 9-1 in a White Hart Lane rout.

One third-round tie, Swansea's game at Newcastle, lasted only eight minutes before fog forced an abandonment — 63,480 paid over £8,000 for the privilege and 61,064 returned the following Wednesday afternoon to see the Magpies win 3-0. The tie grossed nearly £16,000 for the 98 minutes and those receipts were very sweet consolation for the Welshman. At that time each club took one-third of the receipts with the rest going to the FA pool.

Co-starring in the most sensational FA Cup ties since the war, in which only six of the 16 home teams won, were Rotherham United, Walthamstow Avenue, Gateshead and Halifax Town. Newcastle's three-wins-in-a-row ambitions were shattered at St James's Park before 54,000 when, after new centre-forward Vic Keeble had put them in the lead, goals from wingers Walley Rickett and Jack Grainger (two) gave Rotherham a shock win.

At Old Trafford, Walthamstow Avenue's Polish goalkeeper, Stanislav Gerula, was carried shoulder-high from the pitch after his heroic display. With 15 minutes left the amateurs were one down to a goal from Manchester United's 18-year-old Eddie Lewis. In a rare Walthamstow's attack the Essex and England cricketer Trevor Bailey was brought down. From the free-kick the ball reached Avenue's England amateur international forward Jim Lewis, who coolly beat United goalkeeper Wood for a most improbable equalizer. There was no happy ending for the Avenue as they were beaten 5-2 in the replay at Highbury, but the aggregate attendance for the two ties was 87,530 and they collected around £4,000 as their share.

Gateshead reached the fifth round for the first time as the last hope for Tyneside with an amazing 2-1 win at Hull City, who made a habit of falling to 'minnows' in the Cup. Halifax Town showed that their win over First Division Cardiff in the previous round was no fluke by repeating the feat over Stoke. Their single-goal triumph was watched by over 35,000 at The Shay and well before the end thousands of West Riding voices were booming out 'Ilkla Moor Baht 'At' to celebrate.

One tie at that stage became a real marathon as Chelsea and League leaders West Bromwich slogged through four games totalling 420 minutes. The games were variously played in gales, ice, frost, puddles and finally snow at Highbury where Roy Bentley (twice), Eric Parsons and Bobby Campbell scored in a emphatic 4-0 victory. In all, 158,417 hardy souls paid £22,200 and when it was all over, bottom-of-the-table Chelsea had to play in the next round three days later.

Eight and a half hours of Cup-tie football and three gruelling games in a week meant that exhausted Chelsea were no match for Birmingham City at Stamford Bridge in the fifth round and they crashed out 4-0. Two goals for City's free-scoring South African centre-forward Ted Purdon ensured the passage of the Second Division side to meet Spurs.

Playing for Chelsea at this time was an 18-year old amateur left-winger who needed the permission of his headmaster at Hendon Grammar School on each occasion. Miles Spector was the name and he had a hand in three of the Chelsea goals to earn accolades from the Press: "One of the coolest left-wingers I have seen since Cliff Bastin," was a typical reaction.

Walthamstow Avenue's Jim Lewis beats Ray Wood from the penalty-spot in the Cup replay at Highbury, but Manchester United emerged 5-2 winners.

Halifax fell at this stage, on three inches of snow at home to Spurs before another 30,000 crowd, but Gateshead went through against Plymouth and reached the last eight for the first time. Second Division Everton knocked out Manchester United, 2-1 at Goodison Park where the 77,000 crowd's goalscoring hero was young Dave Hickson, the new blond centre-forward. The leaders of the attack were certainly the stars that season and in that round Bolton's Nat Lofthouse put out Luton, Arsenal's Cliff Holton headed the vital first goal in their victory at Burnley, and Villa's Dave Walsh scored twice at Rotherham to eliminate the Yorkshire giant-killers.

In the quarter-finals, Hickson scored the only goal of Everton's tie against Aston Villa and Lofthouse scored the all-important goal for Bolton for the third successive Cup match, this time at Gateshead's Redheugh Park, to eliminate the gallant Third Division North side.

After drawn games at St Andrew's (1-1) and White Hart Lane (2-2) against Birmingham, Spurs finally secured their semi-final place at Molineux after three bitterly fought contests. There was much acrimony from Arthur Rowe as his bruised and battered Spurs were hit by the hard-tackling Blues.

The tie of the round was at Highbury where 69,158 fans witnessed a dramatic finale as Blackpool recorded their first-ever away victory over Arsenal in one of their finest displays ever. The London Press, in unusually generous vein to a Northern team, conceded that the

Allan Brown has just scored Blackpool's winning goal in the FA Cup sixth-round tie against Arsenal at Highbury. Now he lies in agony after breaking his leg in a collision with goalkeeper Jack Kelsey.

Seasiders were 'a majestic football machine toying with the Gunners as if they were the merest novices'.

All the action in this epic match was reserved for the last ten minutes. First, Ernie Taylor scored for Blackpool, only for Logie to equalize, but Allan Brown was the undisputed man-of-the-match with his bursts of speed and tenacity. Brown's afternoon ended on a note of personal tragedy, when six minutes from the finish, he crashed over the top of Arsenal's keeper Jack Kelsey as he scored the winning goal. The audible crack signalled that his left leg had been broken in two places, six inches below the knee, and he was carried from the pitch with all knowing that, for the second time, the Scottish international would be denied a Wembley Cup Final appearance. The victory shattered Arsenal's 'double' hopes after they were so well placed in the League at the time and with games in hand.

The Bolton-Everton semi-final at Maine Road, Manchester — an all Lancashire 'derby' — created tremendous interest. Everton's chances rested on the new-found ability of centre-forward Hickson to profit from the fast flighted crosses of wingers Ted Buckle and Tommy Eglington. The Toffeemen had a fine, inspiring skipper in wing-half Peter Farrell who was supported magnificently on the other flank by Cyril Lello. Everton went out that March afternoon in a further attempt to become the first club from the Second Division to win the FA Cup for 22 years.

In the event, Everton were baffled and demoralized by the rhythmic Bolton teamwork in the first-half and had conceded four goals, including two to Lofthouse. They shook themselves out of their nerves but after Clinton had missed a penalty for the Merseysiders after the break, three goals from Parker (two) and Farrell left Bolton desperately but successfully defending their 4-3 lead. The proven old Lancashire qualities of dourness, stubbornness and indomitable courage were never better displayed football wise than in that afternoon in front of 75,000 breathless supporters who witnessed one of the most remarkable Cup battles.

Blackpool had reached the penultimate stage in a more impressive manner than any of the other three semi-finalists, under the granite command of captain and centre-half Harry Johnston. Now they had to overcome the classy combination of ball-players from Tottenham to ensure an all-Lancashire Final.

The quarter-final had been a tragedy for Allan Brown in Blackpool's triumph and now the semi-final tragedy involved the Spurs and England classical right-back, Alf Ramsey. In the probably most diabolical piece of bad luck ever to befall a team or a player, Ramsey made a grotesque error of control and judgement in the last seconds of the game to give Blackpool the winning goal and send them to Wembley. In supreme irony, Ramsey had been the game's best player but with the two teams locked at a goal apiece in a repeat of the 1948 semi-final he made a hash of a simple back-pass to his goalkeeper Ted Ditchburn and Blackpool's Jackie Mudie nipped in to score easily. Within seconds the game was over and Ramsey was an inconsolable, dejected figure.

The crowd of 68,221, paying £20,084 — then record receipts at the ground of a League club — at Villa Park saw a magnificent match with Spurs generally the masters, with Baily hitting the crossbar and McClellan a post. Blackpool scored first through a header from Perry but Duquemin shot a fine goal to equalize after half-time. The team in tangerine rode their luck and then capitalised in the most fortunate manner in that fateful last minute.

The 1953 FA Cup Final gripped the public imagination as it had not been gripped by a football match since the war. It was not difficult to perceive one special reason for this unprecedented and fervent interest which centred around the cult figure of Stanley Matthews. The general concensus was that this would be his last chance of a Cup-winners' medal in the mistaken belief that his career was nearly over. The fact of Billy Meredith playing in a Cup semi-final in his 50th year had been overlooked.

In Coronation year, the whole country — except Bolton, of course, — willed Matthews, at 38 years of age, to attain his long-treasured ambition — a winners' medal. Even a First Division Championship medal had eluded him at Stoke City and Blackpool and the latter club had already been to Wembley twice in the post-war years, losing to Manchester United in 1948 and Newcastle in 1950. Now a strong Bolton side with a good team spirit stood in the way of the old maestro.

Bolton were led by Scottish international Willie Moir, the brains of the team and a fine goalscorer, and Harold Hassall was known for his powerful, loping run and strong shot. Malcolm Barrass was an out-and-out stopper flanked by Johnny Wheeler, a fine attacking wing-half. To add to that, Johnny Ball and Ralph Banks were a good combination of full-backs.

For Blackpool the defensive wall was built around Harry Johnston, but two fine full-backs in Eddie Shimwell and Tommy Garrett had emerged. The two inside-forwards, Ernie Taylor and Jackie Mudie, were talented and creative but the unlucky Brown's absence as a goalscorer was more than compensated for by the astonishing qualities of Stan Mortensen. This was certainly a stronger all-round and more compact Blackpool team than had appeared at Wembley previously.

All over the country, thousands had bought their first television set ready to watch the Coronation, so for many that 1953 Cup Final was their first glimpse of live football 'on the box'. What they, and the Queen and the Duke of Edinburgh in the stadium, saw was the softest of Wembley goals in the second minute, when Bolton's Lofthouse saw the Blackpool goalkeeper, George Farm, let a mis-hit tame shot hit him on the shoulder and bounce into the net.

Bolton's misfortunes started in the 18th minute when half-back Eric Bell was struck by a hamstring injury and became a passenger on the left wing. After Mortensen had equalized for Blackpool, Bolton regained their lead through Willie Moir after 38 minutes. After half-time, Wanderers went 3-1 ahead as the injured Bell hobbled in to head past Farm and it seemed as if Bolton had one hand on the trophy. With 22 minutes remaining, Bolton looked certain winners, despite having Bell a passenger and Lofthouse and Banks carrying injuries.

However, in the most stupendous of finishes, the Blackpool side came to life as if galvanised. Matthews was leading a tidal wave of attacks on the Bolton goal and, inevitably, Mortenson scored in the 66th minute after a looping centre from the maestro eluded Hanson. Even now, at 3-2 it seemed safe for Bolton as the game entered its last three minutes. At this stage Mudie, the Blackpool inside-forward, was brought down just outside the Bolton penalty area and Mortensen hit a thunderbolt of a shot from the free-kick into the net for the equalizer. The pale inspirational centre-forward became the first player to score three goals in a Wembley Cup Final.

Stan Mortensen (far right) looks happy. Blackpool teammate Bill Perry has just scored the winning goal in the legendary 'Matthews Final'.

That feat was eclipsed by the piece of pure football trickery produced in *Boys' Own Paper* style by the 38-year old Matthews, in the very last minute of the match. For the umpteenth time in that last quarter of an hour, the ball was whipped out to him by little Ernie Taylor and Matthews was comprehensively beating the full-back Ralph Banks and two other defenders to head for the by-line. A perfect pass — although Matthews slipped as he crossed the ball — inside found Bill Perry, the South African left-winger, who hit the ball into the net from ten yards.

It was the sort of victory a schoolboy dreams about and those who saw it at the time or have seen it subsequently on film will never forget it. Everybody forgot Bolton — all that mattered was that

A winners' medal at last. Stanley Matthews receives his from the young Queen Elizabeth II.

Matthews had dominated, controlled and finally won the match and his medal in the most exciting fashion. After a cartilage operation earlier in the season, Mortensen had scored a hat-trick to add to his other goals in every round, but little Ernie Taylor was an unsung hero with his slide-rule passes out to Matthews. The two goalkeepers, Farm and Hanson, in contrast had most unhappy afternoons.

In the most sentimental of years — Queen Elizabeth II was crowned, Britain conquered Mount Everest, Gordon Richards won his only Derby — the most loved footballer in England had performed feats of prodigious brilliance in a game that went into the legends of football. The magnificant, unbelievable melodrama had been blessed with a remarkable finale. Whether this owed anything to the fact that one of the linesmen was a vicar — the Rev S Davis from Oxford — we shall never know.

As the League season went into its last month, before the Final was played, a four-horse race had developed between a well-organized Burnley, a stylish Preston North End, the ageing but hugely experienced Arsenal and the forceful, athletic Wolves.

Indeed, Burnley looked like the winners when they went to the top of the table in March. Two scheming inside-forwards in Jimmy McIlroy and Bill Shannon fed two lively wingers in England international Billy Elliott and Jack Chew. Spearheading the attack was the leggy, tearaway centre-forward Bill Holden, another typical leader of the day in the Lofthouse-Ford mould. At the back could be found the reliable Tommy Cummings at centre-half and an up-and-coming half-back in Jimmy Adamson.

Preston, under manager Will Scott, were to come within an inch of taking the title. There was a feeling that they relied too much on the supreme talents of Tom Finney, but that gave no credit to the prolific goalscoring of Charlie Wayman. Jimmy Baxter was a crafty inside-forward feeding Angus Morrison, a natural left-winger. Tommy Docherty and Australian Joe Marston were the bedrocks of their defence.

Preston's Deepdale ground was the scene of the most tragic of accidents which that spring put an end to the short, brilliant but controversial career of Sheffield Wednesday's Derek Dooley. He challenged for a 50-50 ball with the Preston goalkeeper and his right leg was broken. Within days most of the leg had to be amputated after gangrene had set in as a result of an infection from a cut earlier in the game.

Another centre-forward, amongst many, in the news was the Barnsley leader, Tommy Taylor. His special talent had attracted a number of £20,000-plus bids from First Division clubs and in the end Taylor moved to Manchester United for £30,000. Busby staggered his fellow managers by this fee for an untried youngster from the Second Division, but his legion of admirers rated him as a natural ball-player, fast off the mark with effortless grace, and deadly shooting. His early goalscoring entry into the United side was evidence of his worth and within five weeks of his transfer, Taylor was included in the England party for the summer tour.

Also making the headlines was another young teenager, Frank Blunstone, on the left wing at Chelsea after his £8,000 move from Crewe. When Chelsea gained a memorable double over Spurs, a 3-2 win which eased their relegation worries, it was Blunstone who coolly beat Ted

Arsenal goalkeeper Jack Kelsey gets down low to save a shot during the game against Spurs at Highbury in February 1953. Over 69,000 saw Arsenal win 4-0 on their way to another Championship.

Billy Holden, Burnley's centre-forward, heads his side's only goal in their 5-1 defeat at Molineux in April 1953.

Ditchburn for the second goal. Blunstone was reported to have eight brothers and five sisters but his debut was marred by the coincidental accidental death of his eldest brother in a car crash.

The last week of the season produced the most thrilling conclusions to the Championship and relegation issues in the top division as the mathematicians came into their own, particularly those with the feel for averages. The 'goals against' total had to be divided into 'the goals for' was the formula extensively explained by the Press as the fans took pencil and paper and tried a few permutations for themselves.

On the Wednesday, Preston completed their fixtures at Derby County and a disputed penalty by Tom Finney — stroked past Rams goalkeeper Ray Middleton — put them two points above Arsenal at the very top. Derby were consigned to relegation on that result and that at Chelsea, where the Pensioners scraped to safety on the strength of a 3-1 win at Stamford Bridge against Manchester City. Stoke City went down, also as a consequence of that Chelsea result.

Now the action moved to the Friday Cup-Final eve and to Highbury where Arsenal had to beat Burnley to carry off the title on goal-average. Burnley had talent money to play for, so it made for a stirring tussle before 51,586 spectators. After eight minutes, Burnley's Stephenson capitalized on a mistake by Swindin in the Arsenal goal, but a minute later the Gunners' wing-half Alec Forbes scored his first goal of the season with a deflected shot to equalize. By half-time it was 3-1 after further Arsenal goals from ace marksman Doug Lishman and the scheming Jimmy Logie. The second-half was controlled by Burnley and when Elliott scored to make it 3-2 it meant an agonising last 15 minutes before Arsenal could claim the Championship for a record seventh time.

That nerve-racking match, played in torrential rain on a sea of mud, in such contrast to the beautiful weather and superb pitch awaiting the Wembley contestants the next day, made the Arsenal champions by the tenth part of a goal, with a goal-average of 1.51 against Preston's 1.41, with both teams on the 54-points mark. Afterwards, in an emotional scene on the main steps outside Highbury's East Stand, the indomitable Joe Mercer told the waiting crowd that he had decided to hang up his boots for good. It was a pity that Mercer could not keep his vow, however. He was tempted to play on and had to finish his career the next season, in hospital with a broken leg.

In the Second Division, Sheffield United were promoted as champions and this owed much to their prolific goalscoring — 97 goals in all shared out amongst such as Alf Ringstead (22), Harold Brook (17) and Len Browning (17). Invariably, the creator was the evergreen Jimmy Hagan and in the rearguard was the Bramall Lane 'find of the season,' young left-back Graham Shaw, who joined his brother, Joe. Now Sheffield had double representation in the First Division for the first time since 1933-4.

Huddersfield returned to the First Division, as runners-up, under the expert guidance of the Scot, Andy Beattie. The defence of Jack Wheeler, Ron Staniforth, Lawrie Kelly, Bill McGarry, Don McEvoy, and Len Quested was unchanged for the entire 42 matches and in the process conceded only 33 goals. Their attack had its best post-war campaign, scoring 84, and Jimmy Glazzard claimed 31 of them.

The most romantic success-story came from the West Country where tall, quietly-spoken manager Bert Tann led Bristol Rovers out of the Third Division South for the first time. The team was assembled for less than £1,000 and was finally reckoned to be worth ten times that figure. None was more valuable than Geoff Bradford, who notched a club-record 34 goals, one more than his fellow forward Vic Lambden's record. With attendances frequently up to 30,000 and averaging 23,000, the Rovers were able to resist several offers for their players. In any event, Tann's success was based on a happy family policy based on all the players securing the top wage of £14. This was boosted by the squad collecting more bonus money than any other League line-up, particularly in the 27 games-without-a-defeat record for the club. It was over 20 years since the city of Bristol had a team in any but the Third Division.

Whilst Southampton and Barnsley were being relegated, there were celebrations at Oldham where the Latics returned to the Second Division after a lapse of 18 years, following a tense struggle with Port Vale and Grimsby Town at the top of the Third Division North. Their secret was consistency and great strength in defence under the experienced generalship of player-manager George Hardwick. In attack, the tall, balding centre-forward, Eric Gemmell, was the star with 23 goals in 27 League games.

As far as England's 1952-3 international season was concerned it seemed at the start as if there would be few problems after the previous summer's successful visits to Italy and Austria. The team that defeated Austria in Vienna in May was selected without change for the opening international against Northern Ireland, against whom England had their narrowest escape in years. Only a good goal from Billy Elliott, from Jack Froggatt's centre, three minutes from the end, after the attacking centre-half had made a great run down the right-wing, denied the Irish. Inspired by Peter Doherty, their team manager, the Irish had been leading 2-1 until that point, thanks to two goals from Glasgow Celtic's Charlie Tully.

Wales, appearing at Wembley for the first time, attracted a sell-out crowd and receipts of £43,600, which were a record for any football match in this country. The Welsh were outclassed in a 5-2 defeat and the two stars were Lofthouse, with two goals, and centre-half Froggatt, who was carried off on a stretcher, but returned on the left wing to score with a brilliant bullet-like header. A fortnight later, Belgium were feeble competitors at Wembley on a cold, sleety November afternoon and were crushed 5-0 in a one-sided game before 68,000.

In the five months which elapsed before England appeared at Wembley again for the annual fixture against Scotland there was an increasing clamour and a renewed public campaign for Stanley Matthews, at 38 years of age, to be recalled. His unique brand of trickery and unhurried calmness meant that Matthews could not be judged by ordinary standards. When the party for the summer tour of the Americas was announced before the Cup Final, Matthews was not included and John Berry of Manchester United and Tom Finney seemed to have taken the wing positions. Within days of his incomparable performance in that 'Matthews Final', the Football Association had the courage to admit they were wrong and invited him to join the party. In the event, however, Matthews had to refuse, due to a nagging thigh injury which had needed an injection to enable him to play in that Cup Final.

England and Scotland shared four goals with the Scots snatching a draw in injury time after they had played three-quarters of the game at Wembley with ten men after left-back Sammy Cox was carried off. It was a dramatic, pulsating international and surprise selection inside-forward Ivor Broadis, from Manchester, City was the pick of the English forwards, as well as hitting a superb goal. The left-wing partnership of the two cousins — Redfern Froggatt from Sheffield Wednesday and Jack Froggatt — was not rated a success however.

As a prelude to the World Cup qualifying rounds, England toured North and South America that summer and, despite beating Chile and the United States, were beaten by the World Champions, Uruguay, and could only draw with Argentina. In 1953, the Football Association celebrated its 90th anniversary but by now the country had realised that it had lost its football mastery. The Continentals had finally shattered the myth that England were still 'the masters' and they just 'the pupils'.

The final damning evidence was provided in the next season, first by a celebration match against a FIFA team with the best European players, without the Hungarians. England escaped with a 4-4 draw, thanks to a dubious last-minute penalty scored by Ramsey. Then came the watershed — the game which obliged England to accept for all time that they were no longer the overlords of football.

The 6-3 defeat by Hungary on home soil on that dark November 1953 afternoon was a stunning blow to the game in this country. The Hungarian forward line was the most graceful and deadly that any country had fielded up to that time. England were outplayed by the great Hungarians — 1952 Olympic Champions and unbeaten for 25 matches. The tarnished state of our football was evidenced by the failure to find an effective combination or method to beat the Magyars' winning streak. Now English football, by that match alone, seemed to stand, in technical terms, in bleak contrast to the social and technological advancements which were all around it. As now, England's performances in the international arena reflected both the strengths and weaknesses of the domestic game.

The late Geoffrey Green in *The Times* summed up the defeat succinctly: "Yesterday by 4 o'clock on a grey winter's afternoon within the bowl of Wembley Stadium, the inevitable had happened. To those who had seen the shadows of the recent years creeping closer and closer there was perhaps no real surprise. England were at last beaten by the foreign invader on solid English soil."

The lessons of that defeat were to be slow in the learning in the coming years and it had become vital for the game to shake off its general insularity. Such a move involved a change of heart — a quality not easily found in English football at that time. The managers, directors and officials, brought up in a game which had for so long enjoyed the undivided and devoted loyalty of the fans, had seen little need to look abroad.

An editorial in *Charles Buchan's Football Monthly* was typical of those elements of the media who attacked football's handful of 'Europeans' who 'admire everything that is foreign and sneer at everything that is British'. The magazine reproduced pictures from abroad showing a football riot with police charging supporters on terraces in Italy. The pictures were published to underline the editor's arguments that 'such terrible scenes could not occur in our land' and the assertion, "In Britain partisanship does not descend to bitterness. It reflects our tolerant way of life — here it is a good and healthy emotion."

There was no doubt that the English game still remained profoundly strong at the grass-roots of the community, still rooted in the school system and widely popular at amateur level. The professional game was contracting as the hard face of post-war austerity had given way to the clear signs of material prosperity. The more prosperous society was able to channel its spare money and energies into new areas of social and recreational activities.

In 1952-3, attendances at Football League games fell by two million and in the following year by an even more alarming four million. Initially, the decline had been slight — from the all time high of 41.3 million spectators in 1948-9, the numbers fell to 39 million in 1951-2. Now the figures were to fall markedly and steadily each season and never again would the game see the regular 50-60,000 attendances of those halcyon lost days. On its return after the war, the game had been able to capture unprecedented crowds by simple force of habit and the overwhelming need of people for relief.

Now the 1950s were to be a different age in which the American nation exerted a persuasive and lasting influence on the other peoples of the free world with its 'mass culture'. The influence of the wealthy status-conscious America was being felt towards the mid-1950s and their mass-consumerist economy became the model for our society. Britain was catching up in the prosperity-stakes and took to electric blankets, washing-machines, refrigerators and the like in a big way. The youth-culture came to the fore, epitomised by the 'Teddy-boys' and headed by their heroes — Marlon Brando and James Dean. In the midst of all this, the game seemed incapable of adapting to the changing environment in which it found itself. Football was to struggle on into a new age of practially universal club insolvency, dwindling crowds and chronic indecision.

During the 1952-3 season, the Arsenal-Hibernian and London-Berlin friendly matches played under floodlights at Highbury had established both the arrival and the value of floodlit football. Over 100,000 people turned out for these fixtures but whether floodlit football was to be the long-awaited panacea which would solve the ever-present problem of congested fixture lists or falling attendances was still to be resolved. Only time would tell whether the novelty value would wear off, whether it enabled mid-week matches in the League or Cup to be played in the late evening, whether it could ever adequately replace daylight football, particularly in the light of inclement weather and the attractions of television and the fireside. At the end of the season it was reported that only 13 clubs in the League possessed floodlighting facilities, and only three of those were in the First Division.

For the players, the maximum wage gradually rose from its pre-war rate of £8 per week to £20 per week during the season and £17 in the summer by 1961. It was estimated that about a quarter of players were on the maximum by 1953. Those who were not had some compensation by the way of signing-on fees, benefits after five and ten years with a club and sometimes even business help from club directors, often in the form of providing houses. In addition, the more prominent players earned cash by journalism or by advertising products. In 1951 Stanley Matthews, for example, earned £20 per week for endorsing football boots made by the Co-operative Wholesale Society.

Looking back now, it can be seen that the pre-war insularity had firm historical roots, orginating in the early rise and influence of the English game and its undisputed superiority up to 1914. Throughout the inter-war years, English football never questioned the firm belief in inherited superiority which attitude was compounded by administrative isolationism and shored up by the buoyancy and strength of the domestic game. Now the reality of football abroad and the relative decline of the English game were fully appreciated. Now, after years of no more than embryonic international football, club football with a European framework was on the horizon. When the European Cup was set in motion in 1955, English clubs were conspicuous by their absence, Chelsea having been persuaded by the Football League not to enter for fear of interfering with their domestic commitments.

By the 1960s, English football was to its credit making determined efforts to close up the gap and the removal of the maximum wage in 1961 and the industrial emancipation of footballers in 1963 determined much of the course of football in the subsequent decade. Austerity had given way to prosperity nationally and through the subsequent decades football had enormous problems but was burdened by unimaginative leadership, outdated direction and a general undermining of the spectator appeal by so many extraneous factors.

Now to a degree football has become 'respectable' again and, thanks to television, has universally cut across class lines and united the country during the 1990 World Cup finals. The enormous enthusiasm generated was proof that the game and its personalities can still appeal to the social sensibilities of even a conservative English society.

These halcyon days of professional football, related in the previous chapters, will not return, but despite all the changes the basic character remains the same. It remains the game of ordinary people — the people's game — but through the 1980s it had been hijacked by the football hooligans, the agents and the politicians. The roots of the game had been forgotten. The collective nationhood of the game needs to be restored before it can once again be part of the spirit of the age. With the knowledge that overall attendances have shown an increase for each of the past five season, perhaps football is in sight of regaining its place among the most eminent of social institutions.

The Teams

Manchester United

THERE was no more popular team during the first post-war decade than Manchester United, but their success and popularity was to be found in a combination of several factors. From a club without a ground and deep in debt, Matt Busby fashioned a team which, in 1948, won the FA Cup and then, in 1952, lifted the League Championship. The latter team still included six members of the Cup-winning side.

Those 1948 and 1952 teams began a pattern of success for Manchester United — First Division titles in 1956, 1957, 1965 and 1967, FA Cup successes in 1963, 1977, 1983 and 1987 and the European Cup in 1968. The early post-war United, by their quality play, loyalty and commitment to their manager, set a high level of consistent performance which meant that no other team matched their record of having topped 50 points in each of the six seasons after the war. United were lifted to a level of public acclaim and esteem never previously achieved by the club, which had spent most of the pre-war decade adrift in the Second Division in the shadow of Manchester City. Indeed, between the wars United were continually in financial difficulties and being relegated and promoted three times.

Busby was the first to admit that he inherited a small nucleus of talented players whose careers had been blighted by six years of war. Some had already played League football, whilst others had blossomed in service and wartime soccer. The players bequeathed to Busby by his predecessor, Scott Duncan, included Johnny Carey, Henry Cockburn, Jack Rowley, Johnny Morris, Stan Pearson, Allenby Chilton, Joe Walton, Charlie Mitten, John Aston and goalkeeper Jack Crompton. Donning a track suit, Busby was to be found out on the training field working with those players, in a move way ahead of its time.

Busby showed shrewdness in the transfer market throughout his long tenure at Old Trafford and never more so than in his very first capture — that of 30-year-old Jimmy 'Brittle Bones' Delaney, who went to Old Trafford in February 1946 from Glasgow Celtic. The slight, balding Delaney became such a vital component in the United attack that he could reasonably be described as one of the most remarkable bargains in the game's history. Not only considered to be well past

Manchester United's 1948 line-up. Back row (left to right): Johnny Carey, John Anderson, Jack Crompton, Allenby Chilton, Henry Cockburn, John Aston. Front row: Jimmy Delaney, Johnny Morris, Arthur Rowley, Stan Pearson, Charlie Mitten.

his best, after apparently being at his peak in Celtic's Scottish Cup victory of 1937, but also with a long history of injuries, Delaney was Busby's only purchase and proved to be a speedy and elusive winger for nearly five years. He regained his old confidence and his Scottish international place and thrived in Manchester.

Busby spent the 1945-6 season constantly searching for the right blend and balance in the side. In the process, nearly 40 players made first-team appearances as the pre-war senior players and the wartime players were all given a chance to prove themselves. All were juggled around until they found their true positions and there was constant experimentation to find the right combination. The conversion of Carey and Aston from inside-forwards to full-backs and Chilton from wing-half to centre-half were three of the most successful outcomes as the foundations were laid for the first post-war League season.

The 1946-7 season showed that most of the players had found their niche and that their popular manager had brought the best out of them. Swift, flowing football, which was immediately attractive to the hordes who flooded to their adopted 'home' at Maine Road, and a disciplined teamwork brought the First Division runners-up spot. There were many memorable games and United had already begun to build up a reputation for the speed of their attack and the swift inter-changing of positions by the forwards. Support for the team, home and away, was simply staggering.

By now Busby had great confidence in his first-team squad of almost 20 players and was sure that the club was poised for success as the 1947-8 season opened. His confidence was not misplaced as United not only finished as runners-up for the second consecutive year but also won the FA Cup. Their run of victories in that Cup campaign were simply sensational — in every round they were drawn against First Division opposition, every game was technically 'away' from home and every one was won by at least two goals. Aston Villa, League Champions Liverpool, Cup holders Charlton Athletic, Preston North End and high-riding Derby County were defeated before Blackpool were beaten in what has been described as Wembley's finest Final.

Each of the Cup winning squad was a unique character in his own right. Jack Crompton, the quiet man, was loyal and dependable rather than spectacular. One of six local-born players in the side, Crompton made a speciality of penalty-saving. In the 1947-8 season he made the headlines by saving the first three penalty-kicks he faced, from

internationals Don Welsh of Charlton. Tommy Lawton of Chelsea and Jimmy Hagan of Sheffield United.

The captain and right-back, John Carey, was an ideal, thoughtful leader and he and Busby had a mutual respect and understanding which was priceless to the team's cause. As one of their greatest-ever players, Carey had the ball-skills and composure of an inside-forward with great positional sense. His all-round ability meant that he was able to fill ten different positions, including goalkeeper. The mention of Carey in the club's minutes on his retirement says it all: 'By his outstanding personality as a true sportsman, the honours he had won as an international and in club matches, he had covered his career with glory and set a shining example to all who follow him.'

John Aston, his partner at full-back, made 290 League and Cup appearances for United, won 17 England caps and was the club's first World Cup player before his career was ended in 1954 by tuberculosis. Aston had been converted from inside-forward and his defensive abilities were seen to great advantage in the 1948 Final when he kept Blackpool's Stanley Matthews quiet. The regular England place which he had secured was sacrificed when he moved to centre-forward in 1950 to deputize for the injured Jack Rowley. The talented young Roger Byrne took the opportunity to make his mark in his place in the defence.

Allenby Chilton, the centre-half, took a measure of criticism from the fans as United's weak link but Busby was one of his staunchest supporters. As a classic, typical stopper centre-half, Chilton was strong in the tackle and powerful in the air but had a tendency to give away free-kicks or penalties for which United seemed always to be punished. Towards the end of his career Busby showed his faith in the Wearsider by making him captain, after Carey's retirement, and his experience came in useful to nurse the early 'Busby Babes'. Chilton was the hard, ruthless type of skipper who dictated the play with his attitude and did not suffer shirkers gladly.

Henry Cockburn was a wily, stocky left-half, who was adept at organizing the United defence, and a ferocious tackler. More than that, he was an accurate distributor of the ball and his talents were rewarded by 13 England caps. Indeed, he took over Joe Mercer's left-half spot in the England team immediately football resumed after the war. On breaking a jaw in October 1953, Cockburn was replaced by the prodigious talent of Duncan Edwards and his long reign in the position for United, which stretched back over 243 appearances, was over.

At right-half the experienced veteran, Jack Warner, was replaced by reserve-teamer John Anderson for the 1948 FA Cup Final and he made his name by scoring one of the second-half goals which brought the Cup to Old Trafford for the first time since 1909. His stay in the team in the next season was short-lived and Anderson finally moved to Third Division South club, Nottingham Forest.

It was United's forwards who were the stars, however, with Rowley and Pearson as the main goal-getters, relying on the service and crosses from the free-running Delaney and Mitten on the wings. Rowley was nicknamed 'Gunner' for the ferocity of his shooting and was the archetypal centre-forward of the period. Big, strong and muscular in his approach, Rowley could also play anywhere in the forward line and was renowned for his mobility, moving from wing to wing to leave the other forwards to go down the middle.

Stan Pearson scored many important goals for United in those League and Cup triumphs, making a great contribution to their tally of goals towards Wembley in 1948. The goal which broke the 2-2 deadlock in the Final was reckoned to be one of his finest. Nobody gave more pleasure to the hundreds of thousands who flocked to Maine Road than Pearson — lethal shots, clever headed flicks, sweeping passes and endless energy made up his repertoire.

The other inside-forward, ebullient Johnny Morris, benefited from personal tuition from Busby after he had joined United as a 15-year-old, but after the 1948 Cup triumph Morris was sold unexpectedly to Derby County for a record fee. Morris was the subtle type of forward who formed a brilliant partnership on the right with winger Delaney. For all his finesse Morris took his share of goals, scoring 32 in 83 appearances from 1946 to 1949 as evidence of his shooting power. His quick brain and swift reactions were ideal for an attack which was based on first-time passing and constant movement.

The left winger, Charlie Mitten, was a confident, impudent player whose main attributes were his speed, particularly when cutting inside the full-back, and his pin-point centering of the ball. Mitten was remembered by his contemporaries as one of the most accurate kickers of a ball and this was reflected in his deadly accuracy from the penalty-spot.

The team which started off after the war with six or seven local lads and an assortment of diverse talents had formed a great under-standing and spirit and were encouraged to play football the natural way. In the process, United's 1948 team was acknowledged as the most attacking and brilliantly entertaining side

in the country until the emergence of the revolutionary Tottenham side.

Six of the players who had won FA Cup medals in 1948 were in the United side who added League Championship medals in 1952-3 — Carey, Chilton, Cockburn, Pearson, Rowley and Aston. That title was won by a total of 24 players who gave United their due reward for such an amazingly high level of consistent performance in the League in the immediate post-war era.

Mitten had severed his links with Old Trafford by his Bogota trip and the colourful skilful winger was initially difficult to replace, but speedy young Roger Byrne eventually took the position with great success. On the other wing, John Berry — bought from Birmingham City for £25,000 in the summer — was the new outside-right and the little man showed the speed and skill which was to earn him England international recognition. Classy and reliable goalkeeper Reg Allen had been recruited from Queen's Park Rangers for £11,000 to replace the ever-patient Crompton, but eventually illness cut short his career. The Bradford inside-forward John Downie became Morris' successor at inside-right for an £18,000 fee.

United continued to catch the imagination of the football-mad nation in 1952 and 95 goals were the product of their all-out, creative attack. Rowley was a prolific scorer with 30, giving notice of his threat when scoring three hat-tricks in the first three weeks of the season. United's tally was the best goalscoring since neighbours City had taken the title in 1936-7.

That 1951-2 season saw the emergence of several young players who had been spotted, recruited and nurtured by the efforts of chief scout Louis Rocca, Jimmy Murphy, the reserve-team manager, Bert Whalley, the youth-team coach, Tom Curry, the trainer, and Bill Inglis, his assistant. Such as Tommy McNulty, playing at full-back when Aston was required at centre-forward, Don Gibson and Jeff Whitefoot at wing-half (the former was later to become Busby's son-in-law), Mark Jones and Jackie Blanchflower at centre-half, were the forerunners of the famous 'Busby Babes'.

Busby's inherent belief in the certainty of good football's eventual reward and his firm but fatherly managerial style were crucial, but now he showed his uncanny eye for the possibilities in each young local player. A poor start to the 1952-3 season, when United were paired with neighbours City at the bottom of the First Division, forced Busby's hand. The old order had to change and Busby had no apparent hesitation in breaking up the established side.

The flow of fresh young talent into the first

team seemed endless as, one by one, the many talented youngsters on the books were given their chance. The men who had brought United their first post-war successes had to be disappointed as they were gradually eased out to make way for the likes of winger David Pegg, defender Billy Foulkes, centre-forward Tommy Taylor, bought from Barnsley for £30,000, the prodigiously talented wing-half Duncan Edwards (only 15 when the season opened), and inside-forward Dennis Viollet. Other than Taylor at 21, all were still teenagers but United were still able to finish in eighth place in the First Division, albeit their lowest position since the war.

The talented, experienced, but now ageing squad of players who had brought United such success, acclaim and financial security in those early post-war years now had to disperse but, as his assistant Jimmy Murphy put it, "This mature team was our golden asset; because it gave us time and breathing space to look around and build for the future." In the modern era there have been many Manchester United sides with gifted individuals, but none that was so well co-ordinated, self-disciplined and full of enjoyment of the game itself with most having no regard for the rewards. The former was born out of the understanding of each other's game — almost a sixth sense, the discipline learned from the forces, the enjoyment out of the atmosphere and spirit engendered by Busby and of their determination to make up for their lost war years.

Blackpool

ON THE day that war was declared and League football abandoned for the duration, Blackpool sat at the top of the First Division with three wins out of three games. Subsequently, wartime football brought some of the best players in the game to the Bloomfield Road ground as the seaside resort was used as a major training centre for forces personnel. One such player was Stanley Matthews, in his first and significant attachment to the town, although he was still registered with Stoke City. With a host of guest players Blackpool won the League North Cup and beat the South Cup winners, Arsenal, for the 'Championship of England'.

From those wartime beginnings, through to the mid-1950s, were the years of splendour for Blackpool, years when a whole constellation of stars, of whom the incomparable Matthews and Mortensen were the brightest, lit up the football scene and reached Wembley three times.

Only the League Championship eluded the grasp of the squad, although they went close more than once, even finishing third in 1951. In 1948 they were beaten 4-2 by Manchester United in a classic Final; in 1951 they were beaten again, this time 2-0 by Newcastle United and the virtuoso Jackie Milburn; but finally, and in their finest hour, overcame Bolton Wanderers in the 'Matthews Final' of 1953.

Throughout this period the team was managed by Joe Smith, who had played for Bolton Wanderers in the 1920s and who had been appointed Blackpool boss in 1935. The successful association lasted until 1958 and the frank, blunt Smith proved to be a strong character who was a tremendous judge of a player. Typical of the management style of the period, Smith groomed or recruited players whom he judged were equipped to do specific jobs in the team and then let them get on with it. This was never better illustrated than in his astute handling of Matthews. Smith always gave the maestro the freedom, of mind and style, that left his genius unfettered, in complete contrast to his manager at Stoke, Bob McGrory.

Matthews remembered that Smith 'loved life almost as much as he loved football — he would puff on his cigar and tell us that he didn't care if we lost by six goals so long as we went out and entertained him'. Matthews further recalled a typical pre-match instruction: "Get a goal up before half-time if you can, so that I can enjoy my cigar."

In the first season of League football after the war, Blackpool finished fifth in the table but it was the signing of 32-year-old Matthews which transformed their future. The investment of £11,500 in the master winger — who had assured Smith that he could make it for another couple of years — early in the 1947-8 season was paying immediate dividends. Blackpool progressed steadily towards their first appearance at Wembley in the Cup and Stan Mortenson, alongside Matthews, profited from his arrival and never underestimated his good fortune in being able to develop such an unique partnership.

Mortensen, of course, was one of the unforgettable characters of the era. The way he played expressed the nature of the man. Courageous, strong and with great tenacity, Mortensen's loyalty to Blackpool was absolute and his efforts for their cause were non-stop and inexhaustible. All this disguises his great talents — great acceleration, heading ability and a great shot made him the complete marksman.

It had been a straightforward decisive run to the 1948 semi-final — Leeds United, Chester, Colchester United and Fulham easily beaten on

Blackpool's 1953 side. Back row (left to right): Johnston, Fenton, Shimwell, Garrett, Brown, Farm, Kelly, Crosland. Front row: Joe Smith (manager), Matthews, Taylor, Mortensen, Mudie, Perry, J.Lynas (trainer).

the way with 15 goals scored and none conceded. Then Second Division Tottenham were finally overcome at Villa Park after extra-time, thanks to three typically opportunist goals from Mortensen. In the Final against Matt Busby's Manchester United, Blackpool were brimful of confidence — mainly on the strength of having Matthews and Mortensen in their team, quite simply the best combination of creator and scorer of goals in Britain at the time.

On the Friday before the 1948 Final, Matthews had been presented with the Footballer of the Year trophy and Mortensen had been voted into second place. Blackpool sprang a surprise that same week by announcing that Mortensen would play at centre-forward to replace Jimmy McIntosh, who had played in all the Cup rounds, and Alec Munro would be brought in to replace Mortensen as Matthews' right-wing partner.

In the event, United's defensive strategy prevented the ball reaching Matthews and after a bright start he faded from the game. Mortensen played his heart out and scored a goal to join the select band of then only four players who had scored in every round of the Cup. Outside-left Walter Rickett had played brilliantly when eclipsing Matthews on the day, to give the lie to the feeling that Blackpool were a 'lop-sided' team. It was reported that he had beaten United's Johnny

Carey more often than any other left-winger had done that season.

The 33-year-old Matthews seemed to have missed his last chance of a Cup winners' medal as Manchester United's superior team effort overwhelmed Blackpool in the last quarter of the game. It was indicative of the management approach of the period that Blackpool had no pre-match plan for their first-ever Final, other than to play their football at all costs and rely on the individual talents of such as Matthews, Mortensen and Rickett.

In defence that afternoon, Eddie Shimwell was a strong, determined, tough but not dirty full-back who, in the modern idiom, was prepared to make the occasional foray to prompt the forwards and cross a centre for them. When he scored from a penalty in the 14th minute, he became the first full-back to score in a Wembley Cup Final.

His partner, Johnny Crosland, went on to become an England 'B' international but on the day was an accountant and part-time professional who was brought in at the last minute in place of the unfit Ronnie Suart. It was revealed later that Crosland had never previously played at full-back, his six League appearances having been at centre-half.

The captain, Harry Johnston, was at right-half, before his subsequent conversion to centre-half, and many felt it suited his composed, cultured and thoughtful style more naturally than the purely defensive position. Johnston captained Blackpool for a decade and in all three Cup Finals, and was known as a gentleman with great modesty, but that disguised a determination and strength of will which led him to drive the players hard.

Hugh Kelly was a Scot who was the defensive wing-half to counter Johnston's attacking role. Kelly eventually made 471 appearances in the first-team and became a full international. He was a student of fitness and earned a reputation as one of the sturdiest, hard-tackling wing-halves in football. After the disappointment of missing the 1953 Final due to an ankle injury, Blackpool obtained permission from the FA for a special medal to be cast for him.

The centre-half that afternoon was Eric Hayward, a veteran of pre-war and wartime football with the Seasiders, and his leadership and defensive qualities served the side well in that Final and the next. Not always appreciated by the media, Hayward gave them some ammunition in that 1948 Final by confusing goalkeeper Robinson and allowing United's Jack Rowley to step in and score.

After playing their part in that classic Final, Blackpool had truly caught the public's imagination. In the early days it had been the lure of Matthews which initially drew people to watch Blackpool but, more often than not, they were also pleasantly surprised by the skills of the other players in tangerine. Blackpool were the side to watch and possibly only Arsenal drew bigger crowds to away matches.

By the time Blackpool had skilfully played their way to a second Cup Final appearance in four seasons, in May 1951 after finishing third in the League, goalkeeper George Farm had been signed for a give-away fee from Hibernian, and the opportunist Scottish forward Jackie Mudie had graduated from the Reserves. Another Scot, Allan Brown, had moved from East Fife for £26,000 — the highest fee that had been paid to a Scottish club — to partner South African-born Bill Perry on the left wing, and young Tommy Garrett had won a full-back place beside the mighty Shimwell.

Farm never missed a Cup match for Blackpool in his 11 years at the club and played an important role in the 1951 and 1953 Cup campaigns. The Scottish international was a shy, sensitive individual who saved the most nervous and mistake-ridden performances of his long career for the two Wembley Finals. It was a shame because Farm is remembered by Blackpool fans for his courage and agility, coupled with his relentless intense dedication.

Mudie played in the first team at 19 and little more than a year later partnered Matthews in the 1951 Final against Newcastle. The maestro was quick to praise his young partner. Because of his light build he could move swiftly and he had an eye for the half-chance. This eye was destined to confound Alf Ramsey of Spurs after he hade made a faulty back-pass in their 1953 semi-final — the young Mudie seizing on the loose ball to score the winning-goal. This ability was later to be confirmed on Scotland's behalf for whom he made 17 consecutive appearances in between 1956 and 1958.

Bill Perry was one of the fastest wingers in the game at that time, after having been brought over by Blackpool from Johannesburg in October 1949, and his irrepressible form made him a regular in the run to Wembley in 1951. With his speedy runs, accurate crossing and goals, often scored on the run. Perry was described aptly as the man who 'moves like a springbok and shoots with the kick of a rogue elephant'. The left wing of Brown and Perry was a combination which was to figure prominently in the most momentous years in Blackpool's history. Perry, at 20 years of age, became the first South African to play in a Wembley Cup Final.

Allan Brown was a strong courageous forward who had the most astonishing misfortunes to miss both the 1951 and 1953 Finals through injury. After Brown had damaged a knee at Huddersfield, his deputy George McKnight was given a try-out and he had the same misfortune. This meant that Bill Slater, an England amateur international had to be drafted into that 1951 Final side at the last minute, and sadly looked out of his depth in the inside-left position.

After a run of 20 games without defeat in the League, Blackpool were clear favourites to beat Newcastle. To everyone who was not a Geordie, the hope was that at long last Matthews would pick up the only honour to have escaped him. They all reckoned without one Jackie Milburn and his two memorable opportunist goals.

Blackpool had played disjointedly and the winners' medal had eluded the two Stanleys and Harry Johnston for the second time. When a knee injury kept Matthews out of the Blackpool side for almost three months of the next season, in which the team finished ninth in the League and were eliminated from the Cup at the first hurdle, it seemed as if the maestro's days were numbered. Significantly, however, by the start of the 1952-3 Cup campaign, Matthews was showing something of his old form and Mortensen had recovered his form and confidence after weeks out of action with cartilage trouble.

The run to Wembley included single-goal victories over Sheffield Wednesday, Huddersfield Town and Southampton. The home win over Huddersfield was secured by a 40-yard 'lob' by left-back Tommy Garrett which happily fell into the net two minutes from time. Garrett was a poised and intelligent defender, unusually stylish in that position for the period, who had made the position his own after the departure of Ron Suart to Blackburn.

Brown had broken his leg at Highbury in the process of scoring the winner against Arsenal in the sixth round, and then Hugh Kelly was injured to give the reliable Ewan Fenton his Wembley chance at right-half. Fenton was known for his shrewd passes and thoughtful, steady approach to the game and went on to captain Blackpool in the 1956-7 season.

Compensating for Brown's absence in the attack was the diminutive Ernie Taylor, who had played for Newcastle in that 1951 Final. Taylor came to Blackpool in October 1951 at the height of his creative and mischievious powers and many felt that manager Joe Smith never made a better capture. Taylor blended well with Matthews, showing uncanny understanding of the maestro's needs and judging his passes to the inch.

The 'Matthews Final' of 1953, as it has since been dubbed, was Blackpool's finest hour. Every neutral fan in the country willed Blackpool to win and there was a feeling that they just could not fail for a third time. Bolton Wanderers, their opponents, clearly had a huge emotional barrier to break down but when they raced into a 3-1 lead with 20 minutes left, it was the cue for the most dramatic climax ever to a Wembley Final. The praise for one Stanley knew no bounds in the days and weeks after as the Press wallowed in the sentimentality. The other Stanley, Mortensen, had played his part equally by becoming the first player to score a hat-trick in a Wembley Final.

If Blackpool were lucky in the star forwards they could call on in that era, they were equally fortunate in their captain, Harry Johnston, who was the natural leader and hard-driver every team needs. The proudest chapter in their history also coincided with the longest and most successful reign of any manager in Blackpool's story. It was no coincidence that from the time that Joe Smith was appointed in August 1935, the club was on a path to greatness, inspired by his unique character.

After those great days, Blackpool's star gradually faded and the team grew old together and lesser players replaced them. Blackpool still continued to produce stars in the coming decades, men like Jimmy Armfield, Alan Ball, Tony Green and Emlyn Hughes, but the return of those old glories now look completely beyond their reach.

Newcastle United

IF YOU were a youngster being taken into the hotbed of football at St James' Park, Newcastle, in the early 1950s, then you were raised on massive crowds, a myriad of memorable goals, phenomenal Cup success and a legendary centre-forward. In 1951 and 1952 the predominant colours worn by an English side were the stark black and white stripes of the Magpies and in successive years they came to Wembley to win the Cup. The colours were synonymous with all-out attacking football and a powerful Cup-fighting force who were galvanised as each round brought Wembley nearer.

The people of the North-East had been brought up on a tradition of the best in football, whether it was at Sunderland, Middlesbrough or Newcastle. In those early 1950s it was Newcastle's anthem *The Blaydon Races* which was raised in triumph to salute the exhilarating football which swept the Magpies to Cup success. Football had always seemed to half belong to the Tyneside masses and in those days it most certainly did.

During the war years their shrewd director Stan Seymour, a former Newcastle United outside-left who appeared in the 1924 FA Cup winning side, had gathered in future stars from across the North-East from the local colliery villages — men such as Charlie Wayman and Tommy Walker in 1941, Ernie Taylor from Sunderland in 1942, Bobby Cowell and Jackie Milburn in 1943, and finally Charlie Crowe in 1944. When the war was over, Seymour wielded the cheque-book in his relentless quest to rebuild the Newcastle team.

Seymour's unequalled record as a talent-spotter was enhanced by his signing of Joe Harvey and Len Shackleton from Bradford City for £4,250 and £13,000 respectively, Roy Bentley from Bristol City for £8,500 and Frank Brennan from Airdrie for £7,500. When United resumed in the Second Division after the war, it was with a mixture of the old and the new. The youthful Milburn was on the right wing, partnered by new man Bentley but with pre-war stars Albert Stubbins at centre-forward and Tommy Pearson on the left wing.

In finishing fifth in the Second Division in 1946-7, United were the best supported team

Newcastle United in 1952 with the FA Cup. Back row (left to right: Ted Hall (secretary), Cowell, Harvey, Simpson, Brennan, McMichael, Ted Robledo, Norman Smith (trainer). Front row: Walker, Foulkes, Stan Seymour (manager), Milburn, George Robledo, Mitchell.

in the country. Despite their lower division status, the average home attendance at St James' Park was 49,336 and new manager George Martin, from Luton, led the Magpies to an FA Cup semi-final. By then Stubbins had moved to Liverpool for £13,000, but his loss was mitigated by the 30 goals from Wayman that season on his move to centre-forward.

That semi-final at Elland Road, lost 4-0 to Charlton Athletic, was particularly significant to United's and Milburn's future. There was clearly trouble in the St James' Park dressing-room and it surfaced that day when Wayman was dropped for the match. More than that, two or three players had threatened that week to leave United if houses they had been promised by the club did not materialise. Milburn later remembered: "That was the last time there was any real discontent in the club because we all learned from the Charlton debacle. The club learned that you cannot mess about the players and the players learned that you can't mess about the supporters."

Wayman's exclusion led to Martin switching Milburn to centre-forward and this was a move which, in itself, was to create a legend. Wayman, the naturally gifted goalscorer, was subsequently sold to Southampton for £10,000 and Milburn, with some initial nursing from Shackleton, settled into the position to make it his own. His tearaway runs and strong

shooting immediately tore defences to ribbons as many a centre-half found his speed and power too much to handle. The sensitive, highly-strung Milburn was on his way to legendary status.

The 1947-8 season saw the eagerly-awaited promotion secured and this time United's home support increased to an average of 56,351. Their home record was impeccable with 18 wins out of 21 starts, but for all that Martin chopped and changed the side and again it could not be said to be a happy dressing-room. Ironically it was a Cup tie defeat by Charlton which again brought things to a head and subsequently the entire forward line, the highest scoring line in football at the time, was dropped. It seemed as if every player of note had either asked for a move or was reported to be on the point of doing so.

In the course of the promotion season only Brennan, Milburn and Harvey had played more than 26 games each in the complete campaign and in the process star forwards Bentley (to Chelsea), Shackleton (to Sunderland), Pearson (to Aberdeen) and Wayman had been sold. Shackleton's stormy two seasons with United, punctuated with flashes of genius and party-tricks and having as its highlight his six goals against Newport County on his debut, had been brought to a typically dramatic finale by his transfer to Sunderland, of all places, for a record fee. Bentley, the debonair former naval officer with the thoughtful, cultured style, went on to greater things in the capital, for Chelsea and England.

The Second Division clubs were very sorry to see Newcastle promoted; most of all they would miss their 20 per cent share of the St James' Park gate money. That 1948-9 season brought a fourth place, only one point behind runners-up Manchester United, but more important, several prominent deals were struck which proved decisive. Goalkeeper Jack Fairbrother was bought for £7,000 from Preston, the Robledo brothers — Ted and George — from Barnsley, winger Bobby Mitchell from Scotland and full-back Alf McMichael from Linfield.

When manager George Martin moved to Aston Villa in December 1950, he was not replaced and the assertive Stan Seymour took complete control of team affairs with trainer Norman Smith as his aide. By then United had already created a club record by going through the ten opening games without defeat and the double was within reach. The players and supporters were obsessed with the FA Cup, however, and its glamour clearly held more appeal than the long slog to secure League honours. When the 1951 Final was reached, Newcastle were five points behind the leaders, Tottenham, with a game in hand. In the two months and 11 games before the Wembley Final, only one was won.

The 1951 FA Cup Final triumph was the best and most thrilling of Newcastle's three Wembley successes in the decade. In view of their poor League form they had arrived as outsiders to beat in-form Blackpool, but Milburn dominated. He added two brilliant goals of differing styles to the others scored in every other Cup round. Both Milburn and the captain, Joe Harvey, later confessed that the 1951 Final team was the best of the United great Cup sides of the decade.

Jack Fairbrother in goal was known as a sound unspectacular performer whose secret lay in his positional play. Remembered as a mischievous personality and for his policeman's white gloves, Fairbrother rarely played a poor game but by his style he did not often make headlines. His full-backs at Wembley were Bobby Cowell, a solid, tough former pit-boy, who went on to play in all three Wembley Finals and who became the first United player to receive a testimonial; and Bobby Corbett, a sharp-tackling back who was sold to Middlesbrough within a few months.

Joe Harvey at right-half was a former company sergeant-major with a fearsome reputation who relished a dour struggle and drove his players relentlessly. Milburn admitted that the rest of the team were scared of him but there was no doubt that his 'bullying' brought the right response. His partner on the left was local boy Charlie Crowe, who was an honest and industrious worker recruited by Seymour during the war.

It was true to say that Scottish centre-half Frank Brennan was another of the tough, granite-like archetypal stoppers of the period. He took to the field with just one idea in mind — the stopping of all attacking moves down the centre of the field. In the event he was usually awesomely successful in his aim.

Tommy Walker on the right was an orthodox direct-running winger who was partnered by the impish creative Ernie Taylor. Taylor, of course had the distinction of playing in three Cup Finals for three different clubs.

On the other flank, George Robledo partnered Bobby Mitchell in a great combination of scoring power and elegant skills. The Chilean-born Robledo was known as 'the bronze bull from Chile' in a tribute to his strength, but he was also a master at subtle positioning with a nose for goals. Mitchell was a typical Scottish winger with his close, artistic dribbling. But to add to that he was an accurate crosser of the ball with a fine left-foot shot.

That team remained intact only for 12 months before Fairbrother broke his collarbone, to end his career at the age of 30, and Taylor, Crowe and Corbett were transferred after demanding moves from Seymour. Despite the friction, United went to eighth in the First Division and were the country's top scorers with 98 goals. George Robledo was prolific with 39 goals, even dwarfing Milburn's 28 in that 1951-2 season of further Cup success.

The 1952 Final was reached afer a series of titanic, heart-stopping struggles. Against Aston Villa at home, United were 2-1 down with ten minutes left but Mitchell's magic inspired a sensational 4-2 win. In the next round at Tottenham they swept the Champions aside and then came one of the greatest ties of all time and arguably Milburn's finest hour. The 4-2 win at Fratton Park over Portsmouth was the showpiece of United's season with Milburn climaxing his display with a hat-trick.

The Final was spoilt by the injury to Arsenal's Wally Barnes and it was a hollow victory in a grim, gruelling match lit up only by Robledo's fine opportunist winning goal. Only McMichael and Brennan performed to their full potential, but Mitchell was disappointingly selfish in his play, despite the perfect cross which brought the winner.

Ronnie Simpson was in goal, having been bought from Third Lanark, and he made up for his lack of inches with great agility and reflexes. Simpson of course subsequently returned to Scotland to keep goal for Celtic, playing in a European Cup Final at the age of 36 — a full 15 years after that 1952 Cup Final appearance.

Alf McMichael was an Irishman who went on to play for his country with distinction and he put on a fine display of firm tackling and good distribution that afternoon to subdue the fiery Arsenal winger, Freddie Cox. Ted Robledo was at left-half to make it two brothers in the same Wembley team. Billy Foulkes, at inside-forward, had been signed from Chester that season and he was a skilful ball-player without the creative expertise of Taylor. Nevertheless, Foulkes earned international honours with Wales that season and even scored, with his first touch at that level, against England.

There were to be great changes within the Newcastle camp before their third Wembley appearance in 1955. Joe Harvey retired, the Robledos returned to Chile, Brennan was sacked after a row and whilst all this was going on, Duggie Livingstone, after managing the Belgian national side, had been appointed, leaving Seymour to take a back seat. The 1952-3 season was particularly disappointing and whilst United finished in 16th spot, Milburn was sidelined after a cartilage operation.

The signing of the aggressive Jimmy Scoular the next season was significant, to add to those of centre-half Bob Stokoe, centre-forward Vic Keeble and wing-half Tommy Casey. As captain, Scoular drove Newcastle to another Wembley triumph against Manchester City and only Milburn, Mitchell and Cowell were still in the side. It was rumoured that the controversial, abrasive Livingstone had dropped Milburn from his original Wembley side but had to reinstate him on Seymour's insistence. Milburn repaid his faith by scoring a leaping header after only 45 seconds and United won 3-1 with further goals from Mitchell and Hannah.

Newcastle were renowned for their brash, swaggering style both on and off the field and the forthright, plain-speaking Seymour was more than a match for the demands of some of his temperamental strong-minded players. It was Seymour who initially had built, nurtured and guided the Magpies to their great feat in taking the Cup in those successive years, a feat not achieved since Blackburn Rovers did it in 1890 and 1891. The dominant influence of Seymour, self-appointed as the 'honorary

team-manager', had brought those uncompromising teams together and welded together the rock-like qualities of such as Cowell, Harvey and Brennan to the power and goalscoring of Robledo and Milburn and the elegance and skills of Taylor and Mitchell.

It all added up to an exhilarating mix of aggression and artistry which was based essentially on flat-out attacking forays. The ball was seldom worked backwards but played forward, ever forward, in incessant waves. The value of the fanatical Geordie support, home and away, cannot be overstated as they too always put Wembley in their sights as part of their revived tradition.

Those Tyneside glory days were brought to St James' Park by some glamorous, some just plain resolute, but always larger-than-life characters who put the Newcastle club amongst the elite in the game and revived their long-standing tradition, established in an earlier part of the century, as renowned Cup fighters. After that 1955 success the Magpies had to wait another 14 years for a further knock-out trophy — the European Inter-Cities Fairs Cup. It was no wonder that the fans found their continual failures in the FA Cup through the 1960s so hard to stomach, after those heady days in the previous decade.

Portsmouth

THE resignation of Jack Tinn, one of the most colourful managerial characters in the game, at the end of the 1946-7 season, ended one eventful chapter in the history of Portsmouth Football Club and heralded the start of another. Tinn, with his famous 'lucky' spats — half-joke, half-supersitition — had been appointed secretary-manager in May 1927 after the club had won promotion to the First Division. He had taken Pompey to Wembley three times and it was third time lucky in 1939 when odds-on favourites Wolves were thrashed 4-1. In truth, though, Pompey mainly struggled to retain their First Division status during Tinn's 20-year reign at Fratton Park.

It was Tinn, however, who during the war years recruited a number of players who were to bring the club such success when football resumed. Jimmy Dickinson, Jimmy Scoular, Jack Froggatt, Peter Harris and Len Phillips were spotted and served in the Forces locally; Duggie Reid was secured from Stockport County for £5,000; Ernie Butler from Bath City for £100; and Harry Ferrier from Barnsley for £1,000. The team that Tinn had built, with

Portsmouth, League Champions for the second year running. Back row (left to right): Jimmy Scoular, Bill Hindmarsh, Duggie Reid, Ernie Butler, Jimmy Dickinson, Bill Thompson. Front row: Peter Harris, Ike Clarke, Harry Ferrier, Bert Barlow, Jack Froggatt. Thompson, normally a reserve full-back, hit two goals in the last game of the season to ensure Pompey the title.

the likes of Bert Barlow and Reg Flewin from pre-war and the addition of only one newcomer, Ike Clarke, was to win the First Division title for two years in succession and had cost less than £10,000.

In that first post-war season, Pompey finished half-way up the League despite being at the bottom on Boxing Day. A marvellous run-in the second-half of the season ensured their safety and only one match was lost from January to the end of the season. More important, amongst the 22 players used, Duggie Reid, who made his mark with 29 goals, had made his League debut along with Dickinson, Harris, Froggatt and Phillips as service duties permitted. The seeds of the great Championship side were being sown. As the last match was played, the charismatic Tinn announced his retirement but Pompey did not have far to look for his successor.

When Bob Jackson was appointed as manager it was a case of 'bow-tie replacing spats' to reflect their hallmarks. The new manager had played for a number of clubs, including Tranmere Rovers and Bury, and scored closer on 400 goals in his career. Jackson had been chief scout, after gaining experience as scout, then coach, with Bolton Wanderers and manager of Southern League Worcester City. He made his first significant signing when securing the powerful centre-forward Ike

Clarke from West Bromwich for £7,000. In Jackson's first season, inconsistency was the main feature but crowds averaging 30,000 at Fratton Park were evidence of the attractive play of the rapidly-maturing young brigade of rising stars.

As the 1948-9 season opened, the barometer was certainly set fair for the start of Pompey's coming of age year in the First Division. It was the South Coast club's Golden Jubilee year and, sensing the team's potential, the Pompey chairman called for the anniversary to be marked by the winning of the Championship. The response was immediate as Portsmouth made their best-ever start to the top division and when they went to the head after taking 22 points from a possible 36, it had been 12 years since they were in that exalted position. When the Jubilee was celebrated in November 1948, it was noted that since Tinn had handed over to Jackson, all three Portsmouth teams — League side, Reserves and 'A' team — had lost only one match in 42 and scored more than 100 goals. Those statistics were testament to Tinn's efforts to strengthen the club's playing resources over the war years.

Jackson was a warm, thoughtful character who presided unobtrusively over many of the players he had spotted as Tinn's chief scout. The team thrived under Jackson's paternal tenancy, summed up by 'Bow-tie Bob' thus:

"I do everything I can within the rules to keep the boys happy and contented." The uncomplicated collection of players were not subjected to motivational or tactical team-talks and often made contingency plans amongst themselves to counter an opposition threat. They were highly self-motivated, knew what was expected of them on and off the pitch, and Jackson needed have no concern for their corporate attitude.

Pompey's avowed intention in early post-war was to develop not buy and individuality in the form of star players was replaced by a team spirit at a club which was run more like a family concern than a gigantic business concern. Clearly Pompey were not a rich club and manager Jackson was adamant: "We have no intention of playing fast and loose in a crazy transfer market."

The electrifying atmosphere at Fratton Park on 27 November 1948 for the 'birthday' match against mighty Arsenal inspired Pompey to put on a superlative display for a crushing 4-1 victory over the Gunners which set off a triumphal march towards the clinching of the title in the 39th match of the season. Only 18 players were used but six of those made ten or fewer appearances and the magnificent Pompey machine, completely underrated by the national critics, rolled smoothly from one success to another.

Clearly, under Jackson's benign managership the right blend had been found but, above all, Pompey were never anything but a team. There were at this stage no recognized stars in the side. The side played beautiful attacking football, always seeking to make the ball do the work, always handsome to watch, always playing to a strategic plan with the wingers, Harris and Froggatt, as the springboards. Pompey were also quite capable of 'looking after themselves' in any physical contest.

The bedrock of the team was the defence, the most resolute and resilient in the business at the time, where two strong, steady but not over-ambitious full-backs in Rookes and Ferrier coupled with a stumbling-block of a centre-half in Flewin, who was no mean tactician. Phil Rookes and Harry Ferrier had been astutely recruited from the North by Tinn, from Bradford City and Barnsley respectively, but local man Reg Flewin was an experienced, aristocratic stopper who was an England wartime international. Pompey's president at the time, Field Marshall Montgomery, always stressing the value of strong leadership, approved of Flewin's authoritative captaincy and would correspond with him to urge and encourage his team.

In goal Ernie Butler was a tall, underrated 'keeper who was agile without being acrobatic and never seemed to have to resort to the dramatic. Somewhat unappreciated by the fans, his worth was soon recognized when he was missing from the side.

The half-back line was the key, where the rugged terrier-like Jimmy Scoular was aggressive and powerful in the tackle. Later to win Scottish international honours, Scoular was rated by no less an authority on the subject as the late Duncan Edwards as the finest tackler he ever saw, but he was also an essentially attacking constructive half-back. For all his class, he came in for much criticism for his hardness and in this the volatile Scoular was compared to the fearsome Arsenal half-back of pre-war days, Wilf Copping.

Scoular's style and temperament vastly differed from that of his fellow wing-half Jimmy Dickinson, whose quiet and orderly play mirrored a well-mannered and diffident personality. Dickinson's polished and composed style and his remarkable consistency were great assets to Pompey, and later to England. His faultless defensive play was coupled with an almost telepathic understanding of Scoular's attacking instincts. At outside-left, Froggatt also owed much of his goalscoring success to the continuous service he received from Dickinson behind him.

It was Dickinson and outside-right Peter Harris who were first recognized by the international selectors, but Harris had to compete for an England place with such men as Stanley Matthews and Tom Finney. Harris was a penetrative, goalscoring winger with great speed and opportunism. Off the mark, he had the speed of the sprinter McDonald Bailey, and the ball played inside the full-back for him to run on to was a deadly weapon in Pompey's attacking repertoire. In those two Championship years, and after, Harris was a prolific scorer — 17 goals towards the first title and another 16 the following season.

The big-hearted six-footer, Duggie Reid, was a bustling, raw-boned striker known for his fearsome pile-driver of a shot. Reid had developed into one of the game's most consistent scoring forwards after converting from full-back. He exactly matched Harris's scoring record in those two unique seasons for Pompey and it was significant that over three-quarters of the goals scored were spread between Harris, Reid, Clark and Froggatt, who were all in double figures on each occasion.

At the age of 32, Ike Clarke was a most astute signing and he was the type of muscular, powerful centre-forward who could pass effectively and hold the line together in those days when the number-nine was expected to play well upfield. His record of 49 goals in 116 appearances for Pompey spoke for itself and his contribution was invaluable before his move to manage Yeovil in 1953.

Inside-forward Bert Barlow had been signed in the last pre-war season and the slight, retiring man had been one of the heroes of Pompey's winning 1939 Cup Final team. His 29 appearances in the first Championship team were proof of his creative skills but he moved to Leicester the following season as his war-ravaged career came to a close.

Len Phillips was the ball-playing schemer in the team and his contribution was often under-valued at the time by supporters who craved speed of movement before creative build-up. The former Marine, who later went on to earn England recognition before a knee injury, sustained whilst training with the national squad, ended his unfulfilled career, was the 'brains' of the attack and added his share of goals. In an era of great artistic inside-forwards, Phillips rated among the best, standing close behind such greats as Carter, Logie, Mannion and Morris.

Out on the left wing was the stocky, blond, rumbustious 'Jolly Jack' Froggatt with his strong-running and fine shooting which also attracted England's attention. The popular Froggatt showed his versatility by successfully converting to centre-half in the 1950-51 season to fill the vacancy left when Flewin suffered appendicitis.

Playing to the ceiling of their ability before massive support at Fratton Park, where crowds averaged 36,000 and were dotted with the white caps of sailors in port, Pompey's secret lay simply in that great team spirit. The players remembered grudging respect from the newspapers and they were upset about accusations of over-robust, unsporting play from the London-based national Press. What was certain was the players' deeply enthusiastic commitment to Pompey. The 'Iron Men of Portsmouth', as they were known, never knew when they were beaten. As Dickinson once reflected: "If we were a goal down, even two, nobody worried. We just got on with the job, fought back and usually won".

Whilst the 1948-9 season will always be remembered for Pompey's Jubilee League Championship, their Cup run brought crowds flocking to Fratton Park in numbers which will stand unchallenged in their record books for all time. The semi-finals were reached for the fourth time in Pompey's history and they were red-hot favourites to dispose of Leicester City

from the depths of the Second Division. Their realistic hopes of becoming the first side in the century to achieve the 'double' were shattered, though, by a surprise 3-1 defeat. It was typical of that group of players that their response was to produce two stunning 5-0 victories, over Newcastle and Wolves, to put the title firmly in their grasp and bring the Championship to the South Coast for the first time.

In the following season, Portsmouth were as good as ever, although their triumph in the League was on goal-average and was not clinched until the final game. Their feat of winning the title two years in succession was gained by virtually the same well-tried line-up. Only sturdy Bill Hindmarsh at full-back was a newcomer, replacing Rookes, but the defence was disrupted by the loss of Flewin for three months. In the event, the superb defensive record of only 38 goals conceded in 42 matches saw them home when all the calculations had been completed at that momentous finale.

The title was achieved by a well-timed and storming 12-match unbeaten run to finish the season. The final match still had to be won, however, and in a hysterical atmosphere, a 5-1 victory over Aston Villa put Pompey two-fifths of a goal better off than Wolves. A hat-trick from the irresistible Duggie Reid made him the hero of the hour and enabled Portsmouth to hold off the fierce competition from Wolves and Sunderland.

During the season, Dickinson, Harris and Froggatt had all been capped for England. Scoular received a tardy call from Scotland two years later as the football world finally recognized the talent to be found in the royal-blue shirts and white shorts. Soon the 'big-name' clubs were making sizeable bids for the Pompey stars, but all were successfully resisted.

The next season Pompey set themselves the colossal, and as it transpired unobtainable, task of taking the title for a third successive time. The going was much harder as opponents looked to match the Champions physically and the cause was not helped by seemingly continuous injury and sickness problems. The will to complete the hat-trick was never there and the age pendulum was beginning to swing against the club's progress and the club's fading drawing-power was reflected in diminishing attendances. That 1950-51 campaign, despite seventh place, was inevitably an anti-climax after the high excitement of the title wins. In future seasons the battle-cry of the famous old 'Pompey Chimes' was to be heard less often booming down from the Fratton terraces.

After a creditable fourth place in 1951-2, Pompey were never the same again and too much reliance was placed on the original side which had brought such success. Young players were not recruited or groomed successfully and new manager Eddie Lever was not given the purchasing power to rectify the situation. Pompey flirted with relegation in the ensuing years before finally succumbing in 1958-9 in a quite horrific campaign under manager Freddie Cox.

There followed two decades of decline for the proud club and the drab character of that period was in complete contrast to the colourful nature of Pompey's post-war era and to the outstanding individuals, devoted to the club, who had lit up those two never-to-be-forgotten seasons.

Arsenal

NO club approached the challenge of the post-war years with a greater tradition of success in pre-war than Arsenal. In the years before war broke out, the Highbury club had proved themselves the best side in England by winning the League Championship five times in eight years, including a unique triple success with two FA Cup wins thrown in for good measure. From the time of his appointment in 1925, the incomparable Herbert Chapman had literally revolutionised Arsenal and football in general, and lifted a struggling and honourless club to be the most famous in the world before his sudden death in January 1934.

The Gunners were always considered as the model football club and stood on a pedestal within the game. Raich Carter, then an England inside-forward and Sunderland captain, remembered : "They were not merely a great side. They towered so much above every other club. We were in awe of them." It was no wonder that when football restarted after the war, the football public looked towards them in high expectation. Not only was their reputation a big handicap but the pre-war side had also disintegrated — unavailable through war service, injury or retirement.

The task of restoring the debt-ridden North London club's eminence was in the hands, initially, of the former journalist George Allison, who leaned heavily on his trainer Tom Whittaker. Allison, with his dictatorial approach, had a sharp mind and a business-like approach but did not compare with his successor in the way of man-management. Allison relinquished the job due to ill-health at the end of 1946-7 season in which Arsenal had made a disastrous start, finding themselves in next to bottom place by December.

That whole 1946-7 campaign was transformed by Allison's inspired signing of

Arsenal with the FA Cup in 1950. Back row (left to right): Tom Whittaker (secretary-manager), Scott, Swindin, Barnes, Billy Milne (trainer). Front row: Denis Compton, Goring, Forbes, Mercer, Lewis, Leslie Compton. On ground: Logie, Cox.

two veteran stars who were thinking of retiring. Ronnie Rooke, at 35, was signed from Fulham to take up the centre-forward berth and enable Reg Lewis to move to inside-forward. Joe Mercer, at 31, was invaluable as captain on and off the field and was a great steadying influence. By the end of the season, Arsenal had begun to settle down into a good side and finished a respectable 13th.

In 1947-8, Whittaker's first season in charge, Arsenal had climbed back up to the top as Champions and set two new records: first they had conceded only 32 goals, fewer than any previous Championship team had ever conceded; second, they had called on no more than 19 players. The Gunners had been unbeaten in the first 17 games, starting with six successive wins, and, indeed, were leaders for the whole campaign, losing only six of the 42 games. Inspired by the craggy Rooke's bustling, non-stop style and his 33 goals, the title was clinched with four games left and the Highbury club finished seven points ahead of closest rivals, Manchester United.

The Championship had been won nine years earlier with five of this latest successful squad — the Compton brothers, Reg Lewis, the veteran George Male in his last season, and George Swindin. At right-back was Laurie Scott, who was one of the fastest defenders in the League. His sophisticated, cultured play in the Hapgood tradition earned him 17 consecutive England caps in the first two post-war seasons before he moved to Crystal Palace as player-manager in 1951. His partner was Wally Barnes, who had proved his recovery from a serious wartime knee injury by his dependable play allied to determined tackling.

The red-headed right-half, Archie Macaulay, signed from Brentford for £10,000, had started his career in Scotland as a forward in pre-war days and was a brilliant ball-player with magnificent balance. His hard-tackling was an asset to the defence but often his fiery, quick-tempered displays did not endear him to opposition supporters. His style complemented the controlled, mature, now purely defensive play of Mercer on the other flank.

Initially, the steady Alf Fields was at centre-half but a serious injury gave the majestic Leslie Compton the chance to claim the position after his release from cricket commitments and his conversion from full-back. With his strong, solid tackling, as the immobile stopper figure, any opposing centre-forward really knew he was in a game.

In the forward line, Don Roper on the right wing was a powerful, robust goalscorer who had been signed from Southampton and who was to prove his versatility and worth to Arsenal in the coming seasons, on the other wing and even at full-back. His partner, Jimmy Logie, was the schemer of the side and Rooke in particular benefited from his astute passes. The neat and subtle touches, following in the footsteps of the great Alex James, were the highlights of Logie's play during the period when he was one of Arsenal's most consistent performers.

Reg Lewis was known for his skilful positioning and quick-thinking and his 103 League goals in his 154-match Arsenal career stretching from 1937 were evidence of his scoring ability. Lewis positively blossomed in the big games and never more so than in the 1950 Cup Final, when he scored the match-winning goals. His heading ability marked him out as dangerous in the air, to add to his skills on the ground, and it was surprising to note that Lewis did not come into the international reckoning.

On the left wing for most of the 1947-8 campaign was the speedy Scot, Ian McPherson, who had been signed from Notts County the year before. Temperamental, but a gifted ball-player for all that, McPherson lost his place to Denis Compton after the latter's full recovery after a serious knee operation at the end of the cricket season. The whole-hearted, brave play of the more famous Compton brother was an inspiration to the Gunners in the run-in to the title.

The only significant signing in that period was that of the red-headed Scottish international wing-half Alex Forbes, for £13,000 from Sheffield United. The man with the fierce tackle originally gave up football with Dundee to play ice-hockey, but was persuaded back to the game. Forbes was a brilliant attacking half-back, and also a tower of strength in defence, who struggled to contain his aggression such that he was often in trouble with referees and opposition supporters alike.

The next season saw the arrival of the 6ft-tall former Marine Commando, Doug Lishman from Walsall for £10,000 and he proved a particularly fine opportunist in the coming years, topping the scoring list in five of his eight seasons at Highbury. Lishman soon got his chance when Logie was injured and there was a change alongside him at centre-forward after Rooke's departure. The blond youngster Harold — but always known as Peter — Goring was introduced after his move from Cheltenham Town and proved a skilful and stylish leader.

The team which took its next honour at Wembley in 1950 also included the powerful winger Freddie Cox, a short-term but infinitely valuable buy from Spurs. Cox was the inspiration behind the run to Wembley and it was his once-in-a-lifetime shot which won the semi-final in extra-time against Chelsea. The Final brought a deserved but quite forgettable 2-0 victory, but the trophy was won by a combination of the Gunners' experience and good fortune.

Until late in season 1950-51, Arsenal had great hopes of winning the League again but injuries took a heavy toll of their key players. Cox, Logie, Lionel Smith and Roper were casualties and, more important, the 38-year-old Mercer was ordered to take a rest after playing six matches in ten days. Lishman's absence with a broken leg for four months was a crucial factor but he still finished as leading scorer. At the end, the Gunners had to concede the Championship to Manchester United. As landmarks Smith, Leslie Compton and Daniel had earned their first caps; and 72,408 fans, Highbury's biggest post-war crowd, had seen the fourth-round FA Cup tie against Northampton Town.

When the next 1951-52 season came to a climax, Arsenal were to be found attempting to pull off the double but at the death failed on both counts. More injuries not only handicapped them in the League but also limited their chances at Wembley against Newcastle United, even before a ball had been kicked. New centre-half Daniel played with a broken wrist and Logie and Lishman were not fully fit. Barnes twisted his knee in his 58th game of the season and Arsenal's ten men fought until five minutes from time before succumbing to Robledo's winner.

The next season the Highbury men got as far as the last eight in the Cup, and after a shaky start in the League they went on to capture the title for a record seventh time. A stunning 3-1 win over the then leaders, Blackpool, in the autumn sparked off the run up the table which led to them squeezing home on goal-average on the last day of the season, pipping the more attractive Preston North End. Seven of the team were over 30 years of age and the general feeling was that their triumph was down to the paucity of the competition rather than their own stamina, skill and experience.

The Arsenal team had undergone a number of changes since the title had been won five years earlier and included only four of that squad — Swindin, Mercer, Roper and Logie. Swindin, in fact, handed over to the Welshman Jack Kelsey after 14 appearances and the latter was said to have the biggest hands in the game, put to good use in his trade as a blacksmith. Capped for Wales 41 times, Kelsey was a fine, dominant goalkeeper who was honoured as Great Britain's choice against the Rest of Europe in 1955.

Joe Wade had taken his chance well when Barnes was absent for nearly a year and proved a consistent, sturdy full-back. His partnership with Lionel Smith, a former centre-half, blossomed in that title season. Tall and stylish, with powerful headed clearances, Smith earned surprise England recognition after spending some years in the Highbury shadows.

The centre-half was, by tradition, the key component in the Arsenal set-up and when Leslie Compton retired in 1952, the Gunners turned to Ray Daniel, signed as an amateur from Swansea Town in 1946. Daniel made great strides that season, so great that he was capped for Wales after only six appearances and was an unusually clever ball-player for the stopper role. Daniel provided that rare instance of an Arsenal man being unhappy at Highbury throughout that triumphant season and he was soon transferred to Sunderland to give him the move he craved.

Arthur Milton was a blond, good-looking Gloucestershire cricketer who, by his enterprising wing play that season, made a meteoric rise to an England cap to add to his similar recognition at the summer game in the Test match arena. Milton appeared 75 times in his Highbury career before returning to the West Country to help Bristol City to promotion in 1955.

The centre-forward spot had been taken over by the powerful Cliff Holton to give more thrust to the attack. Holton had been converted from a defender by Whittaker and his magnificent build made him a fine, aggressive leader, often compared to Ted Drake. His dynamic shooting brought 19 goals as his contribution to the title success, with Lishman leading the way with 22 in the Arsenal total of 97. Later, Holton proved his versatility by moving to wing-half for the Gunners and when his career finally ended in 1968, he had scored 295 goals in 571 League games and played for five other clubs.

Still on the scene was the incomparable Mercer — full of guile and craft to compensate for his lack of mobility, still too good for many a younger man. He announced his retirement in the midst of Arsenal's celebrations, only for the charming Merseysider to be found playing again the following season.

It was clear that many in the game outside the capital, through the post-war years, were dismayed by Arsenal's dour and utterly defensive game, but it could be argued that this was down to the number of veterans in the side who were plainly physically incapable of matching the lively all-out attacking of such as Newcastle United, Spurs or Manchester United. The key element was their ability to switch from periods of such defensive play to decisive attacking bursts with the wing-halves as the main inspirations. This, of course, typically meant that the Gunners were defending almost all through a match, particularly away from home, only to snatch a sudden goal to secure victory. From such a victory the catch-phrase 'Lucky Arsenal' would be trotted out again.

The 'third-back', the centre-half, was the pivot on which the whole defence hinged. The emphasis lay on defence and whilst the backs looked after the wingers, the middle was covered by that stopper aided by the wing-halves. The whole team defended where necessary but were ready to switch to rapid counter-attack — typically with long, sweeping passes to ensure the surprise element.

Great planning was a prime ingredient of Arsenal's success, based on Chapman's lesson to Whittaker that you can plan to win a football match. As a result, nothing was left to chance in the pre-match discussions but it was the old methods which were at the root of their thinking. Pride and team spirit were stressed and instilled and it was said that one rarely found an Arsenal man who was dissatisfied with his lot or wanted to leave. When he was at Arsenal, Tommy Lawton commented: "If a player wants to get a transfer from this club, you can take it from me there's something very wrong with the player."

Whittaker had tried to emulate his success with Mercer and Rooke by signing the 34-year-old Lawton in 1953-4, but it did not work out so successfully. With the likes of Mercer and Logie in retirement and many of the squad facing the wrong side of 30, Arsenal were soon to pay for their lack of encouragement for youth and little emphasis on rebuilding.

Arsenal stagnated after Whittaker's sudden death and the late 1950s and the 1960s found managers Jack Crayston, George Swindin and Billy Wright struggling to compete, in barren years, with their London neighbours, always conscious of that great tradition of success. The revolution started by Chapman and maintained with such momentum by first Allison and then Whittaker, at the cost of their health for all three, put Arsenal at the forefront of British football. Happily, that tradition has been successfully revived since the double was won in 1971 and the Gunners once again find the football public looking their way expectantly.

Tottenham Hotspur

WHEN war broke out, Tottenham Hotspur had passed through one of the most undistinguished periods in their history and on League football's return seven years later, there was no reason to think that the team from White Hart Lane would not continue to lie dormant and forgotten in the Second Division.

What was not immediately obvious was the pre-war recruitment of teenage talent through the inspiration of manager Peter McWilliam. His scheme was for the young talents to be put through a 'Northfleet nursery' and to this end the groundstaff were registered as playing members of the Northfleet club in the Kent Senior League.

In McWilliam's first spell of management for Spurs, the stern disciplinarian had led them to a Cup Final win in 1921 and promotion to the First Division; and in his second spell he had laid the groundwork for the post-war Spurs to return again to the First Division and take the League Championship trophy for the first time in the club's long history. By the time League football was suspended, the first parts of that side were appearing on the Tottenham scene after being brought on at Northfleet — wing-halves Ron Burgess and Bill Nicholson, goalkeeper Ted Ditchburn, inside-right Les Bennett and winger Les Medley.

Under new manager Joe Hulme, the first three post-war seasons were disappointing, to say the least, considering the promise in the team and the massive crowds thronging expectantly to the fine North London stadium. A disappointing sixth place in the Second Division in the first season was followed by a drop to eighth in 1947-8, but that was mitigated by a Cup run to Spurs' first semi-final since 1922. Only a superb hat-trick by Blackpool's Stan Mortensen put paid to their Wembley hopes, but the ability in the side was there for all to see.

The final pieces in the jigsaw were added during the 1948-9 season with the emergence of the chirpy Cockney, Eddie Baily, at inside-forward and he struck up an immediate rapport with winger Les Medley on his return from Canada. Centre-forward Len Duquemin, from the Channel Islands, had graduated to the first team, where he joined winger Sonny Walters, who had rejoined the staff after his service commitments. A new centre-half in the form of big Harry Clarke from Southern League Lovells' Athletic had been introduced, but any visions of promotion disappeared when 16 matches were drawn and Spurs had to settle for fifth position.

The great Tottenham 'push and run' side. Back row (left to right): Ludford, Ramsey, Nicholson, Ditchburn, Burgess, Withers, McClellan. Front row: Walters, Rees, Duquemin, Baily, Medley, Clarke.

As the 1948-9 season was ending in another anit-climax for Tottenham, the board of directors made a decision which was to have a great bearing on the club's immediate future. The decision was to have a change of manager and the man chosen to replace Joe Hulme was the former Tottenham captain Arthur Rowe. Almost all of Rowe's football life had been associated with Tottenham — the four successful years in charge at Chelmsford City from 1945 until 1949, plus the war years, were the only periods he had been away from the club.

Rowe was quick to introduce his simple but revolutionary ideas to an initially doubtful group of players who were soon joined by the cultured full-back Alf Ramsey, transferred from Southampton. The group, largely made up of 'home-produced' players, were soon convinced of the value of this form of creative football — dubbed 'push and run' — which was in essence an adaptation of the modern Continental style. The all-out attacking style was based on the simple basis of possession football with short passes of 15-20 yards. The ball was always on the move, and it was never held longer than was absolutely necessary as each man ran into open space for a pass made at speed. Correct positioning, accurate passing from everyone in the team — including the goalkeeper — and great skill from the exponents were required.

The long ball, so common in the game at the time, had to be strictly limited and clearly there was to be no place for the individualist. It depended entirely upon every man playing a team game. Several of the players were required to make drastic changes in their own natural styles. The wingers had to play further back than in the normal game and were thus brought more into the game in the light of the inter-changing with the inside-forwards which was an essential part of the scheme.

The wing-halves had to be in a position to take the short ball from the full-backs, ready to push it on to the inside or wing man. Attacks would invariably start from the goalkeeper and be carried from man to man through the defence, the half-backs and on to the forwards, without any recourse to long-kicks.

After continuous practice in the system in pre-season, the team approached the new season convinced of the efficiency of the new style and this confidence was a vital factor during the triumphant season. Going all out for promotion, two early 4-1 wins over Brentford and Plymouth Argyle were followed by a 23-match unbeaten run in which only four points were dropped. The team went to the top on the first Saturday in September and stayed their for the full term, going ten clear points ahead of their nearest rivals, Sheffield Wednesday, at one stage. In that 23-match run,

50 goals were scored, including five against Bradford and seven against Sheffield Wednesday.

The Second Division Championship Shield was presented at the White Hart Lane ground two weeks before the end of the season and the 'new' tactics had won instant acclaim and success. At a stroke, Tottenham had been transformed into the most attractive and original side in the land and home crowds averaging 54,000 greeted their club's rise from the trough in which it had languished.

In goal Ted Ditchburn, who made his League debut in 1946, was an alert and agile 'keeper with good handling. His remarkable consistency was evidenced by his missing only two games in the first seven post-war seasons, including 247 consecutive League appearances. Ditchburn played a full part in starting attacks by his use of the ball and, in particular, by his throw-outs to the full-backs; his almost telepathic understanding with Ramsey, in particular, was a vital starting-point.

Ramsey was at the time the most expensive full-back around and certainly the most creative as he displayed all the skills of an inside-forward. A model of consistency, Ramsey was calm and composed on the field to match his off-field temperament. His perfectly-placed free-kicks led to a number of goals and that composure made him the perfect penalty-taker. Ramsey and Withers were a strong defensive full-back partnership, even if both were somewhat slow on the turn.

Bill Nicholson was as disciplined and professional at right-half as he was to be as a manager in later years. Strong in the tackle, in an essentially defensive role Nicholson could also use the ball well which was of course a prime requirement of the system.

At centre-half Harry Clarke was a tall — 6ft 3in — dominant defender who went directly into the first team on his arrival at White Hart Lane from the obscurity of the Southern League. Many felt that Clarke's heading was his weak point, but his other defensive qualities and distribution compensated for this such that he managed to earn an England cap.

Skipper Ron Burgess was a veteran of ten years at Spurs, as a driving, forceful half-back, but for the sake of the team he had to curb his natural attacking tendencies. The Welsh-man was a shrewd reader of the game and in front of him the Cockney parnership of Baily and Medley benefited immeasurably from his probing. Not only was his leadership positively inspiring, but Burgess was also known for his great consistency of performance and seemingly inexhaustible appetite for work.

Sonny Walters out on the right wing was a fast and direct forward who was always looking for a goalscoring chance. The top scorer in the promotion season with 18 goals, Walters managed another 15 in the 1950-51 First Division championship season. Like his contemporaries of similar style and persuasion, Peter Harris of Portsmouth and Johnny Hancocks of Wolves, Walters found it difficult to gain the national recognition he deserved in the face of the competition from Matthews and Finney.

At inside-right, Les Bennett was locally-developed, a scheming forward with a great capacity for work. This latter quality was particularly valuable in a side where the front players were required to be continually on the move to be ready to receive the ball in an open space.

Len 'Duke' Duquemin was a Channel Islander who had lived on Guernsey during the German occupation and proved to be a hard-shooting skilful leader of the attack with a knack of scoring vital goals with impeccable timing. Many felt that if he could have added a more aggressive forceful streak to his play, a la Ford or Mortensen, then the gentlemanly Duquemin might have scored more goals and earned more recognition.

The other inside-forward, Eddie Baily, thrived on Rowe's new concept and his ball-playing talents and quick intuitive play were tailor-made for the scheme. He and his partner Medley played havoc with opposing defences and the two small, compact men switched positions with such speed and in such harmony that it was difficult to tell them apart. If there was one player in that great Spurs side who really caught the eye, it was Baily with his cheeky, irrepressible play around which much of the attacking seemed to revolve.

Baily and his partner Les Medley were paired together for England four times in recognition of their understanding but not before Medley had tried to carve out a career for himself in Canadian football after the war. Spurs were very glad to welcome him back to White Hart Lane in 1949, to complete a formidable forward line, all of whom, including Medley, were capable of getting into double figures with their goal tallies.

In 1950-51, Tottenham continued from where they had left off as Second Division champions by sweeping to the First Division title and in doing emulated the feats of Liverpool (1905, 1906) and Everton (1931, 1932) in winning those titles in successive years. Spurs began the season with their biggest reverse — losing 4-1 at home to Blackpool — but quickly clicked into gear by swamping Stoke 6-1, Portsmouth 5-1 and Newcastle 7-0 in the next three home games. The latter result was considered by many to be the greatest exhibition of the 'push and run' style which the North London side had by then perfected.

After a successful Christmas period, when five out of six points were secured, Spurs moved into top place and retained that exalted position for the remainder of the season. Manchester United gave them a great run for their money but only one of the last 12 games were lost and the title was won with a fortnight of the season left. Their 60 points was the highest total in the top division since Arsenal's record 66 in 1930-31. Eighty-two goals had been scored and only seven defeats incurred in that magnificent season, before an average home attendance of 55,486.

To the side which who had brought promotion the previous season, Rowe added inside-right Peter Murphy, who had been secured for a big fee from Coventry City after Bennett's recurring injuries. Murphy's speed and stylish play were a bonus, as was the tenacious tackling of Arthur Willis, who regained his left-back position from Withers. Willis had made his debut in 1946 but lost his place first to Sid Tickridge and then to Withers until the latter's injury gave him a chance. How well Willis took that chance was recognized in the next campaign when he, too, earned an England cap.

In 1951-2, Spurs were not quite the same exhilirating force and Manchester United took their chance to secure the title as a result. For all that, Arthur Rowe's team took 20 points from the last 12 games but had to settle for the runners-up spot. Like all great teams, it plainly could not last and the relative decline from those high peaks of performance continued in the next season. Spurs slipped to the tenth place but reached the Cup semi-final, surviving four away ties before losing to Blackpool in a repeat of the 1948 scenario.

By the time Arthur Rowe retired through ill-health, the Championship side was into the veteran stage. New manager Jimmy Anderson began the task of building a new team. The transfer of Danny Blanchflower from Aston Villa for £30,000 was a masterstroke and when Anderson recruited the likes of Maurice Norman and Bobby Smith, the beginnings of the team which would eventually capture the League and FA Cup double within a few years was there for all to see.

Ten years earlier, Rowe and his Spurs side had heralded the rebirth of 'artistic' football in England, football based on team discipline and no little skill. By their success they had blown apart the game's obsession with defensive football. The trend had been set and from then on Spurs would forever be associated with a brand of smooth, attacking football, full of enterprise, enthusiasm and skill.

The Managers

Matt Busby

THE name of Manchester United is known throughout the world and support for the Old Trafford club can be found in all four corners of the globe. But it is true to say that their standing has come about almost entirely thanks to the efforts of Matt Busby.

When he took over as manager on 22 October 1945, the club was on its knees — the ground had been blitzed almost beyond repair, mountainous debts had accrued and only a handful of players were available. United, standing very much in the shadow of Manchester City, were in a desperate state — the dressing-rooms were derelict, there were no offices for staff and no training facilities. Busby had to work from a desk in a coal depot a mile away and the players were forced to train on waste-ground earmarked for a car-park. From those humble beginnings Matt Busby built United into the institution it is today with his unique record of success in the 24 years he sat in the manager's chair.

Busby was born in a pitman's cottage in a small village in Lanarkshire and inevitably followed his father into the mines until the day in February 1928 when he signed for Manchester City. After an unsuccessful spell at inside-forward he was moved back to right-half and his playing career began to blossom. After playing in the 1933 and 1934 Cup Finals, Busby moved to Liverpool and came under his first great influence — that of manager George Kay. Busby always gave credit to Kay for teaching him about man-management — most particularly telling him the value of keeping players on top wages even when they were injured and could not play, and of always rewarding loyal service with a benefit. Busby never forgot the way each and every member of staff at Anfield was treated with kindness, consideration and understanding.

During World War Two, Busby graduated to an Army company sergeant-major and in football to wartime internationals for Scotland, but when peacetime came he was looking to carve out a future for himself off the playing field. Just as Busby was about to accept an offer from Liverpool to become a coach on a five-year contract under manager Kay, the chairman of hard-up, bombed-out

Manchester United, J.W.Gibson, offered him the chance to become their manager.

Liverpool were disappointed and even unsuccessfully looked for a transfer fee from United in the mistaken belief that Busby was moving to Old Trafford as a player-manager. The young track-suited manager led United into the League North in 1945-6, inheriting a side that was 16th place. The first United team under his charge beat Bolton Wanderers 2-1 and read: Crompton; Walton, Roach, Warner, Whalley, Cockburn, Worrall, Carey, J.Smith, Rowley and Wrigglesworth. On that day Johnny Carey was playing his first match for two years, after demob, and Stan Pearson, Allenby Chilton, Johnny Morris and Charlie Mitten were still in the Services. By the end of the season, United had climbed to fourth place and Busby acknowledged that he inherited some wonderful players.

His first priority, setting the pattern for the whole term of his management, was to find young talent to supplement and later to replace the old heads. His first public statement as boss was prophetic — "I am determined that United shall provide the public with the best in the game. It is my intention to develop young players." The assembly line of talent had almost stopped and there was nothing else to be done but find new players and groom them into First Division footballers. In the short term, Busby's first signing turned out to be his best. For £4,000 the veteran winger Jimmy Delaney was recruited from Glasgow Celtic and gave Manchester United six magnificent seasons, being one of the main reasons for the emergence of United as the most successful team in post-war football.

Even by the end of his first season, Busby had created the nucleus of a side which, despite the transitional state of affairs in the club, finished only one point behind the League Champions, Liverpool, in 1946-7. By this time the likes of Chilton, Pearson, Aston and Rowley had become established in the side and the supporters were rolling along in ever-increasing numbers for the home games, albeit at Maine Road. The bank manager was much happier as the club, which had for so many years been saddled with debts, made a profit of nearly £60,000 in Busby's first two seasons.

So confident was Busby in his team's ability that he was moved to predict at the start of the 1947-8 season that United would win the Cup, even though in effect they would have to play every round away from home. Despite a season of brilliant all-out attacking football, United were unable to catch a remarkably consistent Arsenal side in the League, but in the Cup were not to be denied.

The third-round tie at Aston Villa was the epitome of United's early post-war performances. It was the hardest and the most pulsating on their road to Wembley. In the first half United were simply irresistible, handing out a soccer lesson to bemused Villa. The attacking flair and style, which Busby espoused throughout his management career, brought United a 5-1 lead at Villa Park with Stan Pearson and Jack Rowley at the peak of their goalscoring form and the gifted, darting schemer Johnny Morris demoralizing the Villa defence.

The second-half was a tremendous battle with Villa pulling back to 5-4 before Pearson scored a late goal to clinch a stupendous 6-4 victory in one of the great matches of the early post-war period. In the event United went on to beat Blackpool in a Final described by many critics at the time as the finest ever played at Wembley. The classic qualities of the 1948 United team, so expertly assembled by Busby, were never better displayed than in that afternoon's feast of football.

By now Busby had made several positional switches in an attempt to get the maximum efficiency from each player. Allenby Chilton was successfully converted from wing-half to centre-half, but Busby's most gratifying and inspired experiment was the double moving of Johnny Carey and John Aston from inside-right and inside-left to the two full-back positions where they went on to establish themselves as the finest club pair in Britain.

Carey's leadership qualities had been recognised immediately by Busby, who made him club captain, another wise move as the Irishman's wisdom, quiet demeanour and unique ability proved to be the ideal qualities for the position. Busby was always unstinting in his praise for Carey — "It is difficult to do honour to a soccer genius — to his command of the game, his artistry, his greatness."

United displayed their great attacking skills in that 1948 Cup Final to beat Blackpool — Matthews, Mortenson and all — 4-2 to confirm their manager's complete confidence in their ability. In two and a half years, Busby had welded those disparate talents into a superb unit — their artistry complemented by their loyalty and commitment to their manager.

Busby's involvement with the 1948 Great Britain soccer team for the Olympic Games held in London brought him great credit. The British team reached the semi-final after a job of work which Busby always regarded as one of his best. In a matter of weeks he sorted out a winning team from 26 spare-time amateur players from four different countries and many of the United players gave up much of the close-season to assist with the coaching.

United were runners-up again in 1949 and 1951 and, to most people's delight, finally took the Championship in 1952, finishing four points ahead of Tottenham Hotspur. By this time, however, Busby realized that his great team of over-30s was growing old and would soon need to be dismantled and rebuilt. Early in that 1952-3 season, Busby began the process of breaking up the 'old' Manchester United team to build the 'new' from the group of talented youngsters so eagerly waiting in the wings. For the first time Busby showed that typically honest but realistic approach and he was conscious that no useful purpose would be served by putting off the day of decision. He commented at the time, "Panic in the transfer market is usually caused through wringing the last drop of football out of ageing stars."

The message was clear — the likes of Carey, Chilton, Rowley, Pearson and Cockburn and others had to reluctantly be moved on. Young players, who were to become household names — such as Jeff Whitefoot, Jackie Blanchflower, Eddie Colman, Duncan Edwards and David Pegg — were introduced that season and after United had finished fourth, Busby was convinced of their promise: "This young team will be much too good for anything else in the Football League."

And so it was. Two League Championships followed and Manchester United took the first step by an English club in European competition. Then in 1958, the awful Munich air disaster cut down the flower of Matt Busby's vibrant young team and dashed from his hand the ultimate honour in club football. Busby, terribly injured in the air crash, survived not only to walk again but to rebuild another team of stars. This time the European Cup was gained, in glorious style in 1968.

After the break-up of that first great post-war United team, Busby had, typically, never lost sight of the contribution made by the older servants of the club and he was at pains to ensure that their removal was painless. He never sought to gain big fees for any of the displaced stars, making sure, above all, that they were all fixed up with other clubs to their satisfaction. He took consolation from the fact that none of his old players came back to reproach him or the club for the actions taken so fearlessly at that time.

From then on Busby assumed the role of 'father-figure' to this young group of players. The emphasis was on the youngsters enjoying themselves, playing their natural game and concentrating on serving up good football. Busby's commitment to building sides around home-grown youngsters was further explained by him: "From my own playing days I realized how vital it was to encourage the spirit of loyalty. I always wanted players who would think of the club first rather than themselves and the only way to achieve this is with young players."

Busby had displayed his unerring faith in natural talent by his bold decision to give those 'Busby Babes' their head in November 1952. Whilst the players had certain guidelines, the important thing was that they had their freedom. Freedom to express themselves on the field, with no tactical restraints. Busby knew that if they enjoyed themselves, then they were bound to give pleasure in equal measure to the fans and so it proved.

The man of great dignity, warm sensitivity and unerring charm also contained ruthlessness and iron will. He would always show great loyalty to his players and this was at the forefront of his priorities. Busby was not being modest when he once proclaimed, "I've always had success because I've always got people to have confidence in me — players and directors. They have always done their best for me and I've always tried to do the same for them."

History shows that Busby was often a mover for changes and reforms in the game. Always up to date and ahead of his time, it is interesting to note that he either proposed or actively encouraged so many of the advances which were made in the game in post-war years. The record shows that during the years of his great service to the game, which still of course continues to this day, Busby supported the abolition of the maximum wage, canvassed for floodlit football, the introduction of substitutes and protection for goalkeepers. And, of course, he saw the vital need for English clubs to perform on a wider stage.

However, his greatest achievement remains the rebuilding of United after the war, and their subsequent phoenix-like rise to one of the greatest and most successful sides in the world. Truly, Busby combined all the great assets a manager needs. He was an able administrator but, more than that, he had the unique ability to find, buy and mould great players and insist that the game be played his way. Matt Busby achieved a unique peak of public affection and esteem and was rewarded by a knighthood as the greatest and most successful manager in the Golden Age of Football.

Stan Cullis

IT would be true to say that only Stan Cullis matched the managerial achievements of Matt Busby in the post-war years as he made Wolverhampton Wanderers into a great

and attractive force in the late 1940s and 1950s. In a period of 12 years, after winning the Championship for the first time in 1953-4, Wolves entered upon the finest period of their history in which they won the League title three times, were runners-up three times and won the FA Cup twice.

Cullis was born at Ellesmere Port, Cheshire, on 25 October 1915 and played as an amateur for both Ellesmere Port Wednesday and Bolton Wanderers, where he was termed 'too slow', before joining Wolves in 1934. There followed over 30 years of service to the Molineux club as player, assistant manager and manager. In a playing career of over 300 senior games, under the managership of Major Frank Buckley, Cullis was a great inspiration as Wolves' captain and the last of the great attacking centre-halves.

In his exemplary, constructive style, he was known as one of the toughest, bravest players and was a household name as part of the great Britton-Cullis-Mercer England half-back line of wartime days. Cullis' playing career brought him 12 full caps and 20 in wartime and Victory internationals after his first appearance in 1937. He was proud of his reputation as a tough, fierce and uncompromising defender. It was once said that 'if you kicked him in the heart, you'd only break your leg'. Cullis

remembered that as the greatest compliment he ever had paid to him.

Before he hung up his boots Cullis experienced two crushing disappointments in his quest for a medal to crown his fine playing career. By Wolves' surprising 1939 Cup Final defeat by Portsmouth, he missed a winners' medal, but all the Midlands expected him to be consoled by taking a Championship medal as Wolves were poised for their first League title in the late spring of 1947.

In the event Wolves had to beat Liverpool in the last match of the season, held over until a blazing June Saturday in view of the season's extension due to the winter freeze-up. Cullis had announced his retirement one hour before the game which Wolves lost. With that defeat went his last chance of a medal as a player. The disappointment that day only served to increase his resolve to bring honours to the club to whom he was devoted.

There was no doubt that Cullis's retirement was hastened by the frequency of injuries which punctuated the later years of his playing life. He reluctantly concluded that, as he was prone to regular bouts of concussion after prolonged heading, he had to retire prematurely at the age of 30. After rejecting a management offer from Hull City, as a successor to Raich Carter, Cullis readily agreed to play out one last season with a view to moving into the coaching staff at Molineux.

After his retirement he became assistant manager to Ted Vizard, the famous Bolton and Wales winger, who had replaced Major Buckley after his move to Notts County in 1944. Cullis took on the job of guiding Wolves' Central League youngsters. Indeed, Buckley had often nominated Stan Cullis as his successor and in the summer of 1948 this came to fruition.

It was time for Cullis, at 32, to put into practice the many lessons he had learned from Major Buckley and no-one doubted that he had inherited his mentor's fierce drive and strict discipline. Like Buckley, Cullis put great store on fitness, stamina, discipline and club spirit. From the start Cullis showed the same inclination to express and put into practice his decided and forthright views on how the game should be played.

It was immediately clear that Wolves, like Manchester United, were to continue to be representatives of the school of thought in

English football which believed that it was better to rear one's own players inside the club rather than buy them in the transfer market. Buckley had been the first manager to concentrate on youngsters straight from school and Cullis was lucky to inherit the fruits of this network and maintained this tradition by his commitment to an extensive scouting system. The well-organized system of scouts and contacts which covered all of Britain was maintained with increasing vigilance by Cullis.

This system was the most powerful factor behind Wolves' post-war triumphs and the continual flow of brilliant youngsters provided Cullis with immensely virile teams, year after year. In addition, the process of finding players and selling them was itself a profitable one for the club and, indeed, Wolves became the leading 'distributor' of players in the country. The system laid the foundations for the club's position in the football world through those halcyon days and the balance sheets in the Cullis years made very impressive reading. By the same token Cullis did not hesitate to spend money on new players if he found himself short of the right man for a particular position.

The Wolves, always attractive in their old-gold shirts with black edgings, became a menace to their opponents with their 'long-ball' tactics and, like Manchester United and Tottenham Hotspur, lived for incessant attack. They differed from the other two by their approach and the long pass was the main pillar which supported Cullis's approach to football. Whilst some purists suggested that such a pass had the greater chance of interception and required the greater accuracy in execution, Cullis argued that it has the advantage of reaching the opposing penalty-area quickly and more often during a game. Cullis was of the opinion that the mightly Hungarian team, which had overwhelmed England, employed the same methods. He was supported in his theories by plans and patterns produced by an RAF wing-commander, who thus 'proved' the lethality of the long pass.

The Cullis style of pace, power and little artistry did not meet with the approval of the purists but there was no denying that Wolves' adventurous, swashbuckling style of open play provided the thrills and the goals and was essentially British in nature. The Press were inclined, however, to refer to the style as a slightly refined form of 'kick-and-rush'. The wingers were the key-pieces of the Wolves plan and there the pace and penetration of Mullen and the power of dimunitive, tricky Hancocks were crucial. It was, in some ways, a return to the Arsenal of the early 1930s, when wingers Hulme and Bastin were the main executors as they bore inwards in swift pincer movements.

Cullis essentially worked by two maxims — "There is no substitute for hard work," and "All for Wolves." He expected everyone at the club to follow those attitudes and, indeed, until the removal of the maximum wage in 1961 and a marked falling-off in the flow of outstanding youngsters, he earned respect and dedication.

The bald-headed perfectionist, said to be prone to sulks and to be something of a dressing-room tyrant, mirrored the sort of bold, single-minded assertive approach which Brian Clough brought to his managership in the early 1970s. Like Clough, Cullis was envied and at times reviled, but there was no doubt that from his players he largely obtained and earned respect for and understanding of his disciplinary demands and tactical applications. Again like Clough, Cullis did not lack a sense of publicity and was not loath to expound his strong opinions on most matters of football, from his typically austere office.

As a player, Cullis approached every game like a prize-fighter and coincidentally he also believed in balance and footwork — "All footballers should box, with plenty of sparring and shadow-work." Supreme fitness for his players was Cullis' aim and the unfortunate footballers were subject to his 'work until it hurts' form of training. A belief that proper training and peak fitness could cause the abnormal achievement to become a normal one led to the creation of a highly-organized scientific approach to physical fitness. All aspects in the areas of athletics and weight-training were incorporated but coaching of natural talent was also important. It could not be denied that the coaching at Molineux helped to make fine players out of some who might otherwise not have reached First Division standard.

Cullis' part in the development and success of his captain, Billy Wright, cannot be over-stated. His image, manner and permanency were moulded under his manager's great influence. Cullis' advice to

Wright on evaluating opposing centre-forwards, dictating the direction of play and holding his defence together, was priceless. More than that, it was Cullis' shrewd judgement which persuaded Wright to convert to centre-half in 1954 with such conspicuous success for club and country.

Wright was Cullis's captain when, in his first season as manager, Wolves won the Cup in 1949, beating Leicester City 3-1 at Wembley. The two were still in partnership when Wolves, now one of the finest football production-lines the game has ever known, took their first League Championship in 1954 and again in successive years in 1958 and 1959. Then Wolves restored some of Britain's prestige in the memorable floodlit victories over Russia's Moscow Spartak and Hungary's Honved in 1954, games which were prime factors in the inauguration of European competition.

After a further FA Cup win in 1959, Cullis could not maintain his record of success and in September 1964 was sacked, to end his 30-year association with Molineux. Before that blow, Cullis had been subject to sickness brought on by the stresses of the job. After a rest he moved to Birmingham City in the Second Division in December 1965, for a stay which lasted for over four years and laid the ground for their promotion in 1972.

Cullis' philosophy could be found in his stressing of the three great virtues of soccer — 'spirit, tactics and fitness, and the greatest of these might easily be fitness'. He had shown that football which was played the hard way, the simple way and the fast way, if harnessed to a systematic plan, is capable of winning almost any honour.

Arthur Rowe

In 1949, as a preview to the impending season, Charles Buchan wrote: "It is time we had new tactics instead of the present ones . . .which make most of the games of a negative quality." Little did he know that his plea was to be immediately answered by a Tottenham Hotspur team with an exciting and entertaining brand of all-out attacking football, the like of which had not been seen for many a long year.

It was Arthur Rowe who inspired this rebirth of cultured, artistic football and

brought a very welcome breath of fresh air, not only to the famous Spurs club, who were adrift in the Second Division at the time, but to the game as a whole. Rowe was a Spurs man through and through. Born in Tottenham, he had first become associated with the club in 1921 and graduated through the club's nursery sides before signing professional forms in 1929. He went on to skipper the League team from centre-half and won his one England cap against France in 1933-4.

In March 1949, the Spurs directors were growing tired of waiting for success and although almost all the players that were to bring them that success were already at the club — assembled by the manager, former Arsenal and England winger, Joe Hulme — in March, they sacked their manager. And although they advertised the post, Arthur Rowe, who had been developing Chelmsford City into one of the country's leading non-League sides, was always the favourite for the job. In May 1949, he was appointed.

Until Rowe's appointment, Spurs could only be described as a mediocre club, living largely in the shadow of their illustrious neighbours in North London. Under his managership, however, the position and future of Tottenham Hotspur were transformed as they stormed to successive Second and First Division titles in 1950 and

1951 with a magnificent, hugely admired team. Yet the only addition to the playing staff was the Southampton full-back Alf Ramsey, who Hulme had tried to sign just before the March 1949 transfer deadline. No, the difference was not in personnel but in style. Built around the fundamental principle of 'Make it simple, make it quick' the team played what was predominantly a short-passing or 'push and run' football.

In his playing career in the 1930s, Arthur Rowe was known as an uncommonly sophisticated centre-half, at a time when the position was largely occupied by muscular, uncompromising 'stopper-type' defenders, typical of the defensive play of the period. In 1939, when his playing career was ended by a cartilage injury, Rowe set out to travel extensively to spread his conviction that the game was all about simplicity and movement. He was one of the several British players and coaches, including Jimmy Hogan, who made their way to Europe to teach and dispense to the developing football nations.

As war clouds again gathered over Europe, Rowe was working in Hungary, helping their brilliant natural talent to modify their attacking strategies. Indeed, it was reported that he was offered the post of manager to the Hungarian national team but the outbreak of the war came before the offer could be taken up. Instead he returned to Britain, joined up and was eventually put in charge of the Army football team until his demob in 1945, when he was appointed secretary manager of Chelmsford, guiding them to the Southern League Cup in his first season there.

It was no coincidence, therefore, that the 'new' Spurs style coincided most closely with that which could already be found in certain parts of the Continent. The style, propounded extensively abroad by Rowe before the war, retained many of the qualities of the old English and Scottish game. Indeed, the old-time purists were of the opinion that Rowe's strategy mirrored the traditional, classic style of the pre-war Scottish game.

Rowe brought beauty and grace to football, ingredients which were in short supply in an unaesthetic football era. His was based on a simple logic — the more a side retains the ball, thus denying its use to its opponents, the more are the chances to score. In effect, when the ball was won, the aim was to keep it. Rowe's philosophy was concentrated in six words — "Don't kick the ball — pass it."

The system had been piloted successfully by Rowe at Chelmsford City before his appointment at White Hart Lane. It was based on the short pass of no more than 20 yards, the ball never being held longer than necessary. The ball had to be kept always on the move, with each man running into an open space for the short pass made at speed. Correct positioning and no little skill were required. It demanded drastic changes in many players' natural styles.

The attacks started from goalkeeper Ted Ditchburn and the collaboration between him and full-back Alf Ramsey, who was primed to receive, hold and pass the ball, was vital. Rowe preached to his initially doubtful players that there was a psychological advantage to be gained in that 'while you have the ball, you are calling the tune'.

The possession football, played in perpetual motion, was immediately successful and, even when the movement broke down, the defence was good enough to win the ball back and start again. Essentially, Rowe stressed that there was no place for the individualist, that every man had to play a team game with each section of the team dovetailing with the others. This appeared to promote a fine team spirit, but if there was one attribute which Rowe succeeded in fostering, it was confidence or belief in the system and their ability to carry it out.

Spurs swept all before them in their promotion season and it was as 'team of the season' that they returned to the First Division after a 15-year absence. The same special blend of players and the same spirit carried them to the top of the First Division, taking the title for the first time. In the space of three seasons, Spurs had become the most attractive and creative side in the land, attracting massive attendances at their magnificent White Hart Lane ground.

The sensitive, philosophical Rowe guided Spurs to the runners-up spot in 1952 and to the FA Cup semi-final a year later, but in truth the system only prospered for four seasons. By that time, however, Rowe had taken Spurs back into the top echelon and laid the ground for even greater success under Billy Nicholson, one of his pupils. The impetus could not be sustained, largely because the key players were getting older and also because Rowe's health had deteriorated. In the event, after a nervous breakdown Rowe had to resign in 1955, handing over to another long-standing Spurs servant, Jimmy Anderson.

Rowe returned to management in 1961 at Crystal Palace and was immediately successful in guiding them to promotion from the Fourth Division. Once again however Rowe's health forced his retirement.

At the time when English football was slap-dash, unscientific and largely defensive, the style of play, expounded with unyielding convictions, introduced by the innovative Rowe set the right example and pointed the way to Continental methods. The game in that post-war period and subsequently owed him an enormous debt, if only for the enormous pleasure given to countless tens of thousands throughout the land.

Raich Carter

RAICH Carter, born in Sunderland in 1913, was the complete inside-forward of the 1930s and 1940s, both as a schemer and goalscorer. And in April 1948 he jumped at the chance to move from First Division Derby County to Hull City of the Third

Division North, initially as player-assistant manager to Major Frank Buckley. Carter knew that the managership was likely to become vacant in two or three years' time,

but he was surprised to find himself in charge after only one month when Buckley resigned.

Carter had never played outside the First Division and proved to be an enormous playing asset to Hull, setting a supreme example with the emphasis on quality football. The imperious Carter led his team magnificently on the pitch, foot often on the ball, dictating the play and shouting players into position. The Tigers' record-breaking start to the 1948-9 season — nine successive victories — was evidence of his influence and massive record-setting crowds, averaging nearly 40,000, were attracted to the new Boothferry Park ground. At a stroke, attendances increased from the previous season's average of 24,000.

The relentless experimentation of his predecessor — Buckley used a large number of players — came to an end and Carter employed only 12 players that season in a judicious combination of old experienced professionals and young, untried footballers. As a player, the edge had gone from Carter's game at the highest level but in the lower division he was in a class of his own. He always felt that he was at an advantage managing the team on the field rather than from the stand. He made the point that he got a better 'feel' of the play but acknowledged that it gave him no opportunity to see other teams play or seek out new players.

With his hair having turned a premature silver, the 35-year-old Carter was the bristling authoritative man off the field and such a calming, experienced influence in the dressing-room. Two years earlier, after Derby County had won the FA Cup, young Reg Harrison, who came into the Wembley side for the injured veteran, Sammy Crooks, said, "I knew we'd win the Cup. Raich said so."

At Hull, his philosophy of not giving promotion a second thought but concentrating on his admitted aim — "To play high-class football and let the result take care of itself" — bore rich fruit that first season.

An FA Cup run, which took Hull to the quarter-finals after a magnificent win at First Division Stoke, scared Carter and he admitted that he would have shed no tears if his side had been knocked out long before. Their eventual defeat, at home to Manchester United before 55,000, brought great financial benefit and enormous publicity to a city that was desperate to get back on to the soccer map.

Carter was a public figure with a high profile, both locally and nationally, and it was clear that the raising of public morale and interest in the team's success was reflected in increased output in the Humberside industries. The Tigers stormed to the title in the Northern Section, holding off a very good Rotherham team and losing only four of their 42 League matches, all played before massive crowds. It had been a remarkable instant success story for the single-minded master tactician, who had added only former Sunderland colleague, Eddie Burbanks, and the Dane, Viggo Jensen, to Major Buckley's squad.

In a bid to take the club into the First Division, Carter brought 'name' players to Boothferry Park in the likes of Gerry Bowler, Don Revie and Neil Franklin, but the powerful Hull bandwagon slowed right down in the Second Division. It came as no surprise to Carter, who recalled that four out of the last five clubs promoted to the Second had lasted only one season in the higher division.

In the event, Hull became established in the Second but, with hindsight, it was no surprise that Carter resigned in September 1951. It came as a shock at the time, though. "Disagreement on matters of a general nature in the conduct of the club's affairs," was the club's announcement. Carter's enemy, throughout his career, was a certain abrasiveness and it was always apparent that, on or off the field, he was never one to suffer fools gladly.

It was May 1953 before Carter had a second chance in management, at Leeds United, and in the meantime he prolonged his playing career in Ireland with Cork Athletic. At Elland Road, Carter again succeeded Major Buckley and achieved what he had failed to do at Hull. Leeds gained promotion to the First Division in 1956, but here again it was said that his autocratic approach was less productive off the field than on it.

Carter's genius was lost to the game when he was sacked at Leeds in June 1958, and it was not until 1960 that Mansfield Town brought him back to management. His fine work at Field Mill prompted Middlesbrough to offer him a job in January 1963 and that lasted for three years.

The crafty, arrogant inside-forward of the 1930s and 1940s, who by the age of 24 had achieved every honour then available to an English footballer, had single-handedly transformed the depressed Hull City club and for one glorious record-breaking season had brought glamour and excitement to Humberside, not known before or since.

Alex Stock

ORIGINATING from a little North Somerset mining village, Alex Stock played for two years as an inside-forward at Charlton Athletic and Queen's Park Rangers before the war took him into the Tank Corps. Distinguished Army service ended with Stock having to be invalided out after he was wounded at Normandy. It is said that he applied for the player-manager's job at Yeovil Town almost irascibly on a wet, boring afternoon when he could not get out into his beloved garden.

Yeovil were in the Southern League, the weekly wage bill was a maximum of £80 for the part-time professionals. Stock's appointment apparently arose out of a

casual conversation with a Yeovil director during a train journey and he admitted that he took the job as a pure speculation, no more afraid of command than he had been as an Army officer. Indeed, Stock looked back on his Army career as a good grounding for management and carried his high regard for discipline and personal appearance into each of his football clubs.

The young managerial student was paid £7 per week and saw his players only on match-days, remembering that he spent the week worrying if they were keeping fit. In between, Stock carried out all the administrative duties and just about every other job which needed doing. His home match-day began with mowing the grass and marking the lines out on the pitch. In the afternoon, Stock was to be found out on that same pitch as an inspirational captain. Afterwards he would rush out of the dressing-room to envelope-up the players' wages and then count the gate money.

In his three years at Yeovil, Stock was to turn the Southern League side into a household name with an astonishing run to the fifth round of the FA Cup. Their achievement of reaching the third round had not attracted a single line of comment in the national Press, but when the team from the small Somerset country town proceeded to beat Bury 3-1 to earn another home tie, this time against First Division Sunderland, the football world really sat up and took notice.

Stock had made sure that the sloping pitch at The Huish ground had got as much publicity as possible. As he put it, "By the time Bury arrived, the entire country thought we played on the side of a house." Sunderland, too, were defeated by the slope, by Stock's canny tactics and by a team of publicans, glove-cutters, clerks, warehousemen and labourers. Some 15,000 spectators jammed into the tiny ground, with another 5,000 milling around outside, to see Stock put Yeovil ahead after half-an-hour, only for Robinson to equalize for the Wearsiders. In extra-time, Yeovil's Bryant put them ahead again and after a tense last 15 minutes they were through.

The team lying sixth from the bottom of the Southern League had knocked out Sunderland, then eighth in the First Division with an expensively-assembled collection of stars including Len Shackleton. Now Stock's band of part-time footballers, after climbing their Everest, had to travel North in the next round to take on the might of the FA Cup holders, Manchester United.

Stock, the most articulate of the young managers at the time, summed up the experience and put it into perspective afterwards: "We knew that we had played above ourselves, collectively and individually, all through. Now we had to face this United thing. So we went to Maine Road and there were 81,000 people there. I don't mind telling you, a few prayers were said in the dressing-room. We lost 8-0 and we just felt numb. But afterwards, we heard that our share of the gate was more than our entire receipts for the previous season. Suddenly, what had happened on the field was of no significance."

Yeovil were on the map and had established a permanent place in the annals of football. The architect of their success had made his name and moved into League football the next season with Leyton Orient, where he was to stay for ten years except for a disastrous mistaken two months at Arsenal and four months of betrayal and deceit at the hands of Italian club, Roma.

Another great Cup run was engineered by the mercurial, charismatic Stock in 1952, when Orient, just like Yeovil before them, reached the fifth round. They beat Wrexham, Everton and Birmingham City in the process. Orient, in mid-table in the Third Division South, attracted a 30,000 crowd for the home tie against the all-conquering Arsenal. It was a great thrill for the man who had become so attached to the little London club and who, for all his apparent dispassion, felt every aspect of the game so intensely. His day was spoilt, however, by an absurdly easy win for the Gunners over the 'giant-killers' in a terrible anti-climax.

After 20 years of striving, Orient finally won the Southern Section championship under Stock in 1956. He moved to Queen's Park Rangers in 1959 before being sacked in 1968. He was then with Luton Town and Fulham before returning to QPR as a director and then caretaker manager. In 1979 he was apppointed manager at Bournemouth and finally retired in 1981, although continuing with the South Coast club as a director.

For the man who was only happy with football people from that fateful day when he stepped into the Yeovil job, his greatest triumph was also reserved for the FA Cup, when he led unfancied Second Division Fulham to the Wembley Final in 1975. Again he had taken something small and, for a brief but brilliant period, moulded it into a much bigger and better object.

There will always be a corner in football history for Alex Stock. Not in the limelight with the big names, but reserved for those with the Midas touch with little clubs. A modest and often highly sensitive person, Stock worried to such an extent that he was often troubled by asthma in those stressful periods so frequent in a manager's life. If there was one word that Stock liked to be associated with it was 'respect'. There can be no follower of the game or player of his during his 35 years of management who would not accord him his right to same.

Jimmy Seed

JIMMY Seed spent 43 years in football as a player and a manager before his enforced retirement in 1956, and it all started in Durham where he was brought up a couple of miles from the Sunderland ground. As a schoolboy, his hero at Roker Park was inside-forward Charlie Buchan, playing in a Sunderland pre-World War One team which was the outstanding side of that time. Seed realized his great ambition to play for his local side in April 1914, but very soon had to go to France to fight for King and Country. In the trenches he was gassed and that seemed to spell the end of his football career at the age of 23.

After his recovery, Seed moved out of the

League to play in the Welsh League for Mid-Rhondda but soon had a call back to the big-time. It was Tottenham Hotspur who gave him the chance to resurrect his career as a clever, creative inside-forward and he had a very happy eight-year stay at White Hart Lane, during which time he was capped five times for England. Tottenham won the FA Cup in 1921, with a 1-0 victory over Wolves at Stamford Bridge, and when they transferred Seed to Sheffield Wednesday in 1927, it was probably the worst deal in their history. Spurs were relegated, while Seed went on to skipper Wednesday to two League titles.

Seed's career ended at Sheffield Wednesday after his move north in 1927 and soon his thoughts were turning to management.

His first managerial job came as the result of an offer from Herbert Chapman, the great Arsenal manager, to take charge of the Clapton Orient club with a view to its use by the Gunners as a 'nursery' for young players. Seed was attracted by the move to the Third Division South club and took over as secretary-manager in 1932, only to find that eventually the Football Association would not sanction the scheme. Seed, as a young and inexperienced manager and adminsitrator, was left 'holding the baby'. It turned out to be a very sick child indeed and Seed 'muddled through', as he put it, and was pleased to finish his first season with a balance of £5.

Seed's whole future was transformed, however, in September 1933 when he was approached by the Gliksten brothers to take over at Charlton Athletic, then also in the Third Division South. The Glikstens were determined to put Charlton on the football map with a massive injection of cash and this saved a club, which had spent years in the grip of financial trouble and strife, from ruin. Initially it was an exciting adventure for Seed, as the Glikstens put their cash towards launching the 'new' Charlton.

Despite all the cash injections, secretary-manager Seed and his directors always pursued a policy against big-spending on players and this was maintained throughout his 23-year tenure at The Valley. Seed was determined to discover rather than buy stars and in the pre-war period he concentrated his scouting on the North-East. Some 30 players were recruited from the area, including such stalwarts as

Jack Shreeve and Sam Bartram. For many years the biggest fee Seed paid was £3,250 for Don Welsh from Torquay United. Even in the days of regular £20,000 transfers, his biggest outlays were £7,650 to Hearts for Alec McCrae and £8,500 to Millwall for Tommy Brown. Seed recalled that in his 23-year period as manager, he brought in over £170,000 in fees to the club and spent over £55,000 in return. In a period when the cheque-book ruled football, Jimmy Seed proved himself to be an astute 'wheeler-dealer'.

Seed had great success initially, repaying all of the faith of the Gliksten family in him. Within two years 'The Addicks' had reached the First Division. In addition, in their first season in the highest division, the unfashionable club failed by only three points to take the League Championship. To add to Seed's record, his loyal group of players finished fourth in 1937-8 and third in 1938-9 before World War Two intervened. In the course of the drive to the First Division, Seed had made a profit of £7,000 and attendances at The Valley had averaged 30,000. Despite all this, Charlton were not given a good Press by London football writers dazzled by Arsenal's successes. Charlton's achievements were often dismissed as a 'lucky phase' but this gave no credit to Seed for the ability and team-spirit in his side.

Cup success was on the menu in the first post-war season, although in the 1946 Wembley Final, Charlton were completely overrun and demoralized by the class of Derby's Carter and Doherty. They hung on until extra-time before being defeated by a three-goal Derby burst. To Seed's credit, his Charlton side were back at Wembley the next season. It was not an entertaining match but that mattered little to Seed when he took the FA Cup to the rebuilt Valley for the first time. The little winger Chris Duffy, bought from Leith for £330, cracked in a great shot in extra-time to score the only goal of the game.

Seed was accused of encouraging negative football and the main thrust of his tactics was that the defence of any successful side started with the inside-forwards. As a master tactician, much of his thinking formulated in the latter stages of his playing career. Seed was one of the movers behind the 'W' formation. The inside-forwards were forced to abandon their natural attacking role and drop back to pull their weight in defence.

His partnership with trainer Jimmy Trotter lasted 22 years and Trotter became the top trainer in the country, succeeding Tom Whittaker in charge of the England team.

Despite Charlton having won every honour except the League Championship, the club still found it difficult to compete with their London neighbours, whether it was Arsenal, Chelsea or Spurs, and Seed acknowledged that the lack of adequate covered accomodation at The Valley and poor transport communications did not help his cause. The early 1950s found Seed under increasing pressure to make ends meet as dwindling attendances and increasing entertainments tax added to his problems.

When he realized that he had to strengthen the side in the post-war period, Seed turned to South Africa, mindful that there were a number of young Springbok players anxious to move into a higher grade of football in Britain. Inside-forward Syd O'Linn and wing-half Dudley Forbes from Capetown arrived in December 1947 to start the first link in Charlton's South African chain. In all, 13 players came over with ambition and talent and saved Seed paying what he considered ridiculous transfer fees plus the inevitable personal inducements which infringed Football League law.

The elegant Eddie Firmani was possibly Seed's finest signing from South Africa, costing only the boat-fare from the Cape in February 1950. Unheard of in this country, Firmani was eventually transferred, after great success at The Valley, to Sampdoria in Italy for £35,000 and even collected £5,000 for himself. Lanky John Hewie was an all-purpose player who settled at full-back and was later to play outstandingly for Scotland when it was discovered his father was Scottish. Stuart Leary was a great success at inside-forward and even became as accomplished at cricket, playing regularly for Kent. The only goalkeeper to be recruited from that source was Albert Uytenbogaardt — nicknamed 'Humphrey Bogart' by the fans — who, despite his talent, could not displace Sam Bartram in goal.

Bartram was signed without a fee and went on to keep goal from 1934 for a period of 22 years. In Seed's time he was never dropped from the first team. Seed always had a soft spot for the loyal, gutsy goalkeeper whose name became synonymous with Charlton and the two had followed a similar pathway to The Valley via the North-Eastern coal-pits and the terraces of Roker Park.

Seed had the distinction of signing two players who made more money out of the game in a few seasons than stars like Matthews and Finney. One was Firmani, as a result of his move to Italy, and the other was a young Swedish centre-forward Hans Jeppson.

Jeppson had led Sweden's forwards in the World Cup finals in Rio in 1950. When Charlton were struggling around Christmas 1950, the tall, handsome Swede happened to arrive in London to study business methods on behalf of his firm for three months. Seed moved smartly to sign him on amateur forms and by the move transformed their season. From fourth-from-bottom and in danger of relegation, Charlton moved to mid-table security on the strength of Jeppson's nine League goals in 11 appearances. More than that, the Swede brought a touch of much-needed glamour and inspiration to the beleaguered Valley club.

As a direct result of his impact at Charlton, Jeppson was signed as a professional by Italian First Division club, Atalanta, in August 1951 and the Swede received an unprecedented £18,000 for himself.

Jimmy Seed, the silver-haired North-Easterner who could always be seen at games chewing and puffing anxiously on a huge cigar, found the stresses and strains of management overbearing and detrimental to his health in his last years at The Valley. Things came to a head in the early part of the 1956-7 season when, after a disastrous five-match run had been climaxed by an 8-1 defeat at Sunderland, Seed was sacked. The remarkable partnership of the 'Two Jimmies', as they were known, had been broken but Trotter, in sole charge, could not prevent Charlton being relegated to the Second Division. They found themselves in that division for the first time since their Seed-inspired elevation in 1935-6.

Seed had seen many changes and, as one of 'the old school', was often resistant to those changes since that day in April 1913 when he left the pits to take up football as a career. As a manager he plainly admitted that what success Charlon achieved during his time in charge was gained mainly by loyalty. He always

believed that team spirit was the first essential but, alas, his departure from Charlton was less than amicable. Seed's unfortunate experience led him to turn down two offers of further management and he went into semi-retirement, assisting Bristol City with their scouting.

Tom Whittaker

TOM Whittaker, the son of a soldier, was born in Aldershot in July 1898 but grew up in Newcastle where he attracted the attention of the local club. World War One intervened, however, and Whittaker had to give up his apprenticeship in marine engineering after he had been called up by the RAF, for whom he graduated to squadron-leader and earned the MBE. It was in services football that the young wing-half was spotted by Arsenal, for whom he signed as a professional in 1920.

By his own admission, Whittaker 'never became a great footballer' but it was the start of 37 years in the game with Arsenal, whom he also served as third-team player, assistant trainer, trainer, assistant manager and finally secretary-manager before his premature death in 1956. He made 64 League appearances for the Gunners before his playing career was brought to an end when he suffered a serious knee injury on the FA's Australian tour in June 1925.

Whilst Whittaker's destiny was being decided, Arsenal were considering applications for the post of secretary-manager and the successful applicant was one Herbert Chapman. So began the golden era for Arsenal under Chapman which brought an amazing run of success in the ten seasons before the outbreak of World War Two — five times League Champions and twice FA Cup winners.

Whittaker had been encouraged by Chapman to pursue a course, which lasted for a year and included the study of anatomy, massage, medical gymnastics and electrical therapy, with a view to joining the training staff at Highbury. When it was completed in 1927, Whittaker became one of Chapman's hand-picked staff as second-team trainer and then, early promotion to take care of the first-team. Typically, Chapman was firm in his proposition: "I am going to make this the greatest club ground in the world — and I am going to make you the greatest trainer in the game."

Whittaker's expertise, particularly in the field of physiotherapy, led to him earning the title of 'The Man with the Magic Hands' and the word spread in sporting circles, before and after the war, of the special care and treatment available in the spacious treatment rooms at Highbury. Whittaker found himself in constant demand from stars of other sports — jockeys, boxers, golfers and tennis players could be seen variously around Highbury's marbled halls seeking attention. It was not unknown for players from other clubs to ask him to look at their injuries. His most famous and regular 'patient' was Denis Compton, whose equally famous knee required constant care and which care kept him in cricket at the highest level for many years.

Whilst he was still the trainer for the Gunners, such was Whittaker's eminence in the game that he was appointed temporarily as the first England 'team manager' in 1946, before Walter Winterbottom took over as chief coach/team manager the following season. After Chapman's death between the wars, Whittaker served under his successor George Allison and shared many of his managerial duties. It was good experience for Whittaker, often to be given the responsibility of looking out for and negotiating for new players.

When Allison retired, Whittaker was the obvious choice by virtue of the wealth of experience and knowledge gained in his 20 years at Highbury behind the scenes. Whittaker's first moves at the start of that 1947-8 season were to sign Archie Macaulay from Brentford and Don Roper from Southampton and to appoint Joe Mercer as the permanent captain. Immediately, Whittaker, his right-hand man Mercer, and his experienced squad set up a club record for an unbeaten start to the season, including six successive games without conceding a goal. Later in the season, Whittaker clinched the astute signing of Alex Forbes from Sheffield United to complete his squad which, made up of only 17 players, took the First Division title in his first term as secretary-manager.

Whittaker's success prompted an offer from the Milan club in Italy to move abroad as their trainer-coach with the provision that he could name his own terms and conditions. This was turned down out of hand and so was an offer of the Italian team manager's job made two years later. These refusals reflected a devotion to duty and to the Arsenal club second to none in British football circles. A devotion and unswerving commitment which was summed up on his admission, "I owe too much to Arsenal to leave the club," and which almost certainly contributed to his death.

After a summer trip in 1949 to Rio in Brazil, the Gunners came back to lift the FA Cup the next season and Whittaker's inspired signing of Tottenham's Freddie Cox had much to do with it. Cox was reported to be 'finished' at White Hart Lane and was being barracked mercilessly by the Spurs fans. For Arsenal his enthusiasm and dash on the wing played a big part in their two trips to Wembley in three years.

Whittaker made no secret of his admiration for the talents of both Stanley Matthews and Wilf Mannion and at various times made strenuous if unsuccessful efforts to bring their talents to the capital. In an attempt to boost season-ticket sales before the start of the 1951-2 season, at a time when Arsenal's relatively poor showing in the previous season had for once compared unfavourably to the resounding success of Tottenham Hotspur, who had romped away with the First Division title in the most attractive fashion, Whittaker made Blackpool a £20,000 offer for Matthews. The great man apparently wanted to move but to Whittaker's eternal regret Blackpool refused to release him.

In the event, that 1951-2 season found Arsenal's ageing squad confounding the critics and pursuing a League and Cup double. Up until ten days before their Cup Final appearance, the Gunners were in the hunt for the League title and were beaten at Wembley eight minutes before the end of the match. The club with the tag 'Lucky Arsenal' found everything conspiring against them in their 'double' bid. Three walking wounded — Ray Daniel, Jimmy Logie and Doug Lishman — played in the Final in which Wally Barnes's injury put paid to their chances of at least lifting the Cup.

The man with the eye for the astute inspirational signings, from those of Mercer, Forbes, Barnes, Macaulay, Rooke in the early days, through to those of Cliff Holton, Peter Goring, Derek Tapscott and Vic Groves in the later days, pulled off one of his greatest coups in 1953 with the signing of 33-year-old Tommy Lawton. The move came as a thunderbolt to the football world but Lawton's colourful personality, so good for the box-office, put 10,000 on the next home attendance and gave the Arsenal inside-forwards the service they seemed to be lacking.

Arsenal were by now very big business and boasted massive profits in those post-war years, but this only served to increase the pressure on the man for whom the North London club was his life. The strain on his nerves took its toll over the years and Arsenal attempted to supply some relief for him by the appointment of Alec Stock from Leyton Orient as his assistant in the summer of 1955. Stock threw up the job after 53 days and, as a result, Jack Crayston was given the title of team-manager and Bob Wall assumed more of the duties of secretary.

Whittaker, the burly figure with the horn-rimmed spectacles and thinning hair, was a great planner in much detail, heavily influenced by the disciplines and theories of his mentor, Herbert Chapman. Essentially his theories, as far as tactics were concerned,

centred on his exposition: 'you cannot plan how to organize a goal but you can plan and legislate to prevent them as well as trying to help your players to score. In effect you go on to the field with one point, prevent the other side from scoring and you still have the point at the end and two if you have managed to score.''

Whittaker believed that 95 per cent of goals came from defensive mistakes and, with the stopper centre-half regime at the root of his thinking, concentrated on what he termed 'the marshalling of forces into a triangle in front of the net which is the danger area'. He was one of the first to recognize the value of individual training for players on special skills, was always keen to undertake foreign tours, taking the Gunners to Brazil and Russia — the latter for the first post-war visit of a British football team, and pioneered the fitting of oxygen apparatus in the dressing-room.

As one of football's visionaries, Whittaker agitated for the use of floodlights as a spectator aid, had strong views on the need for substitutes, welcomed the advent of televised matches, proposed that a ceiling be placed on transfer fees and insisted that players should receive higher wages to put them on a parity with other industries. Like Chapman before him, he was a visionary

After one of Arsenal's worst-ever periods, during which they fell to 19th position and suffered a 7-1 defeat at Sunderland, Whittaker collapsed in the summer of 1956 and the heart condition which was diagnosed soon led to his death whilst he was still in his late 50s. His contemporaries remembered him as a kind, warm-hearted and human man who was always a trainer at heart and was usually to be found in his shirt-sleeves, as a legacy of his many days spent in the dressing-room area. Like Chapman, Whittaker's total commitment and devotion, which involved working himself to a standstill, had almost certainly killed him.

The ironic aspect of both the Chapman and Whittaker eras was that the Highbury club which was universally labelled with the tag 'Lucky Arsenal' was the one that by the efforts of those two servants left nothing, but nothing, to chance.

The Players

PETER DOHERTY

*Northern Ireland, Glentoran, Blackpool,
Manchester City, Derby County,
Huddersfield and Doncaster Rovers.*

THIS flame-haired Irish inside-forward, who was one of the most gifted and complete players in the game's history, was not only a born dribbler and creative genius but also a tireless player with a high work-rate. Doherty played in English football with Blackpool and Manchester City in the 1930s after initially making his name with Glentoran in Ireland. After moving to Derby in 1944, his unique combination with the silky-skilled, lordly Raich Carter helped win the FA Cup in 1946 and created many goals for forceful centre-forward Jack Stamps. He left Derby the next season — the Rams directors refused him permission to run a pub — for Huddersfield and inspired them to stay in the First Division when relegation appeared certain. As player-manager at Doncaster Rovers, Doherty steered them to the Third Division North title in his first season. Later he went on to manage Northern

Ireland from 1951 to 1962 and, with Danny Blanchflower as his captain, led them to the last eight in the World Cup finals in 1958. Considered to be the most complete inside-forward ever to play the game, Doherty was renowned for his courage, sheer enjoyment of the game and his tremendous competitive spirit. His brilliant and inventive play earned 16 caps for Northern Ireland where his genius was weighed down by the poverty of the material around him. To add to his talent he was a real leader of men who provided a tireless example. Doherty died in 1990.

BILLY LIDDELL

Scotland and Liverpool.

BILLY Liddell was a loyal one-club man who played 492 games for Liverpool and through 23 seasons spent as a part-timer, scored 214 League goals from outside-left and centre-forward. In the course of his playing days he was employed as a youth-worker and accountant and was also a lay-preacher and Justice of the Peace. Turning professional in 1939, Liddell played a big part in Liverpool's 1946-7 League Championship triumph but later had to endure a brief period of Second Division football. Liddell's main virtues were his speed off the mark, strength on the ball and powerful shooting with either foot. He ran with a slight crouch, leaning forward over the ball as he bore in on goal. Many of his goals were from dead-ball situations and only once did he miss a penalty. Liddell earned 28 caps for Scotland and he and Stanley Matthews were the only two players to appear for Great Britain in both 1947 and 1955. War meant that he did not make his League debut for Liverpool until 1946, at the age of 24, but he went on to play until he was 39. Recommended to Liverpool by Matt Busby, Liddell was an idol on Merseyside with a total commitment to the club and a chivalrous, sporting, almost naïve, approach to the game. When Liverpool were struggling in the middle 1950s they were frequently referred to as 'Liddellpool', such was his influence and importance to the Anfield side.

won two League Championship medals, one Cup winners' medal and four England caps. He earned a reputation as the safest goalkeeper in the Football League, with his commanding presence and remarkable consistency. Like many of his contemporaries he began his working life in the pits before signing for Everton in 1929. On Everton's return to the First Division in 1931, Sagar took his place in the first team which he was to hold until 1952 at the age of 42. Such was Sagar's domination of the penalty-area that his Everton teammates nicknamed him 'The Boss'. His courage meant that he sustained more than his fair share of injuries. He fought back from three knee cartilage operations and a dislocated shoulder. Sagar's great loyalty and love of the Everton club never wavered and he looked back on a long career which saw him play with many Goodison 'greats' including Dixie Dean, Joe Mercer, Cliff Britton and Tommy Lawton in his two decades. Ted Sagar died in 1986.

TED SAGAR

England and Everton.

TED Sagar stayed at Goodison Park for almost 24 seasons, making 495 League and FA Cup appearances for Everton, not including wartime matches. In that time he

FRANK SWIFT

England and Manchester City.

THE giant goalkeeper signed for Manchester City aged 17 and within two years, in 1933,

played his first League game. The following season he won an FA Cup winners' medal at Wembley, fainting on the field as soon as the final whistle sounded, such was the ordeal he had faced. Height, reach and cool judgement combined to make Swift an outstanding goalkeeper. More than that, he was not merely a defender but the first line of attack with his fine kicking and throwing. Swift was a giant in more senses than one. Over 6ft tall, he had an exceptionally long reach and huge hands. Despite his size he was agile with cool judgement and, dominating the area he would typically pick up the ball with one hand and throw it out to his forwards. There was a touch of showmanship in his play which Swift admitted he included to please the crowd. Hugely popular, he was an entertainer both on and off the field. First gaining international recognition against Scotland in 1941, he went on to play 33 times for England, being the first goalkeeper to captain an England side, against Italy in 1948. As first-choice 'keeper he played 19 of England's first 20 internationals after the war. He played his last game for City in 1949 and nine years later, whilst in his 40s, he died tragically in the Munich air disaster, travelling with Manchester United as a journalist.

SAM BARTRAM

Charlton Athletic.

SAM Bartram was reckoned to be the finest goalkeeper who never played for England at full international level. With his wavy red hair, he was a wonderful character who was fearless and selfless in his efforts for Charlton Athletic. He is best remembered for his great loyalty to the club which was his life. After starting his days in the North East, Bartram spent 22 years at The Valley and after first playing in goal in 1935 was never dropped from the first team whilst making a club record 583 League appearances between 1934 and 1956. He won an FA Cup winners' medal in 1947 and, in fact, had the distinction of playing in four Wembley Finals in succession after appearances in wartime. Sam Bartram was a showman with his agility and reckless bravery but this hid great ability, determination and a fine sense of anticipation. He was a firm favourite at The Valley and hugely popular with the Charlton supporters. After his 500th League game in 1954, the 'Sam Bartram Gates' were opened at The Valley as a mark of their respect.

Bartram was not every football fan's idea of the perfect goalkeeper and obviously did not appeal to the international selectors. But on his best days there was not a goalkeeper to touch the man who played until he was 40 and took a full part in all of the history-making days of Charlton Athletic, from the Third Division South to First Division and two FA Cup Finals. As a manager he was unsuccessful at York City and then Luton Town before becoming a journalist, until his death in 1981.

TED DITCHBURN

England and Tottenham Hotspur.

TED Ditchburn was the son of a noted boxer and joined Tottenham Hotspur's ground-staff at the start of the 1937-8 season. He gained two wartime caps for England. Making his League debut on Cup Final day 1946, when Spurs beat Newport 1-0, Ditchburn hardly missed a game until his retirement in 1958, displaying his daring and often acrobatic style. Ditchburn's hallmark was his consistency and, after glowing reports of his form in the 1948 period, he gained his full cap against Switzerland, although he looked less than confident in his six internationals for England spread over eight years. A man of powerful physique, who stood over 6ft tall, Ditchburn kept himself in great physical condition and displayed extreme cat-like agility. Enormously popular with the Tottenham fans, he was one of the key figures in the Arthur Rowe 'push and run' team which won back Spurs' First Division status in 1950-51 and went on to win the League Championship a year later. Ditchburn was known as the

best at the art of advancing to block a shot or of smothering the ball at an opponent's feet. He made 418 League appearances for Tottenham, playing until the age of 37, but generally lost out in competition with Bert Williams as successor to Frank Swift in the England goal, largely due to his curious falliblity when appearing for his country.

JOE MERCER

England, Everton and Arsenal.

SIGNED by Everton at the age of 17, Joe Mercer made his debut at Goodison Park in 1932. In the year before the war broke out he led Everton to the League Championship and had been capped five times for England. After the war — during which he won several unofficial caps — Everton clearly thought that the frail but resolute half-back was finished at the age of 31, particularly in the light of a damaged knee. Arsenal, at their lowest ebb for 20 years, bought Mercer for £7,000 and made him club captain in an inspired move which was to resurrect his

career. The Gunners won the League Championship in 1948 and five years later they won it again with Mercer still as captain. Between these two titles they had reached the FA Cup Final twice. It seemed that Mercer had discovered the secret of eternal youth as he went on playing for Arsenal, as a defensive wing-half under the sound and influential management of Tom Whittaker, until he was nearly 40. At the end of the 1953-4 season he broke his leg at Highbury and was carried from the pitch as a sad finale to his fine career. It had been characterized by a great fighting spirit and stamina which defied his spindly and bent legs and spare frame, not to mention his bad knees. Above all Joe Mercer enjoyed playing more than most and could often be seen, as player and later as a manager, with a smile on his face. He had a distinguished managerial career, particularly with Manchester City, before his death in 1990.

JIMMY DELANEY

Scotland, Celtic, Manchester United and Aberdeen.

THIS Scottish international had been out of

football for a year with a shoulder injury at Glasgow Celtic when Manchester United manager Matt Busby took the risk of signing him. Busby's gamble paid off handsomely as Delaney gave United six magnificent seasons. Delaney was nicknamed 'Brittle-bones' but this had some basis in fact. He was once barred from playing for Scotland because, due to a series of fractures, the insurance companies alleged his bones were unusually brittle and would not insure him against injury. Delaney took his place in that first post-war season, in a forward-line also comprising the talents of Johnny Morris, Jack Rowley and Charlie Mitten, who had been introduced by Busby

BERT WILLIAMS

*England, Walsall and
Wolverhampton Wanderers.*

BERT Williams was a fitness fanatic and as a high-class sprinter was one of the fastest men in the game in his 27-year career as goalkeeper. He made his first League appearance for Walsall in 1937, having been signed by legendary goalkeeper Harry Hibbs and, after war service in the RAF, received his first full England cap against France in 1945. Williams became the natural successor to the incomparable Frank Swift and went on to gain 24 caps in all. Ideally built for a 'keeper, Williams was transferred to Wolves in 1945, for a then record fee for a goalkeeper of £3,500, and spent 11 seasons in the first team, helping the Midlanders to their League and FA Cup triumphs. Williams had a spectacular and distinctive style and his speciality was dealing with high centres across the goalmouth where he had a sure and safe touch. His speed off the mark when going for the ball often got Wolves out of dangerous situations. Like all the greats he was immensely brave. Handsome and blond, Williams gave his most memorable performance at Highbury for England against Italy in November 1949 and after the 2-0 win

as part of his rebuilding. Delaney played out on the right wing and was an elusive and tricky customer who provided a string of openings each match for the goalscoring Morris and Rowley. When, in 1952, Delaney went back to Scotland, it was to Aberdeen for £3,500, only £500 less than Busby had paid for him. It was the first of many astute deals for which Busby was to become famous in the ensuing years.

the opposition Press named him 'Il Gattore' (The Big Cat) and the nickname stuck. In the summer of 1952, a shoulder injury threatened his career and he lost all feeling in his left arm for a period. He had a long battle back to fitness but regained his old form and his England place. After retiring, Williams set up a school for goalkeepers and there was no better qualified teacher.

of the finest ball-players in the country, he was almost completely overlooked by the selectors. Shrewd passes split opposing defences and watchers often thought he was lucky to receive the ball in favourable position, but his uncanny reading of the game enabled him to find the room to work. He made the game look so simple — no player 'killed' a ball more quickly. Hagan was a deep thinker about the game and provided the experience and skills to stabilize Sheffield United in the years after the war, before he turned to management with Peterborough United, West Bromwich Albion and then Benfica. He later worked in Kuwait and went back to Portugal to manage Oporto.

JIMMY HAGAN

England, Derby County and Sheffield United.

JIMMY Hagan was an artistic, cultured inside-forward who was at his peak during the war years. As a result, although he made 17 appearances in wartime and 'Victory' internationals, he secured only one full England cap, in September 1948. When the war was over he had to compete with a galaxy of star inside-forwards — Mortensen, Carter, Shackleton etc — for further recognition. Hagan played initially for Derby County from 1935 until Sheffield United signed him in 1938 and he inspired the Blades to win promotion to the First Division that first season. It was a puzzle as to why Hagan had received so few international honours. Despite being one

NAT LOFTHOUSE

England and Bolton Wanderers.

Lofthouse was a miner — a 'Bevan Boy' — in 1945 and the pitwork toughened him up and accustomed him to hard work. After making his League debut for Bolton Wanderers in 1946, Lofthouse went on to play over 400 League games for his one and only club. He was one of the most formidable and feared centre-forwards of the era. Brave, combative and aggressive, Lofthouse was an old-fashioned unsophisticated striker. Goalkeepers had to keep a wary eye out for the man who was known as the 'Lion in Vienna', for a typically brave breakaway goal scored for England in Austria in 1952. A one-club man at heart, Lofthouse's intense loyalty precluded any lucrative move elsewhere. Scoring 255 goals in 452 League games for Bolton, he was leading scorer in 11 of his 13 seasons at Burnden Park and had a great record of 30 goals in 33 internationals for England. Scoring in every round of the FA Cup in 1953, Lofthouse was Footballer of the Year that season to deny the accolade to Stanley Matthews. His service to Bolton continued in several roles on a non-playing basis for many years before his retirement.

23 times for England, missing only one international. Born in Birmingham, Merrick, with the receding hairline and neat moustache, was very strong but was an elegant not showy type of 'keeper. He was known as a consistent and reliable goalkeeper for Birmingham City who was very hard to beat and showed sound judgement, safe handling and good timing. This was evidenced by the meagre 24 goals in 42 matches Merrick and his defence conceded in 1948 as Birmingham became Second Division champions. Merrick was aged 37 when he played his 486th and last League game for Birmingham and the fans at St Andrew's held him in the same regard as Harry Hibbs, his own idol and predecessor. Merrick had the misfortune to be in the England goal that fateful day in November 1953 when the marauding Hungarians shot six past him at Wembley. Six months later Merrick conceded another seven goals in the return fixture in Budapest and was dubbed by the cynics 'Mister 13'. For Birmingham he made 486 League appearances and, typical of many 'keepers of the period, showed great loyalty to his club in the period of service 1946-1960.

GILBERT MERRICK

England and Birmingham City.

WHEN Frank Swift retired, Gill Merrick vied for the England goalkeeper's jersey with another goalkeeper from the Midlands, Bert Williams. Merrick took time to gain international recognition but between November 1951 and October 1954 he played

JOHNNY MORRIS

England, Manchester United and Derby County.

JOHNNY Morris was a modest, dark, curly-haired inside-right, on the small side, but with some of the finesse of a Raich Carter and the shooting power of a Tommy Lawton. He made up one half of the lethal partnership with centre-forward Jack Rowley that ensured the FA Cup went to Old Trafford in 1948. Morris was a 'cheeky' type of forward who could torment and demoralize defences as he darted here, there and everywhere. He was also capable of a regular 20 goals-a-season. After being spotted in Manchester junior football, Morris played in a touring exhibition XI whilst in the services during the war and guested for Charlton and Bolton before returning to United. In his first full season after the war his 20 goals helped Matt Busby's side to finish runners-up in the First Division — their highest position since the 1910-11 Championship year. When Busby and Morris found that, as the former put it, "We had to agree to differ" the scramble for the little man's signature ended with him signing for Derby County for a then record £24,500. At the Baseball Ground his great natural ability endeared him to the Derby crowd and he

continued to demolish the finest defences, earning England caps in the process. He later signed for Leicester City and converted successfuly to wing-half.

WILF MANNION

England, Middlesbrough and Hull City.

AFTER turning professional with Middlesbrough in 1936, Wilf Mannion was playing in their First Division side the next year at the age of 17 and displaying that beautiful balance and immaculate ball-control which were to be his trademarks. Mannion was also a tremendous worker with a dangerous burst of speed, who linked perfectly with Raich Carter for England soon after the war. Mannion was short but sturdy and with his

Wilf Mannion in the thick of the action against Spurs.

blond baby-face looked like a choirboy, but he was one who was never slow to speak his mind, particularly on players' rights. Brushes with authority and the establishment were common and he spent six months out of the game in 1948, without wages after refusing to re-sign for Middlesbrough. He saw their salary offer almost laughable in relation to his talent. Later, Mannion was suspended by the League for refusing to disclose the details of alleged illegal payments. Mannion's best performance was judged to be for a Great Britain side which beat the Rest of Europe 6-1 in May 1947. Tommy Lawton, for

England, benefited greatly from Mannion's creative openings during his 27 post-war internationals. After almost 350 League games and 99 goals for Middlesbrough, Mannion had a brief spell at Hull City before retiring and reportedly falling on hard times, working on the railways and building sites.

RONNIE ROOKE

Fulham and Arsenal.

AFTER an unremarkable career at Fulham, Ronnie Rooke was signed by Arsenal manager George Allison late in 1946 for £1,000 plus two reserve players. The burly, modest centre-forward was 35 years of age and the pundits shook their heads at the

signing. But it was proved to be an astute move and Arsenal were inspired by Rooke's goalscoring exploits and whole-hearted play. Rooke was not everyone's idea of the classic centre-forward but he hit a streak of goals immediately on arrival at Highbury, with 21 in 24 appearances in his first season. In 1947-8 he scored 33 goals and had a foot or head in most of the other 48 scored by Arsenal in their Championship season. The craggy, no-nonsense player benefited greatly from Jimmy Logie's lay-offs and passes but Rooke had great head work, which compared favourably to Lawton's, and speed off the mark which belied his age and build. Rooke's goalscoring record in 1947-8 was outstanding and the best since the arrival of the 'policeman' centre-half in the mid-1920s.

TOM FINNEY

England and Preston North End.

TOM Finney vied with Stanley Matthews as the outstanding player of the era and the loyal one-club man overcame the disadvantage of playing within the Matthews reign. Finney was a very great two-footed player with pure natural ability. Natural acceleration and change of pace were allied to tricky footwork and body swerves. To cap it all he was a proficient goalscorer. As a youngster in Preston he always had a tennis-ball at his toes and on Saturdays studied the

WALLY BARNES

Wales and Arsenal.

AFTER playing as an amateur for both Southampton and Portsmouth, Wally Barnes signed for Arsenal in September 1943 and made his first-team debut almost exactly three years later. Barnes was a polished full-back who was known for his cultured performances but who twice suffered serious injury. With great determination he fought his way back to fitness and won both League and Cup honours with the Gunners during his 267 appearances as well as gaining 22 caps for Wales and also captaining his

craftmanship of Alex James, then playing at Deepdale. After being coached from the age of 15, Finney did not make his League debut until he was 24, due to the war interruption. One month later he made his England debut for the first of 76 internationals, where he played on both wings and at centre-forward. In all, Finney played 431 League games for Preston in five forward positions. Consistency was the keynote as he rarely had an 'off day' and there were no obvious weaknesses. It was said that his greatest contribution was not his goals or his great skills, but the panic he caused in the opposition ranks. Finney's ball-control was uncanny, his passing was accurate, he could shoot well with both feet and he was a fine leader. Quiet by nature, he had a ruthless streak and was a good tactician and team-man. He was strong and scored 30 goals for England to add to his 210 for Preston in 14 seasons in the First Division. Once, an Italian club offered to make him a rich man but Preston refused to release him and the loyal Finney settled back down to the world of the maximum wage. The media and the public never tired of discussing the merits of Matthews and Finney but their respective styles were so different not to bear comparison. What was not in doubt was their unique contributions to the game in the era.

country. After Arsenal had won the FA Cup in April 1950, Barnes suffered a serious knee injury after 20 minutes of the 1952 Final. Arsenal's ten men finally succumbed to Newcastle by a single goal and Barnes missed all of the following 1952-3 Championship-winning season. A well-loved personality, Wally Barnes was a great 'thinker' about the game and later put his knowledge to good use as an early BBC TV football commentator. Before that, however, he had a spell as Wales team manager from August 1959, after trouble with both knees had caused his retirement. Wally Barnes died in September 1975, at the age of 65.

RAICH CARTER

*England, Sunderland, Derby County and
Hull City.*

RAICH Carter personified the complete
inside-forward of this era, at once both a
schemer and a scorer. After being with
Sunderland since 1931 — by the time he was
24 he had won League and FA Cup winners'
medals and England caps — he signed for
Derby County in December 1945, for about
£6,000. Carter and Peter Doherty enjoyed a
brief but brilliant partnership climaxing in
the FA Cup Final of 1946. His elegant control,
defence-splitting passes and great positional
flair led his Sunderland predecessor Charlie
Buchan to call him 'the finest inside-forward
of his generation'. With his silver hair and
arrogant style, Carter had a magnetic presence
but he was a little man, seemingly fragile,
until you took note of the thickness of his
knees and his sharp tackling. With that rare
instinctive play, Carter brought success
wherever he went, to Sunderland in 1936 and

1937, to Derby in 1946 and finally to Hull
City as player-manager in the Third Division
North in 1949. The demonstrative, even
provocative, Carter won 13 England caps, a
total which would have been trebled but for
the war, and scored 216 goals in 451 League
appearances. Still gracing England's forward-
line at the age of 33, he typically saved his
legs by using his head and letting the ball
do the work. After managing Leeds United,
Mansfield Town and Middlesbrough, Carter
retired and the former player of prodigious
talent remained disdainful of modern
coaching and methods.

LEN SHACKLETON

*England, Bradford, Newcastle United
and Sunderland.*

LEN Shackleton was nicknamed 'The Clown
Prince of Soccer' and was known as a
marvellous entertainer who would always

provide something special. Brimming over
with impudence, uncanny skill and ball-
control, Shackleton was originally discarded
by Arsenal as a frail teenager and returned

to his native Bradford at the age of 13. Soon after the war, Shackleton joined Newcastle United for £13,000 and scored six goals on his debut. In the same year, 1946, he moved to nearby Sunderland, who paid over £20,000 for the inside-forward who bore the hallmarks of genius in all his movements. Shackleton had a variety of tricks but, in truth, failed to reach the heights of which his natural skill made him capable. He spent the rest of his career on Wearside striking up a memorable partnership with Ivor Broadis. Shackleton was a curious figure with his hunched-up shoulders and flapping arms but he was always the artist with entertainment his top priority, sometimes to the detriment of the team. With a mere five England international caps, Shackleton was probably the finest player never to win a Cup Final or Championship medal. At the end of his career his natural humour was tinged with a little bitterness when he wrote what at the time was the most provocative autobiography ever to be penned by a star player.

GEORGE SWINDIN

Arsenal and Bradford City.

A YORKSHIREMAN who joined Arsenal from Bradford City in April 1936, George Swindin gave the Gunners continuous service in goal for ten seasons. During this time he earned two League Championship medals and winners' and runners-up medals in the FA Cup. His positioning was his great strength, coupled with his safe handling and superb anticipation. He was known as fearless, solid and undemonstrative without any hint of showmanship, during more than 300 League and Cup games. He represented the Football League on several occasions and could consider himself unlucky not to have been capped at international level, despite the fierce competition for the spot in the period. Swindin and his defensive colleagues at Arsenal had the most uncanny understanding which was crucial in bringing the Championship to Highbury in 1948. Only injury disturbed Swindin's run in the Arsenal line-up. In December 1948, Ted Platt had his chance and then in February 1951, Swindin fractured his wrist and gave good experience to Jack Kelsey, who was to displace Swindin in the 1953-4 season. Swindin made only two appearances in the League that season — the last a sad 7-1 defeat at Sunderland. It was a sorry finale to the career of a fine custodian and servant to the Arsenal club. He became manager of non-League Peterborough United in February 1954, moving to Arsenal for four years and then on to Norwich City and Cardiff City.

DEREK DOOLEY

Lincoln City and Sheffield Wednesday.

DEREK Dooley originally made his League debut for Lincoln City in 1946-7 before moving to Sheffield Wednesday and making his debut for the Owls in March 1950. Dooley was literally a 'one-season wonder' by virtue of his remarkable 46 goals in only 30 games which propelled Wednesday to the Second Division title in 1952. The powerful 6ft 3in bustler with the distinctive red hair was only 23 when he destroyed defences that season with his robust and brave play. He not only shot with awesome power but also had that uncanny knack of being in the right spot at the right time. Inevitably almost, such phenomenal scoring power could not be maintained and Dooley suffered a serious injury. In a tragic accident at Preston in February 1953, he broke his right leg as he collided with the goalkeeper. Earlier in the game he had been cut on the back of the leg and the cut had later become infected as he lay on the ground — otherwise it had been a straight-forward break on the shinbone. Gangrene set in quickly and his

right leg was amputated within days of the accident. In 63 League matches, Derek Dooley had scored 64 goals but one of the most exciting goalscorers of the post-war years had been taken from football without ever playing a full season of League soccer.

TOMMY LAWTON

England, Burnley, Everton, Chelsea, Notts County, Brentford and Arsenal.

TOMMY Lawton's career spanned the war years and but for that he might have broken many scoring records. After starting with Burnley at 17, Lawton was signed by Everton to replace Dixie Dean, whom he emulated and with whom he played in the late 1930s. After three years as their top scorer, war intervened and when peace was restored in 1945, Lawton moved to Chelsea for £11,500, where he stayed for one year of 26 goals. It was a surprise when Lawton moved to Notts County in the Third Division for £20,000, but there is no doubt that both parties were well rewarded for the 31 goals that ensured that County were promoted from the Southern Section and tripled their average attendance. Lawton stayed at Meadow Lane

as captain until he was 33, but after a short period at Brentford was recruited by the mighty Arsenal in the First Division to revive their flagging fortunes for three years. Lawton won 23 official England caps with 22 goals as arguably the finest centre-forward of the period. Known for his masterful, unique heading ability with his spectacular leaps and perfect timing, Lawton was a polished player with all-round ability and a powerful shot. Athletic, with good ball-control and perfect balance, Lawton was unmistakable with his slightly hunched shoulders, long legs and oiled, sleek black

hair with the conventional middle parting. Ideally built at 6ft tall and weighing over 12st, Lawton was a lethal marksman for England and all his six clubs and a magnetic crowd-pulling, charismatic figure right up to his retirement in 1956. In the end he had scored 231 goals in 390 League games as everybody's idea of the perfect centre-forward.

Mannion in various matches against England. Matt Busby was glad of his abilities as a born leader in the Championship success of 1951-2 and at Wembley in the FA Cup of 1947-8. After 306 League appearances, Carey retired at the end of the 1952-3 season to enter management with Blackburn Rovers. Later Carey managed at Everton, Leyton Orient and Nottingham Forest.

JOHNNY HANCOCKS

England, Walsall and Wolves.

BORN at Oakengates in the Midlands, Johnny Hancocks came to Wolves from Walsall in 1946 and, with Jimmy Mullen on the other wing, did much to make the Molineux team the major power of the 1950s. Hancocks was only 5ft 4in tall and wore size 5½ boots, but he was an unusually high-scoring winger who, although he lacked the speed and trickery of most wingers of the

JOHNNY CAREY

*Republic of Ireland and
Manchester United.*

JOHNNY Carey was clearly one of the truly great and versatile players of the period, highly respected and an inspiring captain of Manchester United, who paid only £200 when they signed him from St James' Gate in Ireland in 1936. During 17 years with United, Carey was a natural footballer with great enthusiasm and all-round ability such that he turned out in ten different positions, all except outside-left. His usual position was right-back and his unruffled demeanour, shrewd positioning and undemonstrative yet incisive tackling made him the complete defender. Carey had the constructive ability of a wing-half with the intelligence of an inside-forward. He was a popular choice as Footballer of the Year for 1947-8 and had the honour of captaining the Rest of Europe side versus Great Britain at Hampden Park in 1947. As captain of the Republic of Ireland, Carey had to support a series of weak Irish teams but had been known to shut out Matthews, deal with Finney and dominate

period, compensated by fierce shooting and the delivery of raking crosses. He and Mullen had great penetration with their strong running and made and took a stream of goal-chances. The diminutive Hancocks, who earned three caps and was one of the smallest wingers ever to play for England, had a mighty kick for such a small man and free-kicks and penalties were hit with relentless power. Hancocks was a top scorer but still delighted and, at times, infuriated the fans. His tendency to hang on to the ball excessively frustrated the Wolves' supporters but all was soon forgotten as the Molineux faithful thrilled to his explosive shooting.

NEIL FRANKLIN

England, Stoke City and Hull City.

BORN in Stoke, Neil Franklin joined his home-town club as a right-half but moved to centre-half in RAF football during the war. After first appearing for England in 1945, he played 37 consecutive matches as the best all-round centre-half since Stan Cullis. Franklin was not typical of the big muscular stoppers of the period and showed it was possible to play immaculate football of a type that no other player of his time could match. It was said that his play was so unflappable and free from error that the parting of his well-combed hair was rarely disturbed. Franklin's career was changed and

JIMMY LOGIE

Scotland and Arsenal.

all but ruined by one wrong decision. In May 1950 he was persuaded, at the age of 27, to run out on his contract with Stoke City, turn his back on England's first World Cup adventure and fly to Bogota to play for the unaffiliated Santa Fé club in the rebel Colombian League. Within weeks he had returned to face suspension by the Stoke club, being ostracized by his fellow professionals. A £22,500 transfer to Hull City followed but Neil Franklin's career petered out as he never recouped his old form and lived to regret his decision.

JIMMY Logie was spotted in Scotland by Arsenal and was a teenage Edinburgh bricklayer when he was called to London in 1939 to earn a £10-signing on fee. All 5ft 4in of him was full of brainy, quick-thinking football and he was immediately labelled 'the next Alex James'. Logie was an inside-forward in the true Scottish tradition of the time and typical of the Scots who were coming south — always diminutive and both subtle and imaginative. For all his brilliant dribbling and creativity, Logie was almost totally ignored by the Scottish selectors and gained only one cap. In his Arsenal career he made 296 League appearances with 68 goals to his name, during which two League Championships and an FA Cup medal were won. Logie was honoured with the Arsenal captaincy on several occasions but is best remembered by Arsenal fans for one of his goals — the third and winning goal in the last match of the 1952-3 season. The 3-2 win over Burnley clinched the Championship for Arsenal and ensured for Logie a permanent place in the Highbury hall of fame.

JACK FROGGATT

England, Portsmouth and Leicester City.

JACK Froggatt, born in Sheffield and a cousin of Sheffield Wednesday's Redfern Froggatt, was signed by Portsmouth as a centre-half in 1945 but persuaded manager Jack Tinn to give him a trial at outside-left. Froggatt was an immediate success and his forthright, rumbustious wing-play allied to his powerful finishing was a key factor in Portsmouth's Championship successes in 1948-9 and 1949-50. His 30 goals in 84 games in those two seasons brought him to the attention of the England selectors and he won his first cap in November 1949. In a

club emergency in 1951, Froggatt had to be switched back to the pivotal position and such was his impact there that within months he had been capped in the new position against Scotland at Wembley. Froggatt pointed the way to the return of the dashing attacking centre-half of days gone by and was confident enough to bring the style to the international arena in his nine appearances in the position for England. When 'Jolly Jack' was transferred to Leicester City in March 1954, he went on to give sterling service as an inspiring captain for the Midlands side.

BILLY STEEL

Scotland, Morton, Derby County and Dundee.

BILLY Steel had only a brief three-year career in England with Derby but, like Doherty, Carter and Shackleton, he gave great entertainment from inside-forward. After only nine appearances for Greenock Morton and one international appearance, Steel was selected to play for Great Britian against the Rest of Europe and scored the most spectacular of Britain's six goals. His display led to a scramble for his signature amongst English clubs and Derby County signed the stocky 24-year-old for a record £15,500 to replace Doherty. Steel quickly settled in England, with a rapid rise to stardom, and his ball-control, hard work and influence confirmed him as an extraordinary talent. Not only that, he could be a lethal finisher, particularly for Scotland for whom he scored four out of six in a spell of 25 minutes against Wales. Steel was once described as 'a dancing, industrious player who appeared to be led by his hips' and his immense natural talent was capable of dominating any match. For all that he was often not able to conform to the team plan, remaining an individualist. In his later days at the Baseball Ground, senior Derby players resented his 'star' status and some claimed that he reserved his best games for Scotland or appearances in London, where he was sure

Billy Steel scoring for Derby against QPR in a sixth-round FA Cup tie in 1948.

to get national Press coverage. His pleasant smile also masked a less savoury side to his character and he had a quick temper. After a dispute over terms, Steel left Derby in 1950 for Dundee for £24,000 then the highest fee ever paid by a Scottish club. Steel guided Dundee to two League Cup victories before emigrating to the USA in 1954 when only 31. In England and Scotland, he made only 212 League appearances in seven short years, with 54 goals, but Billy Steel was surely in the top ten of post-war inside-forwards. He died in Los Angeles in 1982.

JACK ROWLEY

England and Manchester United.

JACK Rowley, with Carey, Chilton and Pearson, was one of the pre-war survivors inherited by Matt Busby on his appointment as manager of Manchester United in February 1945. Around them he was to build his attractive and immensely successful post-war sides. Busby's predecessor, Scott Duncan, paid Bournemouth £3,000 for the 18-year-old Rowley in October 1937, as an outside-left. During the war Rowley once scored eight goals as a guest player for Wolves against Derby. Whether at outside-left or centre-forward, he was a star in the United side which finished as Championship runners-up in four seasons out of five from August 1946 to August 1951. Spending most of his career at centre-forward, Rowley switched back to outside-left when John Aston had the number-nine shirt in the 1950-51 season. In all, he gained five England caps playing in three positions. Rowley had the ability to score remarkable goals with sheer

honest-to-goodness power rather than subtlety and he was equally powerful with either foot. Rowley's two goals against Blackpool in the 1948 Cup Final were the highlights of a goal-littered career when he was devastating in combination with Jimmy Delaney. Later, Rowley had two unsuccessful spells in management at Oldham and was also in charge at Wrexham, Bradford and Ajax of Amsterdam.

BILLY WRIGHT

England and Wolverhampton Wanderers.

ONE OF the greatest players of the period, Billy Wright joined the Wolves groundstaff at the age of 14 in 1938-9, made his first-team debut in October 1939 and signed professional in February 1941. In the early months of his apprenticeship he was called into the office of Major Frank Buckley and told that he was being sent home because he was 'too small', but the Major's subsequent early change of mind meant that

a very great captain and servant was not lost to Molineux. Wright was a handsome, blond young man, clean in word and deed, the type who every mother of the time would have wished as a footballing son. He was football's most eligible bachelor of the period — called 'Soccer's Boy Scout' by the Press. His dedication and consistency of performance were unique as he practiced for hour after hour on his own to turn his limited talent into world-class quality. Good on the ground, constructive and firm in the tackle, Wright was a master in the air who was converted from attacking wing-half into a stubborn international centre-half, despite his lack of inches. A fitness fanatic, Wright had wonderful enthusiasm which made him

an inspirational captain who was not the shouting and gesticulating type of leader. Making his debut in the Football League at the opening of the 1946-7 season, Wright made his international debut for England two months later and went on to earn 105 caps. By the age of 24 he was captaining club and country but never let his own reliable performance be affected. As the first Englishman to pass a century of caps, it was a tribute to his stamina, dedication and consistency. An unassuming and delightful person, Wright moved into an executive position in television in the Midlands after an unsuccessful excursion into management with Arsenal. He is married to one of the Beverley Sisters.

ARTHUR ROWLEY

West Bromwich Albion, Fulham, Leicester City and Shrewsbury Town.

AFTER signing professional for West Brom in 1944, at the age of 18, Arthur Rowley achieved little of note at The Hawthorns before moving to Fulham in December 1948. At Craven Cottage he was the goalscoring centre-forward in the prolific Fulham attack, averaging nearly a goal a game, which won promotion to Division One. In the First Division, Rowley was hampered by injury

but, after a move to Leicester City and a switch to inside-forward, he scored 28 goals in his first season, 1950-51, 38 the next season and then 39 in 1952-3 to set a new club record and become the highest scorer other than a centre-forward in any one season. Rowley was big and bulky with little apparent subtlety and finesse, but he had a powerful left-foot shot and a rare knack of scoring goals. In his 19-year career, Rowley, the younger brother of Manchester United's Jack Rowley, became the most prolific scorer in the history of English League football with 434 goals in 619 matches, breaking Dixie Dean's record. Although only three seasons were spent in the First Division, Rowley could point to the fact that he might have produced a larger total if he had made his debut before 1946-7 when he was already into his 20s. As a player-manager at Shrewsbury Town, his last club, Rowley broke all records before retiring and going into management at Sheffield United and Southend United. When he hung up his boots in 1965, Rowley had become the only player to have scored 20 goals or more in 13 successive seasons.

JIMMY SCOULAR

Scotland, Portsmouth and Newcastle United.

JIMMY Scoular was stationed in the Portsmouth area whilst serving in the Navy during the war, when he was spotted and signed by Pompey in 1945. Born in Scotland,

Scoular provided the extreme in temperament to his fellow wing-half, Jimmy Dickinson, in the Portsmouth Championship-winning team. He was quick-tempered, fiery and often in trouble with referees for his aggressive play. For all that, Scoular had a fine attacking style with good passing skills. Long, sweeping cross-passes to release the speedy wingers, Harris and Froggatt, were his speciality. When, in 1953, Scoular became available for transfer, Newcastle United paid £26,000 for his services and he became a steady and loyal captain. He led the Geordies to a 3-1 victory over Manchester City in the FA Cup Final two years later. Scoular played nine times for Scotland and might have won more caps if the selectors had not been worried about his aggressive approach to the game. Later Scoular went into management at Cardiff City and Bradford before retirement brought on by continual problems with ill-health.

JACKIE MILBURN

England and Newcastle United.

JACKIE Milburn — 'Wor Jackie' — was the idol of Tyneside by virtue of his famous exploits for United in the post-war years. From Ashington in Northumberland, after early football in the local colliery team, Milburn wrote to Newcastle for a trial where he was recruited as an outside-right and

where Len Shackleton described him as 'the fastest player I've seen.' This tremendous speed was combined with powerful shooting with either foot and great positional sense. With a unique scoring instinct, it added up to a record of 179 goals in 354 League games for United and ten goals in 13 appearances for England. Many of these came after Milburn had been converted to centre-forward in October 1947, but the fans were unable to agree whether it was really his best position. On the wing, many felt that his speed was put to best use and he never seemed to relish the physical challenges he met in the middle. For all that, Milburn was best remembered for the many valuable and memorable goals scored from centre-forward as he led United to three FA Cup Final triumphs. All his attributes were exemplified when, against Blackpool in the 1951 Cup Final, he first raced through from the half-way line to beat the offside trap and then shoot firmly home for the first goal, and then shot the second goal with a fine drive. If Milburn had a weakness it was said to be in heading, but he contradicted that against Manchester City in the 1955 Cup Final by scoring with a fine glancing header. After a spell with Linfield in Ireland, Milburn had an unsuccessful attempt at League management with Ipswich Town before becoming a journalist and returning to his beloved Tyneside until his death in 1988. The massive turn-out at his funeral and a subsequent musical production of his life reflect the immense affection in which he was held.

TREVOR FORD

Wales, Swansea, Aston Villa, Sunderland, Cardiff and Newport County.

TREVOR Ford joined Swansea as a 17-year-

Blackpool's George Farm is helpless to stop a spectacular goal by Jackie Milburn in the 1951 FA Cup Final.

old left-back, but whilst in the Army during the war was converted to centre-forward. When he put on sufficient height and weight, Ford went on to become one of the most feared of the traditional bustling centre-forwards of the period. Before joining Swansea, Ford had been rejected by Cardiff but it was at Ninian Park playing for Wales that he put on some of his most inspired

performances. Often remembered as a bundle of energy who spent his time harassing and indeed charging goalkeepers at every opportunity, Ford nevertheless had good ball-control and no little skill especially when moving to the wings. Tough as teak on the field, Ford blended that natural skill and his maximum effort into a vivid combination. His tremendous dash and vigour seemed to be worth a goal start for Wales, for whom he scored 23 goals in 38 appearances. When Villa paid Swansea £25,000 for his services in 1947, Ford was at that time the world's most expensive centre-forward and one of the top attractions of the period. The fee was £30,000 on each of the subsequent transfers to Sunderland in 1951 and Cardiff three years later. In the League his final record was of 177 goals in 349 games.

DON REVIE

*England, Leicester City, Hull City,
Manchester City, Sunderland and Leeds
United.*

BORN in Middlesbrough, Don Revie signed for Leicester City in 1943, under manager Johnny Duncan, and learned to deploy his articulate, deep-lying centre-forward role from the Leicester forward Sep Smith. As a teenager his leg was badly broken and Revie suffered a severe nose haemorrhage which caused him to miss the 1949 FA Cup Final against Wolves. Transferring to Raich Carter's Hull City in 1949, for £20,000, Revie went to Manchester City for £25,000 in 1951 and on to Sunderland five years later for a similar fee. All the while, Revie was scheming and making goals for others with his thoughtful and creative, almost revolutionary, form of leadership of the

tactical plan named after him. It was at Manchester City in 1956 that Revie was to finally win a FA Cup winners' medal after being on the losing side the year before. The award of Footballer of the Year in 1955 was a measure of the respect which he earned for his professional and temperate character. After a move to Leeds United in 1958, as a player, Revie became player-manager in 1961 and achieved great success for the Elland Road club before becoming England manager. He left the England job in controversial circumstances, to manage in the Middle East, and after returning to England he did not work in football again before his death in 1989. Don Revie's playing career earned him six England caps, with four goals, and 467 League appearances with 99 goals.

JIMMY DICKINSON

England and Portsmouth.

JIMMY Dickinson joined Portsmouth during the war, after being spotted in Alton youth football, and made his League debut on the resumption of League football. He was an immediate success at left-half as a 21-year-old but his clean-tackling and fine

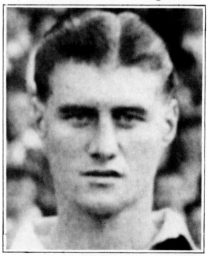

distribution drew many admirers and he won the first of his 48 England caps in May 1949. Quiet, well-mannered and literally never in trouble with referees or his manager, Dickinson was universally known as 'Gentleman Jim'. He was very strong, reliable and correct in everything he did. In

over 20 years of League football, during 764
games, Dickinson was never once cautioned
or spoken to by a referee and he was intensely
loyal to the Portsmouth club. It was not until
the arrival of the precocious Duncan
Edwards that Dickinson was displaced as
England's left-half. His remarkable fitness,
stamina and lifestyle meant he was able to
continue playing for the South Coast club
until 1965. He retired to work for Pompey
in various capacities, including manager,
until his early death from a heart attack in
November 1982 aged 57.

ALF RAMSEY

*England, Southampton and Tottenham
Hotspur.*

ALF Ramsey made his debut for
Southampton in October in 1946, in the
Second Division, but after winning England
honours he lost both his national and club
places to Bill Ellerington and promptly
asked for a transfer. This led to the move
to Tottenham Hotspur, where Ramsey was
to exert a benign and constructive influence
from right-back over the lively 'push and
run' side constructed by manager Arthur
Rowe. Ramsey was a cultured full-back well
ahead of his time as he created attacks and
overlapped in support of his forwards. He
was ideal for the style of the 1950-51 all-
conquering Spurs side with their insistence
on quality passing. Ramsey's kicking and
all-round use of the ball was superb and his
positional sense compensated for his
slowness on the turn and vulnerability to
fast attackers. Ramsey was composed and
calm, but sometimes he was too relaxed. This
almost certainly cost Spurs a Cup Final place
in 1953 when in the semi-final his back-pass

fell short and Jackie Mudie of Blackpool
latched on to the ball and scored the winner.
Arthur Rowe was a great influence on
Ramsey and he learned a lot from the gifted,
imaginative Spurs manager that he put to
good use, first with great success at Ipswich
Town and then with England, whom he
steered to World Cup triumph in 1966. As
a manager Ramsey's approach had a lot in
common with his playing days — the single-
minded, often obstinate pursuit of
excellence.

*Bradford's Gerry Henry is foiled by
Ditchburn and Ramsey during Tottenham's
1949-50 Second Division championship
season.*

ROY PAUL

Wales, Swansea Town and
Manchester City.

ROY Paul was a wartime Royal Marine who was discovered by a Swansea Town scout and made his debut as a tough-tackling wing-half immediately after the war. There was a touch of artistry to add to his honest labour and the combination made him into a valuable wing-half, who proved his versatility by playing at centre-half and inside-forward for Wales. Paul was remembered as an inspirational captain, who brought the best out of international and club teams with his hard, determined play.

The only blot on his record was a brief trip to Bogota, where he discovered that the streets were not paved with gold. Moving to Manchester City in August 1950, for a fee of £19,500, Paul made City's defence into one of the best in the country, eventually leading them to two successive Wembley FA Cup Finals. After the first in 1955, when City were beaten by Newcastle United, Paul resolved to return the next year. This time City beat Birmingham 3-1. Paul led City to promotion from the Second Division before moving to non-League Worcester City in 1957 and played in all three half-back positions. He won 33 Welsh caps, missing only three games between October 1948 and April 1956.

ROY BENTLEY

England, Bristol City, Newcastle United,
Chelsea, Fulham and QPR.

ROY Bentley began his career as an outside-right at Bristol City, but after his move to Newcastle he went on to earn a big reputation and international honours as a

centre-forward. Upon his transfer to Chelsea, for £11,000, Bentley was faced with the uneviable task of succeeding Tommy Lawton and he found it difficult to win over the affection of the Stamford Bridge crowd. Indeed, he was not an immediate success and was dropped from the team at one stage. Bentley was of medium build with light-brown wavy hair and was an inoffensive and quiet character. He was not a typical robust centre-forward and needed someone alongside him to take the knocks. To offset that, Bentley had a roaming, unorthodox style and made unlimited openings for others whilst scoring several memorable goals himself. Bentley was a revelation in the 1948-9 season and clearly the most improved player in the top division. This led to his selection for England that season and a trip to the 1950 World Cup finals. As captain he led Chelsea to the League Championship in 1955, scoring 21 of their 81 goals. Bentley later moved around the capital to Fulham and QPR, converting to centre-half and full-back in the process before going into management at Reading and Swansea.

FREDDIE STEELE

Stoke City, Mansfield Town and Port Vale

FREDDIE Steele began his career with Stoke City in 1934 as an inside-right but switched to lead the attack two years later, topping their scoring list in five of his first seven seasons. After creating a club record with 33

First Division goals in 1936-7, Steele lost his touch in 1939, when he was depressed by a knee injury and personal problems. A psychiatrist spent weeks probing Steele's mind, drawing out his fears and hypnotising him back to confidence. The outcome was that ten goals came in the next five matches. His partner Stanley Matthews observed later: "I wouldn't have believed it possible if I hadn't seen it for myself." As player-manager at Mansfield Town from 1949, Steele took the Stags into the runners-up spot in the Third Division North before returning to the Potteries as player-manager at Port Vale in December 1951. Interestingly, the move was the first case of a player-manager being transferred from one Football League club to another. When Steele made his last League appearance in 1952-3, he had totalled 192 goals in 302 games as one of the top marksman of the post-war period. Steele also looked back on nine England caps in his successful pre-war period. After resigning the Port Vale managership in January 1957, he was recalled by the club to take over for a second time in October 1962.

STAN MORTENSEN

England and Blackpool.

STAN Mortensen was not only the most dynamic player of the post-war years, but also one of the bravest. After suffering head and back injuries in May 1942, during his RAF days when his plane crashed and most of the other members of the crew were killed, Mortensen was told by doctors that he would never play again. Mortensen was English-born with a name inherited from a Scandinavian grandfather and tried his hand at a variety of jobs on leaving school at 14 before joining Blackpool. Often compared with Steve Bloomer, of England and Derby, Mortensen had the same spare frame, sallow complexion — and the great knack of scoring brave, priceless goals. Energy was one of his great virtues and he would chase hard for

openings often taking heavy punishment in the process. Speed, skill and great persistency, allied to a superb temperament, made him the most dangerous inside-forward of his time. His only weakness was lack of height. Much of his career, as the 'other Stanley', was spent in the shadow of his teammate, Stan Matthews. Even after Mortensen had scored a hat-trick in the 1953 FA Cup Final, it was thereafter known as the 'Matthews

Stan Mortensen, brave as ever, battling it out in the air.

Final'. A total of 197 goals in 320 League games for Blackpool and 23 in 25 internationals for England are evidence of his scoring power and on his full international debut it was a storybook start as 'Morty' grabbed four of the ten scored against Portugal. Mortensen's game was so full of humour and drive and he lived life as if determined to enjoy himself. He was disappointed at never winning a Championship medal, at being on the losing side in two Cup Finals and was a member of the England side humiliated by USA in the 1950 World Cup. None of this, though, disturbed his special humour and personality which endeared him to a legion of fans. Stan Mortensen died in May 1991.

BILL NICHOLSON

England and Tottenham Hotspur

AFTER joining Spurs from Northfleet in 1936, when he was an inside-forward, Bill Nicholson made his League debut in October 1938 as a left-back — but subsequently he

became one of the finest wing-halves in the country. As part of the superb 'push-and-run' Spurs side, so ably managed by Arthur Rowe, Nicholson earned First and Second Division Championship medals with one excellent performance after another, but always with the minimum of fuss or flourish. With the fiery and hard-working Welshman,

Ron Burgess, on his left in the midfield, Nicholson was often the mainspring behind those inspirational Spurs forwards with his incisive tackling and accurate passing. It was a wonder that the modest, phlegmatic Nicholson did not make more appearances for England but it was unfortunate for him that the ubiquitous Billy Wright had such a hold on the position through the years 1949-51, when many doubted if there was a more accomplished right-half in the game. Nicholson scored with his first kick for England, against Portugal, but never won another cap. He retired in 1955, after 317 League appearances for his beloved Spurs, to continue to serve the club, in turn, as coach, scout and assistant manager before taking over as manager in October 1958. As a hugely respected manager, Nicholson emulated his mentor, Arthur Rowe, by creating one of the finest sides in the history of English football. He led Spurs to the League and Cup double in 1960-61 and saw them retain the FA Cup the following year and become the first English club to win a European trophy.

DENIS COMPTON

England and Arsenal

THE man who became one of cricket's greatest heroes, through two decades for Middlesex and England, was also a popular and colourful winger through the war years and up to his retirement from football after the 1950 FA Cup Final. Compton signed amateur forms for Arsenal in 1932 and turned professional on his 17th birthday in 1935. When war came he had made 22 appearances in the Gunners' first team and went on to become an established wartime international. Denis Compton and his brother, centre-half Leslie, gained League Championship medals with Arsenal in 1947-8 — a unique distinction in that they also played for the County Champions, Middlesex, in the previous summer. After they played together in Arsenal's FA Cup Final win against Liverpool, Denis retired from soccer to continue his brilliant and charismatic cricket career. Denis was a very popular player with the Highbury crowd and his strength was a natural left-foot allied to a fierce shot and excellent ball control. The crowds loved him for his unorthodox, often erratic but always brave play but increasingly after the war he was handicapped by a long-standing knee injury and often in pain. Statistics show that Denis Compton played in only 54 League and Cup games after the war but the 'Brylcreem Boy', as he was known, was one of the outstanding personalities of the period. The story is told that

Denis, with his knee heavily strapped, was fortified by a stiff brandy at half-time in the 1950 Cup Final, and, after a poor first half, the great competitor was inspired in the second half and left the game on a high note.

HARRY POTTS

Burnley and Everton

HARRY Potts joined Burnley in 1938, as a 16-year-old from Hetton in Durham, and became the 'top shot' of a generally low-scoring Burnley team. In the first post-war season, Potts played a major role in Burnley's bid for the double with 15 goals in 40 matches in the successful promotion campaign from the Second Division. At the end of the same season, Potts was at inside-left in the Wembley FA Cup Final. Charlton Athletic won that Wembley game after extra-time, but not before Potts had seen one of his shots rebound from the crossbar. In the First Division, Potts was again a regular scorer before moving to Everton to join his former Burnley manager, Cliff Britton, for a fee of £20,000. Potts brought his League appearances to 222 before becoming coach at Wolves in 1956. A year later he returned to Burnley as manager and steered them to

the League Championship and another Cup Final appearance. Potts was well-known as an ardent student of the game, who spent hours trying out new moves and shots, being particularly enthusiastic about innovative tactics and coaching. He thought deeply about football at a time when it could hardly be described as an applied science.

CON MARTIN

Eire, Leeds United and Aston Villa

BORN in Ireland, Joseph Cornelius Martin joined Glentoran as a youngster before moving into English football in 1946-7. Leeds United paid £8,000 for his signature but his arrival was too late to save them from relegation. When Martin had a strange lapse of form and was dropped by the Yorkshire club, the Aston Villa manager, Alex Massie, quickly stepped in on 1 October 1948 and signed him for an undisclosed big fee. Martin was a 'defender' but as the game's best utility player of the period was capped for the Republic of Ireland in no less than five different positions — goalkeeper, centre-half, left and right-back and right-half. Remarkably, after two seasons at centre-half for the Midlands club, Martin moved back to take the goalkeeping spot for the 1951-2 First Division campaign. In the most varied of international careers for Eire, Martin was a key figure in the memorable December 1948 victory over England at Goodison Park.

Apart from scoring the first goal from the penalty spot in the 2-0 win, he inspired the Irish defence with the unique qualities which were to serve Villa so well. In 30 appearances for Eire he scored six goals and earned his last cap in 1956,

BERNARD STRETEN

England and Luton Town

IT was one of the major surprises of the early post-war years when Bernard Streten was selected for England in November 1949, to deputise for the injured Bert Williams in goal. Despite being one of the finest

'keepers in the land, the brilliant Streten was completely overlooked by the pundits. His height — 5ft 8ins — was against him and so was his place in the Second Division with unfashionable Luton Town. It was Frank Soo, the wartime England star, who introduced Streten to Luton in 1947 and he soon became an automatic choice. After a century of League appearances Streten made his international debut in England's easy 9-2 victory over Ireland at Manchester. Streten unfortunately had few opportunities to shine in a one-sided contest. Curiously, Streten had an inexplicable loss of form after his one cap and lost his first-team place at Luton to Iorwerth Hughes, whose displays led to him gaining Welsh honours. Streten soon regained his place, however, and his role as an ever-present. The emergence of Ron Baynham as a challenger after Luton had been promoted to the First Division in 1954-5 eventually led to his retirement in 1957. Streten had been one of the real showmen of the post-war era with his acrobatic saves and extrovert nature.

PETER FARRELL

Republic of Ireland, Everton and Tranmere Rovers

PETER Farrell was signed by Everton from Shamrock Rovers in 1946 in a deal which also brought winger Tommy Eglington over from Ireland for a combined fee of £10,000. The sturdy, resilient wing-half went on to

become one of Goodison Park's greatest servants, making 422 appearances between 1946 and 1957. Farrell was known for his biting tackle and accurate constructive distribution but more than that he was an inspirational captain for the Toffees through many often lean years in the First and then Second Division. In 28 appearances for the Republic of Ireland, Farrell's biggest moment whilst playing as an experimental forward, when he scored a rare goal to seal his country's historic 2-0 win over England at Goodison Park in 1949. Farrell saw out the final period of his career at Tranmere Rovers after his appointment as player-manager at Prenton Park in 1957.

IVOR ALLCHURCH

Wales, Swansea, Newcastle and Cardiff

THE tall, golden-haired inside-left was a football natural and clearly the outstanding discovery in Welsh football in this post-war

era. Making his debut for Swansea in the Second Division in 1949-50, Allchurch stayed for ten years, despite many offers from leading clubs. After an impressive debut against England in 1950, Allchurch went on to gain 68 Welsh caps with 23 goals. His finest performance was judged to be in the prestigious fixture in 1951 against the Rest

of the United Kingdom, when his artisitic play coupled with precise passing and astute positioning were seen to full advantage. After helping Wales to the 1958 World Cup quarter-finals, Allchurch moved to Newcastle but never settled and returned to Cardiff two years later. As his career drew to a close, Allchurch was found back at Swansea, playing his final season in 1967 in the Fourth Division. A curious lack of club success with no medals, and only 103 of his 694 League appearances in the top division, did not hide the fact that Allchurch, in the international arena, matched many of the world's leading players for technical ability. At club level he was often in a higher class than most of his colleagues.

IVOR BROADIS

England, Carlisle United, Sunderland, Manchester City and Newcastle United

IVOR Broadis was unique, not only for starting his football career as a player-manager but also by becoming the youngest man in the game to be in charge of a club. Born in Bow, he played wartime football as an amateur with Millwall, Spurs and Carlisle United, joining the latter club when he was stationed in Cumbria in the RAF. In 1946, at the age of 22, he was appointed player-manager at Brunton Park. At the time, Carlisle were in dire financial straits but Broadis revived their fortunes with his inspirational work on and off the field. In the first post-war League season he scored 19 goals from inside-right and by 1947-8, Carlisle had moved up to ninth position in the Third Division North — their best in 17 years. The Broadis management era came to an end the following season, when he was tempted to pursue his desire to play in the First Division and for England. In addition, he was all too aware that his £18,000 transfer to Sunderland in January 1949 would give Carlisle a welcome major cash injection, so with the agreement of the Carlisle Board, he uniquely negotiated his own transfer. His successor was Bill Shankly, taking his first managerial appointment. Broadis, meanwhile, took his place in the expensive North-East outfit with Len Shackleton as his fellow inside-forward. His individual ball-playing and passing skills were further seen at Manchester City, following a £25,000 transfer in 1951. At Maine Road, his partnership with the thoughtful Don Revie was significant. Broadis moved back to the North-East to join

Newcastle United for £20,000 in 1954 and played against City in the 1955 FA Cup Final. Soon he was back at Carlisle, at a fraction of the fee paid for him six years earlier. His ambitions when he left Carlisle had been realized and 14 caps for England in the period 1951-1954 were just reward for his talents. He ended his playing career with Queen of the South before becoming a sports journalist.

MALCOLM BARRASS

England, Bolton Wanderers, Sheffield United and Wigan

IN his early days, Malcolm Barrass, the son of a famous footballer, was known at Burnden Park as a star 'utility man' in the light of the variety of positions he had

occupied. So successful was he at inside-forward during the war years that an England cap was earned for an appearance in October 1945 at inside-left in a Victory international. Later in post-war League football, Barrass was a scoring success from centre-forward in 1948 after a crisis call to replace the injured Lofthouse. It was as a sturdy, dependable centre-half, typical of the period, that Barrass made his name however. Concurrently with Bolton's rise to prominence in the First Division came his first representative honour — selection for the Football League in October 1951. In the same month Barrass became the latest to be tried in England's problem position, against Wales at Ninian Park. He won three caps altogether and played in the 1953 Cup Final. After 12 years with Bolton he signed for Joe Mercer's Sheffield United, later became player-manager of Wigan Athletic and ended his playing days with Nuneaton Borough in the Southern League.

ALF SHERWOOD

Wales, Cardiff and Newport

THIS small but iron-hard full-back had the unusual distinction of having played at schoolboy level at both soccer and cricket for Wales. Sherwood helped Cardiff win promotion from the Third Division South in 1947 and from the Second in 1952 as a hugely popular captain at Ninian Park. Renowned for his courage and fighting spirit, Sherwood was a typical robust full-

back of the day with good positioning and firm tackling. Not only that, he was also a powerful kicker with perfect timing and this made him an expert from the penalty-spot. After gaining his first cap in 1949, Sherwood made 41 appearances out of 44 in the first 11 seasons after the war. Sherwood was also famous as a more than useful deputy goalkeeper and this was evidenced by several brave saves in one international against England after an injury to regular goalkeeper Jack Kelsey. After moving to Newport County, Sherwood earned his last cap in 1957. There was never a more committed Welshman and many famous English wingers felt the full weight of his tackles in the heat of the battles for club and country.

EDDIE BAILY

England, Tottenham Hotspur, Port Vale,
Nottingham Forest and Leyton Orient

THE extrovert, ebullient Baily made his debut for Spurs in February 1946 whilst on Army leave and immediately made a great impression as a ball-playing inside-forward of the highest order. Baily was to play for Spurs for another ten years, being an ideal exponent of the cultured style demanded by manager Arthur Rowe and a key factor in the Championship successes. His partnership with outside-left Les Medley was the main feature of his career and the pair graduated to the England team, so uncanny was their understanding. Baily made his debut against

Spain in the World Cup series of 1950 and went on to earn nine caps. The 'cheeky chappie', as he was known, would weave, swerve and feint through defences and was known for the great accuracy of his passes. More than that, Baily had great acceleration and a fine shot. Baily found fame as a crooner in the capital but after a short spell at Port Vale found a new lease of life at First Division Nottingham Forest before finishing his career at Leyton Orient. Later, Baily returned to Spurs to make a great contribution, as coach with manager Billy Nicholson, to their success in the 1970s and 80s.

RON BURGESS

Wales and Tottenham Hotspur

BORN in a humble mining community in the Rhondda Valley, Ron Burgess was a pit-boy before joining the Spurs junior staff in 1936. After struggling to make the grade as an inside-forward in the Northfleet 'nursery', Burgess successfully converted to wing-half and made his first-team debut in wartime.

Before taking over as captain at White Hart Lane, Burgess gained recognition as the first Welshman to play for a Football League XI and then as left-half in the Great Britain side which beat the Rest of Europe in 1948. Burgess was a hard worker who was geared to maximum effort and complimented the more subtle work of Nicholson on the other flank. Balding, fiery but reliable, he deliberately modified his approach when Spurs started their push-and-run era, cutting out his dribbling in favour of the passing game. A great favourite with the crowds for his dynamic inspiring leadership, Burgess earned 24 Welsh caps, captaining the national side. The rangy Welshman was called 'Marathon Burgess' as a mark of his astonishing work-rate. After spells in management at Swansea and Watford, Burgess's greatest achievement subsequently was to take Hendon to the FA Amateur Cup Final. For some months until his retirement, Burgess managed a 'Soccer Hall of Fame' in the West End of London before its early demise.

HARRY JOHNSTON

England and Blackpool

HARRY Johnston, who first joined Blackpool as an amateur in the 1930s, turned professional and made his League debut in 1937 as an 18-year-old left-half. After military service in the Middle East, he wore England's colours for the first time in November 1946, but his international chances were restricted by the presence of Billy Wright. Johnston skippered Blackpool's three FA Cup Final teams and the high quality of his leadership puts him amongst the finest captains that the game has seen. Known as a gentleman, Johnston was a perfectionist who was devoted to the game and utterly loyal to Blackpool and his manager, Joe Smith, with whom he formed one of the longest player/manager partnerships in League history. From an attacking wing-half, Johnston was suc-cessfully converted to centre-half, where his firm tackling, quiet determination and composure were outstanding. As the mark of a supreme talent, Johnston always seemed to have so much time and his calmness gave strength to the men around him. Johnston preferred to be attacking from wing-half and to further develop his long-throw techniques.

When he retired in 1955, he looked back on 424 appearances for Blackpool, ten England caps and the honour of being elected Footballer of the Year in 1950-51. He went

Harry Johnston's long leg gets the ball away from Roy Swinburne of Wolves.

into management at Reading before returning to his beloved Blackpool in April 1967 as chief scout at the invitation of Stan Mortensen, who had become manager two months earlier. They so nearly took the Seasiders back to the First Division, but it was a short and unsuccessful liaison for two of football's greatest post-war talents.

RONNIE ALLEN

England, Port Vale, West Bromwich Albion and Crystal Palace

RONNIE Allen was born at Fenton in January 1929 and began as an amateur with Port Vale in March 1944 after playing rugby at school. He turned professional in 1946.

The thoughtful young player, whose main assets were his speed, quick thinking and elusive dribbling, developed into a most dangerous and feared striker for West Bromwich after his transfer to The Hawthorns in March 1950. His first England cap was earned as an outside-right on the summer 1952 European tour. He had to wait almost two years before earning four more caps at centre-forward in the face of stiff competition from Lofthouse, Milburn, Mortensen *et al.* Allen eventually netted over 250 League goals for Albion and, after encouragement from manager Vic Buckingham, he was an early exponent of the 'Hidegkuti' style of deep-lying centre-forward. Allen was a leading figure in Albion's FA Cup triumph in 1954, scoring

the winner in the 2-1 semi-final victory over his former club, Port Vale, and a penalty in the thrilling 3-2 win in the Final against Preston. After making over 400 appearances for Albion, he moved to Crystal Palace in 1961 before ending his playing career and joining Wolves as coach in the spring of 1965. Eventually he became Wolves' manager and later managed Athletic Bilbao, Sporting Lisbon, Walsall, West Brom (twice), the Saudi Arabian national team and Panathinaikos.

CHARLIE MITTEN

Manchester United, Fulham and Mansfield Town

CHARLIE Mitten was born in Rangoon. His father was an Englishman who served in a Scottish regiment and his mother was Irish. He signed for United in 1936, when he was an office boy at Old Trafford, and eventually became outside-left in the famous United forward line in four post-war seasons, scoring 92 goals in that period. As a brilliant winger with excellent ball-control and a perfect cross, Mitten reached his peak at the same time as such as Finney, Langton and Froggatt and never achieved international recognition. He had to be content with one unofficial appearance for England, in 1946 against Scotland in aid of the Bolton disaster fund. An immensely fit and always confident winger, quick off the mark with a great shot, Mitten was also an excellent penalty-taker, once scoring a hat-trick from the spot against Aston Villa in March 1950. Against manager Busby's advice he was tempted to go to Bogota in late 1950, to follow in the footsteps of a few English players who included England centre-half Neil Franklin. Things did not turn out too well for the 'rebels' but Mitten honoured his whole contract in Colombia and upon his return was fined £250 and suspended for six months by the FA, despite the fact that his United contract had expired when he signed to play in Columbia. By now there was no chance of reinstatement for Mitten with either United or England after his 'illegal' year in Bogota. Eventually, in December 1951, Mitten was bought by Fulham for a big fee, but he failed to save the Cottagers from relegation from the First Division. He made 156 appearances for Fulham before leaving in 1955, to join Third Division North club, Mansfield Town, as player-manager when he was 31. He managed Newcastle United for five years

before becoming manager of Manchester's White City greyhound stadium and later a licensed UEFA agent who organized travel and accommodation arrangements for football clubs all over the world.

CHRIS DUFFY

Charlton Athletic

SCOTTISH-born Chris Duffy was a sparkling, effervescent little winger who first

became attached to Charlton as a guest player while stationed in the South during the war. He had been discharged from the Welsh Regiment following shock after taking part in the D-Day invasion. Charlton manager Jimmy Seed secured his services after his 'demob' in September 1945, for the modest fee of £330 paid to Leith Athletic. Duffy turned out to one of Charlton's best investments and brought the punch which was lacking in their attack in the early post-war years. In his first season he scored 17 goals and in 1946-7 he was ever present and scored a further ten goals in 42 appearances. The goalscoring winger played for Charlton in three Cup Finals — in 1944 in the South Cup against Chelsea, and in two FA Cup Finals — in 1946 against Derby County and, most memorably, in the 1947 victory over Burnley. Until the latter match Duffy had not caught the eye of the Press or fans outside Charlton, but he became a big name overnight after scoring one of Wembley's most sensational goals. It was the only goal of that Final and came six minutes from the end of extra time — a 14-yard volley hit with tremendous power. Duffy had been inspired in the Cup that year, scoring ten goals in the same number of appearances despite often being accused of greediness. This was all achieved on only one sound leg in the light of cartilage trouble in his right knee. When he lost his form in 1949-50, Billy Kiernan took his place on the wing but Duffy's place in the history of the The Addicks was assured. Charlton, for whom he scored 33 goals in 162 League appearances, were his only League club.

LESLIE COMPTON

England and Arsenal

LESLIE Compton, the man, who forever lived in the shadow of his extrovert, popular brother who captured all the headlines, was the bedrock of Arsenal's Championship victory in 1948 and the Gunners' FA Cup win of 1950, as a typical 'stopper' centre-half. It was manager Tom Whittaker who had the foresight to convert Compton from an undistinguished full-back to centre-half to take over from Bernard Joy after the war. 'Big Les', as he was universally known, was a wicketkeeper for Middlesex for many years but, unlike his brother, was a better footballer than cricketer. The Arsenal defence was built around this solid figure who was bent on stopping the opposing

Arsenal joy. Leslie Compton is mobbed after scoring the equalizer in the 1950 FA Cup semi-final against Chelsea.

centre-forward with strong solid tackling and dominant headwork. Against Wales in November 1950, Les Compton became the oldest Home International debutant when, at the age of 38 years 2 months, he was capped by England in a further attempt to solve their problem position. After his Arsenal debut in 1932, Compton went on to make 253 League appearances before being deposed in 1952 by the young Welshman, Ray Daniel.

STANLEY MATTHEWS

England, Stoke City, Blackpool

BORN in Hanley in the Potteries, Stanley Matthews was groomed in the spartan manner — by early-morning runs and deep-breathing exercises supervised by his father, Jack, a well-known featherweight boxer. As a boy, Stanley earned local fame as a sprinter and then joined Stoke City as a 15-year old amateur and office boy. He turned professional and made his League debut at 17 and, two years later, was playing for

England. It was the start of a football legend. As a young man, Matthews was very quick, especially over the first ten yards, and this, allied to his unique dribbling ability, made him a star performer in pre-war football. In those early years, Matthews was quite a goalscorer, even netting a hat-trick for England against Czechoslovakia in 1937, although in later years he seemed happier making goals than scoring them. In 1947 he moved to Blackpool for £11,000 — there was a public outcry in Stoke — and his aim became increasingly to reach the goal-line and then to pull back a pin-point pass to a colleague running in. The enigmatic winger was able to kill a ball stone dead at any speed, to tempt a defender into a rash challenge, to baffle a marker by the wriggling of his hips, and to bewilder the whole defence with his baffling change of pace and direction. Ball-control became a passion. Matthews was simply the supreme creator

who thrived on taking on and destroying defenders with his trickery — which extended to exquisite feints, to single and double shuffles, defenders falling over, often without Matthews actually touching the ball. He filled grounds wherever he played and the knowledge that he was to appear added considerably to attendances, home and away, in this country and abroad. Always conscious

of his own value, Matthews was one of the first British footballers to exploit his commercial potential. Inevitably, he caused controversy, not of his own making, but as pundits disagreed over his merits, despite his becoming the first Footballer of the Year in 1948. Some thought that, for all his cleverness, he slowed up the attack, some pointed to his lack of goals, to his 'refusal' to head the ball, to his insistence on having the ball passed to his feet every time. Even the England selectors would ignore him at times and when the maestro was omitted from the England-Scotland fixture of April 1953, a newspaper's countrywide poll showed that 85 per cent of readers wanted him restored. Originally he had been a glaring omission from the subsequent tour of the Americas but his legendary performance in the 1953 Cup Final brought a belated change of mind. Matthews eventually decided not to go because he was still suffering from the niggling injury that had needed a pain-killing injection before the Cup Final. That 'Matthews Final' was the most amazing one-man band performance ever seen in a Wembley Final, when Blackpool scored a heart-stopping victory after being 3-1 down to Bolton with 22 minutes remaining. It should be said, of course, that Matthews always disliked the tag of 'his' Cup Final, pointing to the fact that Stan Mortensen scored a hat-trick for Blackpool that day. Stanley Matthews was dedicated to the football and was never at anything other than peak fitness. Known for his own firm ideals, he had amazing will-power and perception which kept him playing longer than anyone else — evidenced by his being the only man to have played First Division football when over 50 years of age. Physical fitness was a fetish throughout and Matthews would insist on training on his own so that it could be fitted to suit his own game. In 1961 he returned to Stoke in the Second Division for £2,500, after his 14 years at the Seasiders had brought them three FA Cup Final appearances and the most successful era in their history. The following season, 1962-3, Stoke chased promotion to the First Division and in their last match of the season, Matthews scored the last goal of his career and the one that ensured that promotion. It was typical of the quiet, polite individualist who was always ready with the command performance for the big occasion and in 1965 he became the first footballer to be knighted, adding that honour to his OBE awarded in 1957. A year later England won the World Cup without playing any wingers at all. His astonishing career had lasted 33 seasons from

Stan Matthews in pensive mood, taking the field for the FA Candian Touring XI against the England World Cup XI in the 1950 FA Charity Shield match at Stamford Bridge. His Blackpool colleague, Harry Johnston, is next.

1932 and in the process he became more than just a footballer, more a legend in his own lifetime. A total of 54 peacetime England caps to add to his 26 wartime appearances were a poor return for the man with the shuffling, stooped dribble who, for all those years, paced the touch-line with his curious, ungainly loping stride. The fantastic body-swerve could not be copied and was simply unique in the way that the likes of Nijinsky, Ranjitsinhji, Charlie Chaplin, Muhammad Ali all had something which others in their fields could not match. Even after he retired, Matthews never drank and never smoked — although in his playing days he was once pictured in an England shirt extolling the virtues of Craven 'A' cigarettes on the pages of *Charles Buchan's Football Monthly*. He also never stopped training, so that he was still playing in retirement in Malta in the 1970s. Only a short unsuccessful venture into management at Port Vale marred his later years, but by then a young winger from Belfast was entering a changed football world.

air disaster. Only one England cap came his way and that in the débâcle against Hungary in November 1953.

ERNIE TAYLOR

England, Newcastle United, Blackpool and Manchester United

ERNIE TAYLOR was one of the smallest forwards to appear regularly in post-war League football, in his size-4 boots. He was in great demand with his nimble brain and visionary passing and it was his prompting and creative play which bore fruit in the goalscoring feats of George Robledo and Jackie Milburn at Newcastle. There was no better examaple than his imaginative exquisite back-heel which presented Milburn with his second goal in the 1951 FA Cup Final. After his move to Bloomfield Road, for a sizeable fee, Taylor wore a Blackpool shirt in the 1953 Cup Final. Here, too, his impact was significant as, in his finest hour, he prompted Stanley Matthews to success against Bolton, using his nimble brain and astute passing skills to great effect in the final 20 minutes of that great drama. In that memorable Blackpool season, Taylor would typically control the play with a short ball to the feet of Matthews, or play a long cross-field pass in front of the sprinting left-winger Bill Perry or thread a searching ball to send Mortensen away down the middle on one of his long runs. In 1958, Taylor, at 31, was recruited by Manchester United for a modest £8,000 to be the father-figure to the team thrown together after the Munich

STAN PEARSON

England, Manchester United, Bury and Chester

SALFORD-born Stan Pearson joined the Manchester United groundstaff as a 15-year-old before the war, under manager Scott Duncan. After four years 'nursing' in the juniors he made his League debut in

November 1937. The youngster, who was 'United-mad' as a boy, had made only two Central League appearances before his promotion but proved to be a quiet, unassuming footballer. When Matt Busby took over as manager after the war, he found Pearson to be dependable week in week out and clearly the brains of the attack. Pearson was a different style to his fellow inside-forward Johnny Morris, not so skilled as a ball-player, but with a wonderful footballing brain and a consistent goalscorer. Busby recognized Pearson as one who could size up a situation in a blink of an eyelid. The goals he scored reflected this — often scoring clever opportunist goals with a glide and flick of the ball with his head. Pearson was particularly remembered for two such short-range goals at Hampden Park against Scotland in 1951-2 season in one of his eight internationals. His partnership with Charlie Mitten on the left wing was a feature of United's 1948 Cup success and Pearson added a Championship medal in 1951-2 before being transferred to Second Division Bury in February 1954. After a subsequent move to Third Division North club, Chester, Pearson became their player-manager, then manager until he left professional football in November 1961. For United he had made 304 League appearances and scored 125 goals.

GEORGE HARDWICK

England, Middlesbrough and Oldham Athletic

WHEN international football resumed after the war, George Hardwick was an automatic choice as left-back and captain for England after his pre-war eminence with Middlesbrough. For the first 13 post-war internationals, Hardwick was a valuable captain with his deep knowledge, his coolness under pressure and his sure kicking. During the war he guested for Chelsea, playing for them in three Cup Finals, and his place as one of the very best full-backs in the game's history was reinforced when he skippered the Great Britain team which met the Rest of Europe in May 1947. After handing over the England captaincy to goalkeeper Frank Swift in 1948, Hardwick led Middlesbrough into the upper reaches of the First Division when the Teesiders were one of the most attractive sides to watch in the country. It was a surprise when he moved to Oldham Athletic as player-manager in 1953, but it cost the Lancashire club £15,000

to secure his services — one of the biggest fees ever paid by a Third Division club at that time. He was their youngest-ever manager and improved the team until it was good enough to win the Northern Section title. Alas, lack of finance at Boundary Park meant that relegation quickly followed and Hardwick later held a number of coaching appointments in England and abroad, including coaching the US Army soccer team

in Germany, before becoming manager of Sunderland in 1964. At Roker Park he gained credit for keeping a poor team in the First Division, after which he took charge of Gateshead. After retiring from football he became chairman of a structural steel company.

PETER HARRIS

England and Portsmouth

LOCAL boy Peter Harris, who was born in Southsea in December 1925, was a joiner by trade before signing for Pompey in October 1944, after being spotted in Hampshire League football with Gosport Borough. He scored on his wartime debut in the League South against an international-laden Aldershot side and in peacetime went on to score 194 League goals for the Fratton Park club. That total, scored from 479 League appearances in the period 1946-1959, is still a club record and looks unlikely to be beaten. Harris finished as top scorer with 17 in Pompey's first Championship-winning side of 1948-9 and notched another 16 the following season when the title was retained. The flying winger, with the astonishing turn of speed, tantalising feints and impeccable ball-control, found himself in competition with Matthews and Finney for the England outside-right spot. As a consequence, despite his consistent club form, his superb finishing skills and the highest rating from his fellow professionals, Harris gained only two international caps and both coincided with disastrous English performances. His debut was against the Republic of Ireland at

Goodison Park in September 1949, when England lost embarassingly 2-0, and the second in the 7-1 massacre by Hungary in May 1954. In November 1959, Pompey fans were stunned to learn that Harris had a serious chest ailment and faced a lengthy stay in a sanatorium. His under-rated and internationally overlooked career was over and the scurrying figure of Harris was no longer seen patrolling the Pompey right-hand touch-line. His health recovered, Harris retired to Hayling Island to manage a restaurant complex.

JACKIE SEWELL

England, Notts County, Sheffield Wednesday, Aston Villa and Hull City

JACKIE Sewell was introduced to Notts County by Major Frank Buckley in 1944, from Whitehaven, and he learnt his trade playing alongside Tommy Lawton in the Third Division South, helping the Magpies into Division Two in 1950. After Sewell had scored over 100 goals in his first four seasons of League football, Sheffield Wednesday manager Eric Taylor persuaded him to move to Hillsborough a few days before the transfer deadline in March 1951. The 24-year old signed for a British record fee of £34,500, which made him the first player to be literally worth his weight in gold. His signing did not prevent Wednesday being relegated to the Second Division, however, but in the next season his partnership with the prolific goalscoring Dooley ensured instant promotion back to the First. Sewell found the price-tag difficult to live with and his lack of self-confidence meant he did not fulfil his potential for the Owls. After 175 League

and Cup appearances (92 goals) Sewell moved to Aston Villa in December 1955 and won an FA Cup winners' medal with Villa in 1957. After a short spell with Hull City, he retired, looking back on six full England caps and an FA tour of Australia. The inside-forward who made all those shock transfer headlines in 1951 was full of craft with a scoring knack which brought him a career tally of 227 goals in 510 League games.

EDDIE QUIGLEY

Bury, Sheffield Wednesday, Preston North End, Blackburn Rovers

IN those post-war years of continual transfer activity, one man who always seemed to be in demand was Eddie Quigley, a player constantly in the headlines because of his prolific goalscoring. After making his name at Bury, Quigley cost Sheffield Wednesday £12,000 in October 1947 — he moved to Hillsborough with team-mate Eddie Kilshaw — and repaid the Owls handsomely with 52 goals in 75 League and Cup appearances. As a result Wednesday could boast one of the finest forward combinations in the First Division and Quigley, Hugh Swift and Redfern Froggatt were in the running for international recognition. Then the British record transfer was shattered by a fee of £26,500 paid by Preston North End for Quigley's transfer to Deepdale. Preston saw him as the ideal foil for Tom Finney at centre or inside-forward, but the two never quite hit it off. A great opportunist, Quigley's build made him look deceptively slow but he always seemed to be in the right place at the right time to snap up chances. Quigley had a spell with Blackburn Rovers before finishing his career back at Bury. Management at Stockport County and Blackburn Rovers followed before he retired.

JOHN CHARLES

Wales, Leeds United, Juventus, Roma and Cardiff City

BORN in Swansea in 1931, John Charles joined the local club's groundstaff where his talent was spotted by Leeds United manager Major Frank Buckley. For the normal £10 signing-on fee, Charles joined Leeds in January 1949 and three months later made his debut at centre-half. One year later, in March 1950, Charles became the youngest Welshman ever to represent his country, at the age of 18. The young towering 6ft 2in tall centre-half or centre-forward made a huge impact as a teenager by his modest bearing, superb temperament and all-round skills in defence and attack. His career was transformed by a permanent switch to centre-forward with 26 goals in his first season and then 42 (a Leeds club record) in the second. No player in the previous 30 years had impressed his personality on the public mind

John Charles (third from left) is unable to stop Arsenal's Reg Lewis scoring during a sixth-round FA Cup tie at Highbury in 1950.

to such an extent. The 'Gentle Giant', as he was known, put his faith in skill and judgement rather than in vigour. The secret of his success lay in his sense of balance and, for such a big man, he had superb control. Despite that, Charles was often accused of not making the most of his physical advantages. His move to Juventus of Italy in 1956 was a great success after one of the most talked-about transfers of the post-war era. A move back to Leeds for three months and then a short return to Roma prefaced the final period of his career at Cardiff City in 1963. Charles was in no demand for managerial vacancies and the man who won genuine world acclaim found life more difficult once his playing days were over.

Football League Tables 1946-7 to 1952-3

– 1946-47 –

DIVISION 1

Team	P	W	D	L	F	A	W	D	L	F	A	Pts
Liverpool	42	13	3	5	42	24	12	4	5	42	28	57
Manchester U	42	17	3	1	61	19	5	9	7	34	35	56
Wolves	42	15	1	5	66	31	10	5	6	32	25	56
Stoke C	42	14	5	2	52	21	10	2	9	38	32	55
Blackpool	42	14	1	6	38	32	8	5	8	33	38	50
Sheffield U	42	12	4	5	51	32	9	3	9	38	43	49
Preston NE	42	10	7	4	45	27	8	4	9	31	47	47
Aston Villa	42	11	6	4	39	24	7	3	11	28	29	45
Sunderland	42	13	5	3	33	27	5	3	13	32	39	44
Everton	42	11	3	7	40	32	6	6	9	22	35	43
Middlesbrough	42	11	5	5	46	33	6	3	12	27	35	42
Portsmouth	42	9	5	7	42	29	7	4	10	24	31	41
Arsenal	42	13	2	6	43	33	3	7	11	29	37	41
Derby C	42	11	2	8	44	38	7	3	11	29	41	41
Chelsea	42	13	4	4	45	39	3	3	15	24	45	39
Grimsby T	42	9	6	6	37	35	4	6	11	24	47	38
Blackburn R	42	9	5	7	23	28	5	3	13	22	25	36
Bolton W	42	8	6	7	30	28	5	2	14	27	41	34
Charlton A	42	7	7	7	30	32	4	5	12	27	39	34
Huddersfield T	42	8	5	8	34	35	5	2	14	19	44	33
Brentford	42	5	5	11	26	35	4	2	15	19	53	25
Leeds U	42	6	5	10	30	35	0	1	20	15	55	18

DIVISION 2

Team	P	W	D	L	F	A	W	D	L	F	A	Pts
Manchester C	42	15	4	2	46	13	11	6	4	32	22	62
Burnley	42	13	6	2	41	15	9	8	4	24	14	58
Birmingham C	42	17	2	2	53	11	8	3	10	21	22	55
Chesterfield	42	11	6	4	37	21	7	8	6	21	23	50
Newcastle U	42	12	6	3	60	27	7	4	10	35	35	48
Tottenham H	42	11	8	2	35	21	6	6	9	30	32	48
West Brom A	42	12	4	5	53	30	8	4	9	35	45	48
Coventry C	42	12	6	3	40	17	4	7	10	26	42	45
Leicester C	42	11	4	6	42	25	7	3	11	27	39	43
Barnsley	42	13	2	6	48	29	4	6	11	36	57	42
Nottingham F	42	13	3	5	47	20	2	7	12	22	54	40
West Ham U	42	12	4	5	46	31	4	4	14	24	45	40
Luton T	42	13	2	6	50	28	3	5	13	21	45	39
Southampton	42	11	5	5	45	30	4	4	13	24	46	39
Fulham	42	12	4	5	42	29	3	5	13	21	45	39
Bradford	42	11	6	4	42	34	3	5	13	23	43	39
Bury	42	7	10	4	42	29	5	2	16	38	49	36
Millwall	42	11	2	8	34	30	3	6	12	22	49	36
Plymouth A	42	11	3	7	45	30	3	2	16	34	66	33
Sheffield W	42	10	5	6	39	28	2	3	16	28	60	32
Swansea C	42	9	6	6	36	30	2	1	18	19	53	29
Newport C	42	9	1	11	41	52	1	2	18	20	81	23

DIVISION 3 South

Team	P	W	D	L	F	A	W	D	L	F	A	Pts
Cardiff C	42	19	1	1	61	10	11	5	5	32	20	66
Queen's Park R	42	15	3	3	45	17	8	8	5	29	23	57
Bristol C	42	13	5	3	53	22	7	6	8	41	34	51
Swindon T	42	13	4	4	51	29	6	7	8	33	44	49
Walsall	42	11	7	3	43	23	6	5	10	31	36	46
Ipswich T	42	11	7	3	38	19	5	7	9	23	34	46
Bournemouth	42	12	4	5	42	22	6	4	11	30	32	44
Southend U	42	12	5	4	44	24	5	5	11	27	36	44
Reading	42	11	5	5	51	32	5	6	10	32	42	43
Port Vale	42	13	2	6	44	27	4	7	10	24	36	43
Torquay U	42	11	4	6	34	26	4	8	9	18	35	42
Notts C	42	11	6	4	39	27	4	4	13	24	36	40
Northampton T	42	11	5	5	46	33	4	5	12	26	42	40
Bristol R	42	11	4	6	37	29	5	4	12	22	40	40
Exeter C	42	11	5	5	39	27	4	4	13	21	42	39
Watford	42	12	4	5	38	28	5	1	15	23	48	39
Brighton & HA	42	9	8	4	35	27	4	4	13	19	42	38
Crystal P	42	10	5	6	30	26	3	6	12	19	36	37
Leyton O	42	9	4	8	35	32	3	4	15	19	43	32
Aldershot	42	8	7	6	30	35	2	5	14	18	43	32
Norwich C	42	8	5	8	40	48	2	3	16	24	52	28
Mansfield T	42	7	6	8	31	35	2	4	15	17	61	28

DIVISION 3 North

Team	P	W	D	L	F	A	W	D	L	F	A	Pts
Doncaster R	42	18	1	2	67	17	15	5	1	56	23	72
Rotherham U	42	20	0	1	81	17	9	6	6	33	36	64
Chester	42	17	2	2	53	21	8	4	9	42	30	56
Stockport Co	42	17	1	3	50	20	7	7	7	28	33	56
Bradford C	42	12	5	4	40	24	8	5	8	22	23	50
Rochdale	42	12	5	4	41	22	7	5	9	39	42	48
Wrexham	42	13	4	4	41	22	4	8	9	24	29	46
Crewe Alex	42	12	4	5	45	31	5	5	11	25	43	43
Barrow	42	11	5	5	34	24	6	2	13	20	38	41
Tranmere R	42	11	3	7	43	34	6	4	11	23	43	41
Hull C	42	12	4	5	36	20	4	4	13	13	33	40
Lincoln C	42	12	3	6	41	27	5	2	14	19	37	39
Hartlepools U	42	11	5	5	43	31	4	4	13	21	42	39
Gateshead	42	12	3	6	39	28	4	3	14	23	44	38
York C	42	11	5	5	42	32	3	4	14	25	49	37
Carlisle U	42	10	6	5	45	37	4	3	14	25	56	37
Darlington	42	12	3	6	48	33	3	3	15	20	47	36
New Brighton	42	11	3	7	37	30	3	5	13	20	47	36
Oldham A	42	9	5	7	34	31	3	4	14	21	49	33
Accrington S	42	11	1	9	39	37	3	3	15	17	55	32
Southport	42	8	6	7	36	35	3	4	14	17	50	32
Halifax T	42	6	5	10	28	41	2	1	18	15	67	22

– 1947-48 –

DIVISION 1

	P	W	D	L	F	A	W	D	L	F	A	Pts
Arsenal	42	15	3	3	56	15	8	10	3	25	17	59
Manchester U	42	11	7	3	50	27	8	7	6	31	21	52
Burnley	42	12	4	5	31	12	8	8	5	25	31	52
Derby C	42	11	6	4	38	24	8	6	7	39	33	50
Wolves	42	12	4	5	45	29	7	5	9	38	41	47
Aston Villa	42	13	5	3	42	22	6	4	11	23	35	47
Preston NE	42	13	4	4	43	35	7	2	12	24	33	47
Portsmouth	42	13	5	3	44	17	6	4	11	24	33	45
Manchester C	42	13	4	4	37	14	5	5	12	15	25	42
Blackpool	42	12	3	6	37	20	5	6	10	20	27	44
Liverpool	42	13	5	3	39	23	3	3	15	26	38	42
Sheffield U	42	13	8	4	44	23	3	2	16	21	47	42
Charlton A	42	13	4	4	37	29	4	4	13	20	37	42
Everton	42	9	4	9	30	22	8	6	7	22	44	40
Stoke C	42	10	5	7	29	23	6	8	7	12	33	40
Middlesbrough	42	9	7	6	26	25	8	2	11	37	44	37
Bolton W	42	11	6	4	37	17	5	5	11	29	32	36
Chelsea	42	7	8	6	25	23	7	2	12	29	36	37
Huddersfield T	42	11	5	5	38	33	4	6	11	23	36	37
Sunderland	42	11	4	6	33	32	2	7	12	22	39	32
Blackburn R	42	8	5	8	35	30	3	5	13	28	42	34
Grimsby T	42	5	5	11	20	35	3	1	17	25	76	22

DIVISION 2

	P	W	D	L	F	A	W	D	L	F	A	Pts
Birmingham C	42	12	7	2	34	13	6	1	11	21	11	59
Newcastle U	42	18	1	2	46	13	6	13	2	56	28	56
Southampton	42	15	3	3	53	30	6	7	8	23	23	52
Sheffield W	42	13	6	2	39	21	7	6	8	27	32	51
Cardiff C	42	12	6	3	36	18	6	5	10	25	40	47
West Ham U	42	10	7	4	29	19	6	7	8	26	34	46
West Brom A	42	11	4	6	37	29	6	7	8	26	29	45
Tottenham H	42	10	5	6	36	24	5	9	7	20	19	44
Leicester C	42	10	6	5	36	28	6	5	10	24	29	43
Coventry C	42	10	5	6	33	16	4	8	9	24	28	41
Fulham	42	6	9	6	24	22	6	7	8	23	24	40
Barnsley	42	10	5	6	31	26	5	5	11	31	36	40
Luton T	42	8	5	8	45	30	6	7	8	24	42	40
Bradford C	42	11	3	7	31	26	5	5	11	35	39	40
Brentford	42	8	6	7	32	22	8	2	11	23	31	40
Chesterfield	42	8	9	4	27	22	3	9	9	22	36	40
Plymouth A	42	8	4	9	44	20	2	13	6	32	52	38
Leeds U	42	12	5	4	44	23	2	3	16	18	40	36
Nottingham F	42	10	5	6	32	31	2	6	13	22	46	35
Bury	42	6	8	7	27	23	3	8	10	31	40	34
Doncaster R	42	7	8	6	23	17	2	3	16	17	46	29
Millwall	42	7	7	7	27	28	2	4	15	17	46	29

DIVISION 3 South

	P	W	D	L	F	A	W	D	L	F	A	Pts
Queen's Park R	42	16	3	2	44	17	10	6	5	30	20	61
Bournemouth	42	13	5	3	42	13	11	5	5	34	22	57
Walsall	42	13	5	3	37	18	7	6	8	33	28	51
Ipswich T	42	16	1	4	42	18	7	2	12	25	43	49
Swansea C	42	14	6	4	48	14	4	6	11	22	38	48
Notts Co	42	12	4	5	47	27	7	4	10	21	32	46
Bristol C	42	11	4	6	48	26	7	3	11	20	33	43
Port Vale	42	11	5	5	32	16	4	8	9	15	27	43
Southend U	42	14	2	5	37	18	3	7	11	14	42	43
Reading	42	10	7	4	34	28	5	5	11	22	30	42
Exeter C	42	10	5	6	34	22	5	5	11	21	41	41
Newport C	42	9	8	4	38	28	5	5	11	23	45	41
Crystal P	42	12	5	4	32	14	1	8	12	17	35	39
Northampton T	42	10	5	6	35	28	4	6	11	23	44	39
Watford	42	6	10	5	31	37	6	4	11	26	42	38
Swindon T	42	8	6	7	21	20	6	2	13	20	26	36
Leyton O	42	8	6	7	31	29	5	4	12	20	41	36
Torquay U	42	8	5	8	40	29	7	0	14	23	33	35
Aldershot	42	5	10	6	22	26	6	3	12	23	41	35
Bristol R	42	7	5	9	39	34	5	5	11	32	41	34
Norwich C	42	8	3	10	33	34	5	5	11	28	42	34
Brighton & HA	42	8	4	9	26	31	3	8	10	17	17	34

DIVISION 3 North

	P	W	D	L	F	A	W	D	L	F	A	Pts
Lincoln C	42	14	3	4	47	18	12	5	4	34	22	60
Rotherham U	42	15	4	2	56	18	10	5	6	39	31	59
Wrexham	42	14	3	4	49	23	7	5	9	25	31	50
Gateshead	42	11	5	5	48	28	8	6	7	27	29	49
Hull C	42	12	5	4	38	21	6	6	9	27	27	47
Accrington S	42	13	1	7	36	24	7	5	9	26	35	46
Barrow	42	9	9	3	24	19	6	6	9	25	21	45
Mansfield T	42	11	7	3	37	24	6	4	11	25	27	45
Carlisle U	42	10	4	7	50	35	8	3	10	38	42	43
Crewe A	42	12	5	4	41	24	4	6	11	20	39	43
Oldham A	42	6	10	5	25	25	8	3	10	38	49	41
Rochdale	42	12	4	5	32	23	3	7	11	16	35	41
York C	42	12	3	6	38	27	3	7	11	27	39	40
Bradford C	42	10	4	7	34	27	5	6	10	26	36	40
Southport	42	7	8	6	30	31	7	4	10	24	39	40
Darlington	42	9	6	6	42	28	4	8	9	30	39	40
Stockport C	42	8	9	4	42	23	4	6	11	21	39	39
Tranmere R	42	10	1	10	30	23	6	6	9	24	44	38
Hartlepools U	42	11	6	4	34	25	2	3	16	20	50	36
Chester	42	10	6	5	44	27	1	3	17	14	42	36
Halifax T	42	4	10	7	25	18	3	3	15	18	49	27
New Brighton	42	5	6	10	20	18	3	3	15	18	53	25

– 1948-49 –

DIVISION 1

	P	W	D	L	F	A	W	D	L	F	A	Pts
Portsmouth	42	18	3	0	52	12	7	5	9	32	30	58
Manchester U	42	11	7	3	40	20	10	4	7	37	24	53
Derby C	42	17	2	2	48	22	5	7	9	26	33	53
Newcastle U	42	12	5	4	35	29	8	7	6	35	27	52
Arsenal	42	13	5	3	51	18	5	8	8	23	26	49
Wolves	42	13	3	5	48	19	4	9	8	31	47	46
Manchester C	42	10	8	3	28	19	5	7	9	19	32	45
Sunderland	42	8	10	3	27	19	5	6	10	22	39	42
Charlton A	42	10	5	6	38	31	5	7	9	25	36	42
Aston Villa	42	10	5	6	40	36	6	5	10	20	40	42
Stoke C	42	14	3	4	43	24	2	6	13	23	44	41
Liverpool	42	10	6	5	25	18	3	8	10	28	25	40
Chelsea	42	10	6	5	43	27	2	8	11	26	41	38
Bolton W	42	10	6	5	43	32	4	4	13	16	36	38
Burnley	42	8	8	5	27	19	4	6	11	16	31	38
Blackpool	42	8	8	5	24	25	3	8	10	30	42	38
Birmingham C	42	9	7	5	19	10	2	8	11	17	28	37
Everton	42	12	5	4	33	25	1	6	14	8	38	37
Middlesbrough	42	10	3	8	37	23	1	9	11	9	34	34
Huddersfield T	42	6	7	8	19	24	6	3	12	21	45	34
Preston NE	42	8	6	7	36	36	3	5	13	26	39	33
Sheffield U	42	8	9	4	32	25	3	2	17	25	53	33

DIVISION 2

	P	W	D	L	F	A	W	D	L	F	A	Pts
Fulham	42	16	3	2	52	14	8	6	7	25	23	57
West Brom A	42	16	4	1	47	16	8	4	9	22	23	56
Southampton	42	16	4	1	48	10	7	5	9	21	26	55
Cardiff C	42	14	4	3	45	21	5	9	7	17	26	51
Tottenham H	42	14	4	3	50	18	3	12	6	22	26	50
Chesterfield	42	9	7	5	24	18	6	10	5	27	27	47
West Ham U	42	13	5	3	38	23	5	5	11	18	35	46
Sheffield W	42	12	6	3	36	17	3	7	11	27	39	43
Barnsley	42	11	6	4	40	18	3	6	12	22	43	40
Luton T	42	10	6	5	32	16	4	6	11	23	41	40
Grimsby T	42	11	5	5	44	28	4	5	12	28	48	40
Bury	42	12	4	5	41	23	2	7	12	26	53	39
Queen's Park R	42	10	5	6	31	26	4	5	12	13	36	38
Blackburn R	42	11	4	6	36	23	4	3	14	17	40	37
Leeds U	42	8	8	5	35	21	4	5	12	20	42	37
Coventry C	42	11	3	7	37	20	4	3	14	18	44	36
Bradford	42	10	5	6	41	26	3	5	13	24	52	36
Brentford	42	7	8	6	24	18	4	6	11	18	35	36
Leicester C	42	7	9	5	40	26	3	7	11	22	53	36
Plymouth A	42	8	6	7	33	22	4	5	12	16	42	35
Nottingham F	42	9	4	6	31	14	2	9	12	19	40	35
Lincoln C	42	6	7	8	31	35	2	5	14	22	56	28

DIVISION 3 South

	P	W	D	L	F	A	W	D	L	F	A	Pts
Swansea T	42	20	1	0	60	11	7	7	7	27	23	62
Reading	42	15	3	3	42	18	10	2	9	35	32	55
Bournemouth	42	15	1	2	42	17	7	7	9	27	31	52
Swindon T	42	11	9	1	38	20	7	6	8	26	36	51
Bristol R	42	13	5	3	42	23	6	5	10	19	28	48
Brighton & HA	42	11	5	5	32	26	4	13	4	23	29	48
Ipswich T	42	13	7	1	53	30	4	4	13	25	47	45
Millwall	42	12	7	2	42	23	5	4	12	21	41	45
Torquay U	42	12	5	4	45	26	5	6	10	20	44	45
Norwich C	42	15	3	3	45	10	1	9	11	22	39	44
Notts Co	42	12	3	6	65	19	7	2	12	37	49	43
Exeter C	42	11	5	5	40	26	4	8	9	23	33	43
Port Vale	42	9	8	4	34	21	5	4	12	17	33	40
Walsall	42	11	5	5	41	28	4	4	13	15	36	39
Newport C	42	9	6	6	41	35	5	4	12	24	38	38
Bristol C	42	8	9	4	28	24	3	6	12	16	33	37
Watford	42	6	9	6	18	21	4	7	10	23	28	36
Southend U	42	5	10	6	33	29	4	6	11	18	22	35
Leyton O	42	9	6	6	33	20	2	6	13	25	51	34
Northampton T	42	9	6	6	26	22	3	3	15	25	42	34
Aldershot	42	6	8	7	26	18	3	7	11	22	30	33
Crystal P	42	7	5	9	27	27	1	6	14	22	49	27

DIVISION 3 North

	P	W	D	L	F	A	W	D	L	F	A	Pts
Hull C	42	17	3	1	65	14	10	8	3	28	14	65
Rotherham U	42	16	4	1	47	17	12	2	7	43	29	62
Doncaster R	42	10	8	3	26	12	10	2	9	27	28	50
Darlington	42	10	3	8	42	36	3	7	11	41	38	46
Gateshead	42	10	6	5	41	28	6	7	8	28	30	45
Oldham A	42	12	5	4	49	28	6	4	11	26	39	45
Rochdale	42	14	3	4	37	24	1	10	10	18	37	43
Stockport Co	42	13	5	3	44	16	3	6	12	17	40	43
Wrexham	42	13	3	5	35	22	4	6	11	21	40	43
Mansfield T	42	12	6	3	39	15	2	7	12	13	33	41
Tranmere R	42	8	9	4	23	18	5	6	10	23	38	41
Crewe A	2	13	2	6	31	27	3	6	12	21	47	40
Barrow	42	13	4	4	27	14	0	9	12	14	35	39
York C	42	11	3	7	49	28	4	6	11	25	46	39
Carlisle U	42	12	5	4	46	25	2	5	14	14	45	38
Hartlepools U	42	10	7	4	34	18	2	5	14	11	33	36
New Brighton	42	10	5	6	34	21	2	6	13	11	39	35
Chester	42	10	4	7	25	19	1	9	11	21	37	35
Halifax T	42	8	6	7	26	19	4	4	13	10	35	34
Accrington S	42	11	4	6	39	23	0	8	13	16	41	34
Southport	46	9	5	10	28	24	2	4	12	17	35	31
Bradford C	42	7	6	8	29	31	3	3	15	19	46	29

– 1949-50 –

DIVISION 1

	P	W	D	L	F	A	W	D	L	F	A	Pts
Portsmouth	42	12	7	2	44	15	10	2	9	30	23	53
Wolves	42	11	8	2	47	21	9	5	7	29	28	53
Sunderland	42	14	6	1	50	23	7	4	10	33	39	52
Manchester U	42	11	5	5	42	23	7	9	5	27	21	50
Newcastle U	42	14	4	3	49	23	5	8	8	28	32	50
Arsenal	42	12	4	5	48	24	7	7	7	31	31	49
Blackpool	42	10	5	6	29	14	7	10	4	17	21	49
Liverpool	42	10	8	3	37	23	7	6	8	27	31	48
Middlesbrough	42	14	2	5	37	18	6	5	10	22	30	47
Burnley	42	9	7	5	23	17	7	6	8	17	23	45
Derby C	42	11	5	5	46	26	6	5	10	23	35	44
Aston Villa	42	10	7	4	31	19	5	5	11	30	42	42
Chelsea	42	7	7	7	31	30	5	9	7	27	35	40
West Brom A	42	9	7	5	28	16	5	5	11	19	37	40
Huddersfield T	42	11	4	6	34	22	3	5	13	18	51	37
Bolton W	42	10	4	7	34	22	0	10	11	11	37	34
Fulham	42	8	6	7	24	19	2	8	11	17	35	34
Everton	42	6	8	7	24	20	4	6	11	18	46	34
Stoke C	42	10	4	7	27	28	1	8	12	18	47	34
Charlton A	42	10	2	9	33	35	3	4	14	20	30	32
Manchester C	42	7	5	9	27	30	1	8	12	9	38	29
Birmingham C	42	6	8	7	19	24	1	6	14	12	43	28

DIVISION 2

	P	W	D	L	F	A	W	D	L	F	A	Pts
Tottenham H	42	15	3	3	51	15	12	4	5	30	20	61
Sheffield W	42	12	6	3	46	23	6	10	5	21	25	52
Sheffield U	42	14	5	2	44	16	5	9	7	24	33	52
Southampton	42	11	8	2	33	16	8	6	7	31	32	52
Leeds U	42	11	5	5	33	16	6	8	7	21	29	47
Preston NE	42	12	4	5	37	21	6	5	10	23	28	45
Hull C	42	11	5	5	39	25	6	6	9	25	47	45
Swansea T	42	11	5	5	34	18	6	4	11	19	31	43
Brentford	42	11	3	7	21	14	4	10	7	23	35	43
Cardiff C	42	11	5	5	28	12	5	5	11	13	32	42
Grimsby T	42	13	3	5	53	25	3	5	13	21	48	40
Coventry C	42	8	6	7	32	24	5	7	9	23	31	39
Barnsley	42	11	6	4	45	28	2	7	12	19	39	39
Chesterfield	42	12	6	3	28	15	3	3	15	15	32	39
Leicester C	42	8	9	4	30	25	4	5	12	25	40	38
Blackburn R	42	10	5	6	30	18	4	5	12	25	42	38
Luton T	42	8	8	5	28	22	2	9	10	13	29	37
Bury	42	10	8	3	37	19	4	0	17	23	46	36
West Ham U	42	8	7	6	30	25	4	5	12	23	36	36
Queen's Park R	42	6	9	6	21	19	5	3	13	19	38	34
Plymouth A	42	6	6	9	25	24	2	10	9	19	41	32
Bradford	42	7	6	8	34	17	3	5	13	17	34	31

DIVISION 3 South

	P	W	D	L	F	A	W	D	L	F	A	Pts
Notts C	42	17	2	2	60	12	8	6	7	35	38	58
Northampton T	42	12	6	3	43	21	8	5	8	29	29	51
Southend U	42	15	4	2	43	15	4	9	8	23	33	51
Nottingham F	42	13	6	2	37	9	7	3	11	30	30	49
Torquay U	42	12	6	3	40	13	7	4	10	26	50	48
Watford	42	10	6	5	26	13	6	7	8	19	22	45
Crystal P	42	12	5	4	35	24	3	9	9	20	30	44
Brighton & HA	42	12	5	4	32	18	4	7	10	25	51	44
Bristol R	42	15	2	4	34	21	4	3	14	17	30	43
Reading	42	11	5	5	48	19	6	3	12	22	45	42
Norwich C	42	11	5	5	44	13	5	5	11	21	50	42
Bournemouth	42	12	6	3	38	13	4	3	14	19	43	41
Port Vale	42	9	7	5	33	30	6	4	11	14	12	41
Swindon T	42	12	4	5	41	19	3	6	12	18	43	40
Bristol C	42	9	8	4	38	27	6	1	14	22	34	39
Exeter C	42	10	3	8	37	36	4	4	13	26	39	35
Ipswich T	42	8	5	8	36	30	4	6	11	21	56	35
Leyton O	42	10	8	3	36	25	2	2	17	17	60	34
Walsall	42	8	8	5	37	16	1	8	12	24	46	34
Aldershot	42	10	8	3	30	18	3	0	18	18	42	34
Newport C	42	11	5	5	50	34	2	3	16	17	64	34
Millwall	42	11	3	7	39	29	3	1	17	16	34	32

DIVISION 3 North

	P	W	D	L	F	A	W	D	L	F	A	Pts
Doncaster R	42	9	9	3	30	15	10	8	3	36	23	55
Gateshead	42	13	3	5	51	23	10	4	7	36	31	53
Rochdale	42	15	3	3	42	13	6	6	9	26	28	51
Lincoln C	42	14	3	4	35	9	7	6	5	25	30	51
Tranmere R	42	13	5	3	35	21	6	6	9	16	27	49
Rotherham U	42	15	3	3	46	21	4	7	10	34	31	48
Crewe A	42	12	6	3	38	20	5	8	8	30	35	48
Mansfield T	42	12	4	5	37	20	6	7	8	29	34	47
Carlisle U	42	12	6	3	39	21	4	7	10	29	30	45
Stockport C	42	14	2	5	33	20	5	3	13	22	32	43
Oldham A	42	10	6	5	32	21	6	5	10	26	28	43
Chester	42	12	3	6	47	33	5	3	13	23	46	40
Accrington S	42	12	2	7	41	21	4	5	12	16	41	39
New Brighton	42	10	5	6	27	25	4	6	11	18	38	39
Barrow	42	9	7	5	27	20	5	4	12	20	33	39
Southport	42	10	5	6	29	18	5	3	13	22	53	38
Darlington	42	7	10	4	35	35	4	6	11	21	34	38
Hartlepools U	42	9	6	6	29	27	5	3	13	23	52	37
Bradford C	42	8	7	6	38	32	4	5	12	23	36	36
Wrexham	42	7	7	7	24	21	3	7	11	15	33	34
Halifax T	42	8	5	8	35	37	4	3	14	23	54	32
York C	42	6	7	8	29	33	3	6	12	23	37	31

– 1950-51 –

DIVISION 1

	P	W	D	L	F	A	W	D	L	F	A	Pts
Tottenham H	42	17	2	2	54	21	8	8	5	28	23	60
Manchester U	42	14	4	3	42	16	10	4	7	32	24	56
Blackpool	42	12	6	3	42	24	8	4	9	37	29	50
Newcastle U	42	10	7	4	36	26	8	6	7	26	27	49
Arsenal	42	11	6	4	47	31	8	3	10	26	25	47
Middlesbrough	42	12	4	5	51	28	6	7	8	25	37	47
Portsmouth	42	8	7	6	38	33	8	6	7	33	35	45
Bolton W	42	11	2	8	32	28	8	3	10	32	33	43
Liverpool	42	9	8	4	31	20	7	3	11	22	39	43
Burnley	42	8	8	5	28	21	6	6	9	20	22	42
Derby C	42	10	3	8	53	33	6	5	10	28	42	40
Sunderland	42	8	9	4	33	22	4	7	10	30	51	40
Stoke C	42	10	5	6	30	20	3	9	9	20	39	40
Wolves	42	9	6	6	44	31	6	2	13	30	30	38
Aston Villa	42	7	9	5	39	29	5	4	12	27	39	37
West Brom A	42	9	7	5	30	23	4	4	13	23	38	37
Charlton A	42	9	5	7	35	31	5	4	12	28	49	37
Fulham	42	8	6	7	30	28	5	5	11	22	40	37
Huddersfield T	42	10	3	8	40	31	5	3	13	24	51	36
Chelsea	42	8	6	7	31	27	4	2	15	22	51	32
Sheffield W	42	9	4	8	43	32	3	4	14	21	51	32
Everton	42	8	6	7	26	35	4	2	15	22	51	32

DIVISION 2

	P	W	D	L	F	A	W	D	L	F	A	Pts
Preston NE	42	16	3	2	53	18	10	2	9	38	31	57
Manchester C	42	13	6	2	53	25	6	8	7	36	36	52
Cardiff C	42	12	7	2	36	17	5	9	7	17	28	50
Birmingham C	42	12	6	3	37	20	8	3	10	27	33	49
Leeds U	42	14	4	3	36	17	6	4	11	27	38	48
Blackburn R	42	13	3	5	39	27	6	5	10	26	34	46
Coventry C	42	15	4	2	51	25	4	3	14	24	34	45
Sheffield U	42	11	4	6	44	28	5	8	8	28	34	44
Brentford	42	13	5	3	47	31	5	3	13	28	44	44
Hull C	42	12	5	4	47	27	4	6	11	27	42	43
Doncaster R	42	10	6	5	37	28	5	7	9	27	38	43
Southampton	42	10	6	5	38	32	5	7	9	26	44	43
West Ham U	42	10	5	6	42	28	6	5	10	26	44	42
Leicester C	42	10	5	6	42	22	5	6	10	26	36	41
Barnsley	42	9	7	5	47	24	6	3	12	27	44	40
Queen's Park R	42	13	3	5	47	24	2	7	12	24	58	40
Notts C	42	9	5	7	37	26	4	8	9	24	34	39
Swansea T	42	14	1	6	34	25	2	3	16	20	52	36
Luton T	42	7	9	5	33	27	2	5	14	24	43	32
Bury	42	9	4	8	33	27	3	4	14	27	59	32
Chesterfield	42	7	7	7	30	29	2	5	14	14	40	30
Grimsby T	42	6	6	9	37	37	2	6	13	24	58	28

DIVISION 3 South

	P	W	D	L	F	A	W	D	L	F	A	Pts
Nottingham F	46	18	5	0	70	17	12	5	6	40	23	70
Norwich C	46	16	6	1	57	17	9	8	6	25	28	64
Reading	46	15	6	2	57	17	6	9	8	31	36	57
Plymouth A	46	16	5	2	54	19	8	4	11	31	36	57
Millwall	46	15	5	3	52	23	8	5	10	28	34	56
Bristol R	46	15	7	1	46	18	5	8	10	18	24	55
Southend U	46	15	4	4	64	27	6	6	11	28	42	52
Ipswich T	46	17	4	2	48	24	6	2	15	21	34	52
Bournemouth	46	15	5	3	49	16	7	2	14	16	41	51
Bristol C	46	13	4	6	41	25	7	7	9	23	34	51
Newport C	46	11	6	4	48	24	8	3	14	29	46	47
Port Vale	46	11	8	4	35	31	5	5	13	25	34	45
Brighton & HA	46	12	4	7	51	30	1	13	9	20	49	43
Exeter C	46	12	4	7	33	20	6	2	16	29	65	42
Walsall	46	12	5	6	32	25	3	5	15	20	37	40
Colchester U	46	11	8	4	43	17	3	4	16	20	59	40
Swindon T	46	13	2	8	38	20	5	2	16	17	47	40
Aldershot	46	13	2	8	37	28	2	8	13	19	60	40
Leyton O	46	13	2	8	36	28	2	6	15	17	47	38
Torquay U	46	10	6	7	39	28	4	3	16	25	53	37
Northampton T	46	8	9	6	36	30	2	7	14	19	37	36
Gillingham	46	10	5	8	41	28	3	4	16	28	73	35
Watford	46	8	5	10	29	25	1	6	16	25	63	29
Crystal P	46	6	6	11	18	24	2	5	16	15	60	27

DIVISION 3 North

	P	W	D	L	F	A	W	D	L	F	A	Pts
Rotherham U	46	16	6	1	55	16	15	3	5	48	25	71
Mansfield T	46	17	4	2	44	19	9	8	6	34	29	64
Carlisle U	46	18	4	1	51	17	7	8	8	28	33	62
Tranmere R	46	15	5	3	51	23	9	6	8	32	39	59
Lincoln C	46	18	1	4	62	23	7	7	9	27	35	58
Bradford	46	15	3	5	46	23	8	5	10	44	49	54
Bradford C	46	13	5	5	55	30	8	5	10	35	33	52
Gateshead	46	17	1	5	60	21	4	7	13	24	41	50
Crewe A	46	11	6	6	38	26	8	4	11	23	34	48
Stockport Co	46	15	5	3	45	18	5	3	15	18	45	48
Rochdale	46	13	6	4	38	21	4	5	14	31	41	45
Scunthorpe U	46	10	7	6	32	24	3	11	9	26	33	44
Chester	46	11	6	6	42	27	6	3	14	20	37	43
Wrexham	46	12	6	5	37	28	3	6	14	18	43	42
Oldham A	46	10	5	8	47	36	6	3	14	26	37	40
Hartlepools U	46	14	2	7	47	24	2	5	16	17	42	39
York C	46	7	12	4	35	24	5	3	16	31	53	39
Darlington	46	10	8	5	35	24	3	5	15	24	53	39
Barrow	46	12	3	8	28	29	4	3	16	23	47	38
Shrewsbury T	46	11	4	8	29	27	4	3	16	14	47	37
Southport	46	9	6	8	29	30	4	4	15	27	42	36
Halifax T	46	9	4	10	28	30	2	8	13	22	39	34
Accrington S	46	9	6	8	28	36	2	4	17	14	65	32
New Brighton	46	10	4	9	27	32	1	4	18	13	58	30

– 1951-52 –

DIVISION 1

	P	W	D	L	F	A	Pts
Manchester U	42	23	11	8	95	52	57
Tottenham H	42	22	9	11	76	51	53
Arsenal	42	21	11	10	80	61	53
Portsmouth	42	20	8	14	68	58	48
Bolton W	42	19	10	13	65	61	48
Aston Villa	42	19	9	14	79	70	47
Preston NE	42	17	12	13	74	54	46
Newcastle U	42	18	9	15	98	73	45
Blackpool	42	18	9	15	64	64	45
Charlton A	42	17	10	15	68	63	44
Liverpool	42	12	19	11	57	61	43
Sunderland	42	15	12	15	70	61	42
West Brom A	42	14	13	15	74	77	41
Burnley	42	15	10	17	56	63	40
Manchester C	42	13	13	16	58	61	39
Wolves	42	12	14	16	73	73	38
Derby C	42	15	7	20	63	80	37
Middlesbrough	42	15	6	21	64	88	36
Chelsea	42	14	8	20	52	72	36
Stoke C	42	12	7	23	49	88	31
Huddersfield T	42	10	8	24	49	82	28
Fulham	42	8	11	23	58	77	27

DIVISION 2

	P	W	D	L	F	A	Pts
Sheffield W	42	21	11	10	100	66	53
Cardiff C	42	20	11	11	72	54	51
Birmingham C	42	21	9	12	67	56	51
Nottingham F	42	18	13	11	77	62	49
Leicester C	42	19	9	14	78	64	47
Leeds U	42	18	11	13	59	57	47
Everton	42	17	10	15	64	58	44
Luton T	42	16	12	14	77	78	44
Rotherham U	42	17	8	17	73	71	42
Brentford	42	15	12	15	54	55	42
Sheffield U	42	18	5	19	90	76	41
West Ham U	42	15	11	16	67	77	41
Southampton	42	15	11	16	61	73	41
Blackburn R	42	17	6	19	54	63	40
Notts C	42	16	7	19	71	68	39
Doncaster R	42	13	12	17	55	60	38
Bury	42	15	7	20	67	69	37
Hull C	42	13	11	18	60	70	37
Swansea T	42	12	12	18	72	76	36
Barnsley	42	11	14	17	59	72	36
Coventry C	42	14	6	22	59	82	34
Queen's Park R	42	11	12	19	52	81	34

DIVISION 3 South

	P	W	D	L	F	A	Pts
Plymouth A	46	29	8	9	107	53	66
Reading	46	29	3	14	112	60	61
Norwich C	46	26	9	11	89	50	61
Millwall	46	23	12	11	74	53	58
Brighton & HA	46	24	10	12	87	63	58
Newport C	46	21	12	13	77	76	54
Bristol R	46	20	12	14	89	53	52
Northampton T	46	22	5	19	93	74	49
Southend U	46	19	10	17	75	66	48
Colchester U	46	17	12	17	56	77	46
Torquay U	46	17	10	19	86	98	44
Aldershot	46	18	8	20	78	89	44
Port Vale	46	14	15	17	50	66	43
Bournemouth	46	16	10	20	69	75	42
Bristol C	46	15	12	19	58	69	42
Swindon T	46	14	12	20	51	68	40
Ipswich T	46	16	9	21	63	74	41
Leyton O	46	16	9	21	55	68	41
Crystal P	46	15	9	22	61	80	39
Shrewsbury T	46	13	10	23	62	86	36
Watford	46	13	10	23	57	81	36
Gillingham	46	11	13	22	71	81	35
Exeter C	46	13	9	24	65	86	35
Walsall	46	13	5	28	55	94	31

DIVISION 3 North

	P	W	D	L	F	A	Pts
Lincoln C	46	30	9	7	121	52	69
Grimsby T	46	29	8	9	96	45	66
Stockport Co	46	23	13	10	74	40	59
Oldham A	46	24	9	13	90	61	57
Gateshead	46	21	11	14	66	49	53
Mansfield T	46	22	8	16	73	60	52
Carlisle U	46	19	13	14	62	57	51
Bradford	46	19	12	15	74	64	50
Hartlepools U	46	21	8	17	71	65	50
York C	46	18	13	15	73	52	49
Tranmere R	46	21	6	19	76	71	48
Barrow	46	17	12	17	57	61	46
Chesterfield	46	17	11	18	65	66	45
Scunthorpe U	46	14	16	16	65	74	44
Bradford C	46	16	10	20	61	68	42
Crewe Alex	46	15	12	19	63	82	42
Southport	46	15	11	20	64	73	41
Wrexham	46	15	9	22	63	77	39
Chester	46	15	9	22	72	85	39
Halifax T	46	14	7	25	61	97	35
Rochdale	46	11	13	22	47	79	35
Accrington S	46	10	12	24	61	92	32
Darlington	46	11	9	26	64	103	31
Workington	46	11	7	28	50	91	29

1952-53

DIVISION 1

Team	P	W	D	L	F	A	W	D	L	F	A	Pts
Arsenal	42	15	3	3	60	30	6	9	6	37	34	54
Preston NE	42	15	3	3	46	25	6	9	6	39	35	54
Wolves	42	13	5	3	54	19	6	8	7	32	36	51
West Brom A	42	13	3	5	35	22	8	5	8	31	41	50
Charlton A	42	12	3	6	47	22	7	3	11	31	41	49
Burnley	42	11	6	4	36	30	7	6	8	26	32	48
Blackpool	42	13	5	3	45	27	6	4	11	34	48	47
Manchester U	42	11	5	5	35	37	7	5	9	35	42	46
Sunderland	42	11	9	1	42	23	4	4	13	26	55	43
Tottenham H	42	11	6	4	55	17	4	5	12	23	32	41
Aston Villa	42	9	7	5	32	27	5	7	10	27	38	41
Cardiff C	42	7	8	6	36	35	7	6	8	22	29	41
Middlesbrough	42	12	4	5	39	34	2	6	13	22	50	39
Bolton W	42	9	6	6	44	33	6	5	10	24	34	39
Portsmouth	42	10	5	6	36	28	4	4	13	30	49	39
Newcastle U	42	10	6	5	35	32	4	4	13	25	37	37
Liverpool	42	10	6	5	35	24	4	2	15	25	54	36
Sheffield W	42	8	4	7	35	28	4	5	12	27	40	35
Chelsea	42	10	2	7	35	26	2	7	12	27	42	35
Manchester C	42	12	2	7	35	29	2	5	14	27	59	35
Stoke C	42	10	4	7	35	26	2	6	13	18	40	34
Derby C	42	9	6	6	41	29	2	4	15	18	45	32

DIVISION 2

Team	P	W	D	L	F	A	W	D	L	F	A	Pts
Sheffield U	42	15	3	3	60	27	10	7	4	37	28	60
Huddersfield T	42	14	3	4	51	14	10	7	5	33	19	58
Luton T	42	15	1	5	53	17	7	7	7	31	32	52
Plymouth A	42	13	5	3	37	24	7	4	10	28	36	49
Leicester C	42	12	6	3	55	29	8	2	11	34	45	48
Birmingham C	42	13	3	5	44	38	8	3	10	27	28	48
Nottingham F	42	11	5	5	46	32	7	3	11	31	35	44
Fulham	42	14	1	6	52	28	3	9	9	29	43	44
Blackburn R	42	12	4	5	42	28	6	4	11	26	45	44
Leeds U	42	13	9	4	42	24	1	6	14	29	39	43
Swansea T	42	9	7	5	42	24	5	7	9	36	55	42
Rotherham U	42	9	7	5	26	30	7	2	12	30	44	41
Doncaster R	42	9	5	7	28	17	3	11	7	30	47	40
West Ham U	42	9	7	5	38	28	4	6	11	20	32	39
Lincoln C	42	9	9	3	41	26	2	8	11	23	45	39
Everton	42	9	8	4	38	23	3	6	12	33	52	38
Brentford	42	9	8	4	36	29	4	3	14	23	47	37
Hull C	42	11	6	4	36	21	3	2	16	21	50	36
Notts C	42	10	5	6	41	31	4	3	14	19	57	36
Bury	42	10	6	5	33	30	5	3	13	20	51	35
Southampton	42	5	7	9	45	44	5	6	10	23	41	33
Barnsley	42	4	4	13	31	46	1	4	16	16	62	18

DIVISION 3 South

Team	P	W	D	L	F	A	W	D	L	F	A	Pts
Bristol R	46	17	4	2	55	19	9	8	6	37	27	64
Millwall	46	14	7	2	46	16	10	7	6	36	28	62
Northampton T	46	18	2	3	75	30	8	8	7	34	40	62
Norwich C	46	16	4	3	56	17	9	6	8	43	38	60
Bristol C	46	13	6	4	62	28	9	9	5	33	40	59
Coventry C	46	15	5	3	52	22	4	7	12	25	45	50
Brighton & HA	46	12	6	5	48	30	7	6	10	33	53	50
Southend U	46	15	5	3	41	21	3	8	12	28	46	49
Bournemouth	46	15	4	4	49	23	4	5	14	25	42	47
Watford	46	12	8	3	39	21	3	9	11	23	46	47
Reading	46	17	3	3	53	21	2	5	16	16	60	46
Torquay U	46	15	4	4	61	28	3	5	15	26	56	45
Crystal P	46	12	7	4	40	26	3	6	14	26	48	43
Leyton O	46	12	7	4	52	34	4	3	16	16	48	42
Newport C	46	12	7	4	43	34	4	3	16	27	41	42
Ipswich T	46	11	8	4	34	24	2	7	14	26	47	41
Exeter C	46	11	8	4	40	24	2	6	15	21	47	40
Swindon T	46	11	6	6	38	33	3	6	14	26	46	40
Aldershot	46	9	8	6	36	29	3	8	12	25	48	40
Queen's Park R	46	8	8	7	37	24	4	7	12	24	48	39
Gillingham	46	10	7	6	30	26	2	8	13	25	48	39
Colchester U	46	9	5	9	40	29	3	10	10	18	47	38
Shrewsbury T	46	11	5	7	38	35	1	5	17	30	56	38
Walsall	46	5	9	9	35	46	2	1	20	21	72	24

DIVISION 3 North

Team	P	W	D	L	F	A	W	D	L	F	A	Pts
Oldham A	46	15	4	4	48	21	7	11	5	29	24	59
Port Vale	46	13	9	1	41	10	7	9	7	26	25	58
Wrexham	46	18	3	2	59	24	6	5	12	27	42	56
York C	46	14	5	4	35	16	6	8	9	25	29	53
Grimsby T	46	15	5	3	47	19	6	5	12	28	40	52
Southport	46	16	4	3	42	18	4	7	12	21	42	51
Bradford	46	13	6	4	37	23	4	10	9	38	38	50
Gateshead	46	13	6	4	51	24	4	9	10	25	36	49
Carlisle U	46	13	7	3	57	24	5	6	12	25	44	49
Crewe A	46	13	5	5	46	24	7	3	13	24	36	48
Stockport C	46	13	8	2	61	26	4	5	14	21	43	*47
Chesterfield	46	13	6	4	40	23	5	5	13	24	40	*47
Tranmere R	46	16	4	3	45	16	5	1	17	20	47	47
Halifax T	46	13	6	4	47	31	3	10	10	21	37	47
Scunthorpe U	46	10	7	6	38	21	4	11	8	24	35	46
Bradford C	46	14	7	2	54	29	0	11	12	21	45	46
Hartlepools U	46	14	6	3	39	16	2	8	13	18	45	46
Mansfield T	46	11	9	3	39	25	1	13	9	16	37	46
Barrow	46	11	6	6	48	20	5	6	12	18	51	44
Chester	46	10	7	6	39	27	5	7	11	25	58	44
Darlington	46	10	7	6	33	27	2	6	15	25	69	37
Rochdale	46	11	4	8	41	27	1	6	16	21	58	34
Workington	46	12	5	6	40	33	1	2	20	15	58	33
Accrington S	46	5	9	9	25	29	2	4	17	14	60	27

How the FA Cup was won
1946-1953

1945-46

First Round

Barnet v Queen's Park Rangers	2-6, 1-2
Barrow v Netherfield	1-0, 2-2
Bath City v Cheltenham Town	3-2, 2-0
Brighton & Hove Albion v Romford	3-1, 1-1
Bromley v Slough United	6-1, 0-1
Carlisle United v South Shields	5-1, 3-2
Chorley v Accrington Stanley	2-1, 0-2
Clapton Orient v Newport (IoW)	2-1, 0-2
Crewe Alexandra v Wrexham	4-2, 0-3
Darlington v Stockton	2-0, 4-1
Doncaster Rovers v Rotherham United	0-1, 1-2
Halifax Town v York City	1-0, 2-4
Hartlepools United v Gateshead	1-2, 2-6
Kettering Town v Grantham Town	1-5, 2-2
Lovell's Athletic v Bournemouth & Boscombe Athletic	4-1, 2-3
Mansfield Town v Gainsborough Trinity	3-0, 2-4
Marine (Crosby) v Stalybridge Celtic	4-0, 3-3
Northampton Town v Chelmsford	5-1, 5-0
Notts County v Bradford City	2-2, 2-1
Port Vale v Wellington Town	4-0, 2-0
Reading v Aldershot	3-1, 3-7
Shrewsbury Town v Walsall	5-0, 1-4
South Liverpool v Tranmere Rovers	1-1, 1-6
Southport v Oldham Athletic	1-2, 1-3
Stockport County v Rochdale	1-2, 1-1
Sutton United v Walthamstow Avenue	1-4, 2-7
Swindon Town v Bristol Rovers	1-0, 1-4
Torquay United v Newport County	0-1, 1-1
Trowbridge v Exeter City	1-3, 2-7
Watford v Southend United	1-1, 3-0
Willington v Bishop Auckland	0-5, 2-0
Wisbech Town v Ipswich Town	0-3, 0-5
Yeovil & Petters United v Bristol City	2-2, 0-3
Yorkshire Amateurs v Lincoln City	1-0, 1-5

Second Round

Aldershot v Newport (IoW)	7-0, 5-0
Barrow v Carlisle United	4-2, 4-3
Bishop Auckland v York City	1-2, 0-3
Bristol City v Bristol Rovers	4-2, 2-0
Bromley v Watford	1-3, 1-1
Darlington v Gateshead	2-4, 2-1
Grantham Town v Mansfield Town	1-1, 1-2
Lovell's Athletic v Bath City	2-1, 5-2
Newport County v Exeter City	5-1, 3-1
Northampton Town v Notts County	3-1, 0-1
Oldham Athletic v Accrington Stanley	2-1, 1-3
Port Vale v Marine (Crosby)	3-1, 1-1
Queen's Park Rangers v Ipswich Town	4-0, 2-0
Rotherham United v Lincoln City	2-1, 1-1
Shrewsbury Town v Wrexham	0-1, 1-1
Tranmere Rovers v Rochdale	3-1, 0-3
Walthamstow Avenue v Brighton & Hove Albion	1-1, 2-4

Third Round

Accrington Stanley v Manchester United	2-2, 1-5
Aldershot v Plymouth Argyle	2-0, 1-0
Birmingham City v Portsmouth	1-0, 0-0
Bolton Wanderers v Blackburn Rovers	1-0, 3-1
Bradford v Port Vale	2-1, 1-1
Bristol City v Swansea Town	5-1, 2-2
Bury v Rochdale	3-3, 4-2

Cardiff City v West Bromwich Albion	1-1, 0-4
Charlton Athletic v Fulham	3-1, 1-2
Chelsea v Leicester City	1-1, 2-0
Chester v Liverpool	0-2, 1-2
Chesterfield v York City	1-1, 2-3
Coventry City v Aston Villa	2-1, 0-2
Grimsby Town v Sunderland	1-3, 1-2
Huddersfield Town v Sheffield United	1-1, 0-2
Leeds United v Middlesbrough	4-4, 2-7
Lovell's Athletic v Wolverhampton Wanderers	2-4, 1-8
Luton Town v Derby County	0-6, 0-3
Manchester City v Barrow	6-2, 2-2
Mansfield Town v Sheffield Wednesday	0-0, 0-5
Newcastle United v Barnsley	4-2, 0-3
Northampton Town v Millwall	2-2, 0-3
Norwich City v Brighton & Hove Albion	1-2, 1-4
Nottingham Forest v Watford	1-1, 1-1, 0-1
Preston North End v Everton	2-1, 2-2
Queen's Park Rangers v Crystal Palace	0-0, 0-0, 1-0
Rotherham United v Gateshead	2-2, 2-0
Southampton v Newport County	4-3, 2-1
Stoke City v Burnley	3-1, 1-2
Tottenham Hotspur v Brentford	2-2, 0-2
West Ham United v Arsenal	6-0, 1-0
Wrexham v Blackpool	1-4, 1-4

Fourth Round

Barnsley v Rotherham United	3-0, 1-2
Birmingham City v Watford	5-0, 1-1
Blackpool v Middlesbrough	3-2, 2-3, 0-1
Bolton Wanderers v Liverpool	5-0, 0-2
Bradford v Manchester City	1-3, 8-2
Brighton & Hove Albion v Aldershot	3-0, 1-4
Bristol City v Brentford	2-1, 5-0
Charlton Athletic v Wolverhampton Wanderers	5-2, 1-1
Chelsea v West Ham United	2-0, 0-1
Derby County v West Bromwich Albion	1-0, 3-1
Manchester United v Preston North End	1-0, 1-3
Millwall v Aston Villa	2-4, 1-9
Sheffield Wednesday v York City	5-1, 6-1
Southampton v Queen's Park Rangers	0-1, 3-4
Stoke City v Sheffield United	2-0, 2-3
Sunderland v Bury	3-1, 4-5

Fifth Round

Barnsley v Bradford	0-1, 1-1
Bolton Wanderers v Middlesbrough	1-0, 1-1
Brighton & Hove Albion v Derby County	1-4, 0-6
Chelsea v Aston Villa	0-1, 0-1
Preston North End v Charlton Athletic	1-1, 0-6
Queen's Park Rangers v Brentford	1-3, 0-0
Stoke City v Sheffield Wednesday	2-0, 0-0
Sunderland v Birmingham City	1-0, 1-3

Sixth Round

Aston Villa v Derby County	3-4, 1-1
Bradford v Birmingham City	2-2, 0-6
Charlton Athletic v Brentford	6-3, 3-1
Stoke City v Bolton Wanderers	0-2, 0-0

Semi-final

Bolton Wanderers v Charlton Athletic	0-2
at Villa Park	
Derby County v Birmingham City	1-1
at Hillsborough	
Derby County v Birmingham City	4-0
replay at Maine Road	

Final

Derby County v Charlton Athletic   4-1
played at Wembley
Derby County: Woodley; Nicholas, Howe, Bullions, Leuty, Musson, Harrison, Carter, Stamps, Doherty, Duncan.
Charlton Athletic: Bartram; Phipps, Shreeve, H.Turner, Oakes, Johnson, Fell, Brown, A.A.Turner, Welsh, Duffy.

Scorers: Derby County — Stamps (2), Doherty, H.Turner (own goal). Charlton Athletic — H.Turner
Referee: E.D.Smith (Whitehaven)   *Attendance: 98,215*

1946-47
First Round

Aldershot v Cheltenham Town	4-2
Barnet v Sutton United	3-0
Barrow v Halifax Town	0-0, 0-1
Bournemouth & Boscombe Athletic v Exeter City	4-2
Bristol City v Hayes	9-3
Brush Sports v Southend United	1-6
Carlisle United v Runcorn	4-0
Doncaster Rovers v Accrington Stanley	2-2, 5-0
Gainsborough Trinity v Darlington	1-2
Gateshead v Bradford City	3-1
Gillingham v Gravesend & Northfleet	4-1
Hartlepools United v North Shields	6-0
Hull City v New Brighton	0-0, 2-1
Ipswich Town v Torquay United	2-0
Lancaster City v Spennymoor United	1-0
Leyton Orient v Notts County	1-2
Leytonstone v Walsall	1-6
Merthyr Tydfil v Bristol Rovers	3-1
Northampton Town v Mansfield Town	2-0
Norwich City v Brighton & Hove Albion	7-2
Oldham Athletic v Tranmere Rovers	1-0
Port Vale v Finchley	5-0
Queen's Park Rangers v Poole Town	2-2, 6-0
Reading v Colchester United	5-0
Rochdale v Bishop Auckland	6-1
Rotherham United v Crewe Alexandra	2-0
South Liverpool v Workington	2-1
Stockport County v Southport	2-0
Stockton v Lincoln City	2-4
Swindon Town v Cambridge Town	4-1
Wellington Town v Watford	1-1, 0-1
Wrexham v Marine (Crosby)	5-0
Yeovil Town v Peterborough United	2-2, 0-1
York City v Scunthorpe United	0-1

Second Round

Barnet v Southend United	2-9
Bournemouth & Boscombe Athletic v Aldershot	4-2
Bristol City v Gillingham	1-2
Darlington v Hull City	1-2
Gateshead v Lancaster City	4-0
Halifax Town v Stockport County	1-1, 1-2
Lincoln City v Wrexham	1-1, 3-3, 2-1
Merthyr Tydfil v Reading	1-3
Norwich City v Queen's Park Rangers	4-4, 0-2
Notts County v Swindon Town	2-1
Oldham Athletic v Doncaster Rovers	1-2
Peterborough United v Northampton Town	1-1, 1-1, 1-8
Rochdale v Hartlepools United	6-1
Rotherham United v Scunthorpe United	4-1
South Liverpool v Carlisle United	2-3
Walsall v Ipswich Town	0-0, 1-0
Watford v Port Vale	1-1, 1-2

Third Round

Charlton Athletic v Rochdale	3-1
West Bromwich Albion v Leeds United	2-1
Blackburn Rovers v Hull City	1-1, 3-0
Millwall v Port Vale	0-3
Northampton Town v Preston North End	1-2
Huddersfield Town v Barnsley	3-4
Sheffield Wednesday v Blackpool	4-1
Everton v Southend United	4-2
Newcastle United v Crystal Palace	6-2
Southampton v Bury	5-1
West Ham United v Leicester City	1-2
Brentford v Cardiff City	1-0
Sheffield United v Carlisle United	3-0
Wolverhampton Wanderers v Rotherham United	3-0
Tottenham Hotspur v Stoke City	2-2, 0-1
Chester v Plymouth Argyle	2-0
Burnley v Aston Villa	5-1
Coventry City v Newport County	5-2
Luton Town v Notts County	6-0
Swansea Town v Gillingham	4-1
Queen's Park Rangers v Middlesbrough	1-1, 1-3
Chesterfield v Sunderland	2-1
Lincoln City v Nottingham Forest	0-1
Bradford v Manchester United	0-3
Walsall v Liverpool	2-5
Reading v Grimsby Town	2-2, 1-3
Bournemouth & Boscombe Athletic v Derby County	0-2
Chelsea v Arsenal	1-1, 1-1, 2-0
Fulham v Birmingham City	1-2
Doncaster Rovers v Portsmouth	2-3
Manchester City v Gateshead	3-0
Bolton Wanderers v Stockport County	5-1

Fourth Round

West Bromwich Albion v Charlton Athletic	1-2
Blackburn Rovers v Port Vale	2-0
Preston North End v Barnsley	6-0
Sheffield Wednesday v Everton	2-1
Newcastle United v Southampton	3-1
Brentford v Leicester City	0-0, 0-0, 1-4
Wolverhampton Wanderers v Sheffield United	0-0, 0-2
Chester v Stoke City	0-0, 2-3
Burnley v Coventry City	2-0
Luton Town v Swansea Town	2-0
Middlesbrough v Chesterfield	2-1
Manchester United v Nottingham Forest	0-2
Liverpool v Grimsby Town	2-0
Chelsea v Derby County	2-2, 0-1
Birmingham City v Portsmouth	1-0
Bolton Wanderers v Manchester City	3-3, 0-1

Fifth Round

Charlton Athletic v Blackburn Rovers	1-0
Sheffield Wednesday v Preston North End	0-2
Newcastle United v Leicester City	1-1, 2-1
Stoke City v Sheffield United	0-1
Luton Town v Burnley	0-0, 0-3
Nottingham Forest v Middlesbrough	2-2, 2-6
Liverpool v Derby County	1-0
Birmingham City v Manchester City	5-0

Sixth Round

Charlton Athletic v Preston North End	2-1
Sheffield United v Newcastle United	0-2
Middlesbrough v Burnley	1-1, 0-1
Liverpool v Birmingham City	4-1

Semi-final

Charlton Athletic v Newcastle United	4-0
played at Elland Road	
Liverpool v Burnley	0-0, 0-1
played at Ewood Park	

Final

Charlton Athletic v Burnley	1-0
played at Wembley	

Charlton Athletic: Bartram; Croker, Shreeve, Johnson, Phipps, Whittaker, Hurst, Dawson, W.Robinson, Welsh, Duffy.
Burnley: Strong; Woodruff, Mather, Attwell, Brown, Bray, Chew, Morris, Harrison, Potts, Kippax.

Scorer: Charlton Athletic — Duffy
Referee: J.M.Wiltshire (Sherbourne)
Attendance: 99,000

1947-48
First Round
Aldershot v Bromsgrove Rovers	2-1
Barrow v Carlisle United	3-2
Bournemouth & Boscombe Athletic v Guildford City	2-0
Bristol Rovers v Leytonstone	3-2
Bromley v Reading	3-3, 0-3
Cheltenham Town v Street	5-0
Chester v Bishop Auckland	3-1
Colchester United v Banbury Spencer	2-1
Crewe Alexandra v South Shields	4-1
Crystal Palace v Port Vale	2-1
Dartford v Bristol City	0-0, 2-9
Exeter City v Northampton Town	1-1, 0-2
Gateshead v Bradford City	1-3
Gillingham v Leyton Orient	1-0
Great Yarmouth v Shrewsbury Town	1-4
Hartlepools United v Darlington	1-0
Hull City v Southport	1-1, 3-2
Lincoln City v Workington	0-2
New Brighton v Marine (Crosby)	4-0
Newport County v Southend United	3-2
Norwich City v Merthyr Tydfil	3-0
Notts County v Horsham	9-1
Oldham Athletic v Lancaster City	6-0
Runcorn v Scunthorpe United	4-2
Stockport County v Accrington Stanley	3-1
Stockton v Grantham Town	2-1
Swindon Town v Ipswich Town	4-2
Tranmere Rovers v Stalybridge Celtic	2-0
Trowbridge Town v Brighton & Hove Albion	1-1, 0-5
Vauxhall Motors (Luton) v Walsall	1-2
Watford v Torquay United	1-1, 0-3
Wimbledon v Mansfield Town	0-1
Wrexham v Halifax Town	5-0
York City v Rochdale	0-1

Second Round
Aldershot v Swindon Town	0-0, 0-2
Bournemouth & Boscombe Athletic v Bradford City	1-0
Bristol City v Crystal Palace	0-1
Bristol Rovers v New Brighton	4-0
Colchester United v Wrexham	1-0
Hartlepools United v Brighton & Hove Albion	1-1, 1-2
Hull City v Cheltenham Town	4-2
Northampton Town v Torquay United	1-1, 0-2
Norwich City v Walsall	2-2, 2-3
Notts County v Stockton	1-1, 4-1
Oldham Athletic v Mansfield Town	0-1
Reading v Newport County	3-0
Rochdale v Gillingham	1-1, 0-3
Runcorn v Barrow	0-1
Stockport County v Shrewsbury Town	1-1, 2-2, 3-2
Tranmere Rovers v Chester	0-1
Workington v Crewe Alexandra	1-2

Third Round
Gillingham v Queen's Park Rangers	1-1, 1-3
Mansfield Town v Stoke City	2-4
Plymouth Argyle v Luton Town	2-4
Coventry City v Walsall	2-1
Rotherham United v Brentford	0-3
Hull City v Middlesbrough	1-3

Crewe Alexandra v Sheffield United	3-1
Derby County v Chesterfield	2-0
Aston Villa v Manchester United	4-6
Liverpool v Nottingham Forest	4-1
Charlton Athletic v Newcastle United	2-1
Stockport County v Torquay United	3-0
Manchester City v Barnsley	2-1
Chelsea v Barrow	5-0
Portsmouth v Brighton & Hove Albion	4-1
Millwall v Preston North End	1-2
Fulham v Doncaster Rovers	2-0
Bristol Rovers v Swansea Town	3-0
Bournemouth & Boscombe Athletic v Wolverhampton Wanderers	1-2
Grimsby Town v Everton	1-4
Blackpool v Leeds United	4-0
Crystal Palace v Chester	0-1
Colchester United v Huddersfield Town	1-0
Arsenal v Bradford	0-1
Southampton v Sunderland	1-0
Blackburn Rovers v West Ham United	0-0, 4-2
Burnley v Swindon Town	0-2
Birmingham City v Notts County	0-2
Bolton Wanderers v Tottenham Hotspur	0-2
West Bromwich Albion v Reading	2-0
Leicester City v Bury	1-0
Cardiff City v Sheffield Wednesday	1-2

Fourth Round
Queen's Park Rangers v Stoke City	3-0
Luton Town v Coventry City	3-2
Brentford v Middlesbrough	1-2
Crewe Alexandra v Derby County	0-3
Manchester United v Liverpool	3-0
Charlton Athletic v Stockport County	3-0
Manchester City v Chelsea	2-0
Portsmouth v Preston North End	1-3
Fulham v Bristol Rovers	5-2
Wolverhampton Wanderers v Everton	1-1, 2-3
Blackpool v Chester	4-0
Colchester United v Bradford	3-2
Southampton v Blackburn Rovers	3-2
Swindon Town v Notts County	1-0
Tottenham Hotspur v West Bromwich Albion	3-1
Leicester City v Sheffield Wednesday	2-1

Fifth Round
Queen's Park Rangers v Luton Town	3-1
Middlesbrough v Derby County	1-2
Manchester United v Charlton Athletic	2-0
Manchester City v Preston North End	0-1
Fulham v Everton	1-1, 1-0
Blackpool v Colchester United	5-0
Southampton v Swindon Town	3-0
Tottenham Hotspur v Leicester City	5-2

Sixth Round
Queen's Park Rangers v Derby County	1-1, 0-5
Manchester United v Preston North End	4-1
Fulham v Blackpool	0-2
Southampton v Tottenham Hotspur	0-1

Semi-final
Derby County v Manchester United	1-3
played at Hillsborough	
Blackpool v Tottenham Hotspur	3-1
played at Villa Park	

Final
Manchester United v Blackpool	4-2
played at Wembley	

Manchester United: Crompton; Carey, Aston, Anderson, Chilton, Cockburn, Delaney, Morris, Rowley, Pearson, Mitten.
Blackpool: Robinson; Shimwell, Crosland, Johnston, Hayward, Kelly, Matthews, Munro, Mortensen, Dick, Rickett.

Scorers: Manchester United — Rowley (2), Pearson, Anderson.
Blackpool — Shimwell (penalty), Mortensen.
Referee: C.J.Barrick (Northampton)
Attendance: 99,000

1948-49
First Round

Barnet v Exeter City	2-6
Bradford City v Doncaster Rovers	4-3
Colchester United v Reading	2-4
Crewe Alexandra v Billingham Synthonia	5-0
Crystal Palace v Bristol City	0-1
Dartford v Leyton Orient	2-3
Gainsborough Trinity v Witton Albion	1-0
Gateshead v Netherfield	3-0
Halifax Town v Scunthorpe United	0-0, 0-1
Hartlepools United v Chester	1-3
Hull City v Accrington Stanley	3-1
Ipswich Town v Aldershot	0-3
Kidderminster Harriers v Hereford United	0-3
Leytonstone v Watford	2-1
Mansfield Town v Gloucester City	4-0
Millwall v Tooting & Mitcham	1-0
New Brighton v Carlisle United	1-0
Newport County v Brighton & Hove Albion	3-1
Northampton Town v Dulwich Hamlet	2-1
Norwich City v Wellington Town	1-0
Notts County v Port Vale	2-1
Peterborough United v Torquay United	0-1
Rochdale v Barrow	1-1, 0-2
Rhyl Athletic v Scarborough	0-2
Southend United v Swansea Town	1-2
Southport v Horden Colliery Welfare	2-1
Tranmere Rovers v Darlington	1-3
Walsall v Bristol Rovers	2-1
Walthamstow Avenue v Cambridge Town	3-2
Weymouth v Chelmsford City	2-1
Workington v Stockport County	0-3
Wrexham v Oldham Athletic	0-3
Yeovil Town v Romford	4-0
York City v Runcorn	2-1

Second Round

Aldershot v Chester	1-0
Bradford City v New Brighton	0-0, 0-1
Bristol City v Swansea Town	3-1
Crewe Alexandra v Millwall	3-2
Darlington v Leyton Orient	1-0
Exeter City v Hereford United	2-1
Gateshead v Scarborough	3-0
Hull City v Reading	0-0, 2-1
Leytonstone v Newport County	3-4
Mansfield Town v Northampton Town	2-1
Notts County v Barrow	3-2
Scunthorpe United v Stockport County	0-1
Southport v York City	2-2, 2-0
Torquay United v Norwich City	3-1
Walsall v Gainsborough Trinity	4-3
Walthamstow Avenue v Oldham Athletic	2-2, 1-3
Weymouth v Yeovil Town	0-4

Third Round

Manchester United v Bournemouth & Boscombe Athletic	6-0
Newcastle United v Bradford	0-2
Yeovil Town v Bury	3-1
Crewe Alexandra v Sunderland	0-2
Blackburn Rovers v Hull City	1-2
Grimsby Town v Exeter City	2-1
Swindon Town v Stoke City	1-3
Barnsley v Blackpool	0-1
Wolverhampton Wanderers v Chesterfield	6-0
Sheffield United v New Brighton	5-2

Nottingham Forest v Liverpool	2-2, 0-4
Plymouth Argyle v Notts County	0-1
Lincoln City v West Bromwich Albion	0-1
Gateshead v Aldershot	3-1
Bristol City v Chelsea	1-3
Everton v Manchester City	1-0
Leicester City v Birmingham City	1-1, 1-1, 2-1
Preston North End v Mansfield Town	2-1
Luton Town v West Ham United	3-1
Fulham v Walsall	0-1
Brentford v Middlesbrough	3-2
Torquay United v Coventry City	1-0
Burnley v Charlton Athletic	2-1
Rotherham United v Darlington	4-2
Portsmouth v Stockport County	7-0
Sheffield Wednesday v Southampton	2-1
Leeds United v Newport County	1-3
Queen's Park Rangers v Huddersfield Town	0-0, 0-5
Derby County v Mansfield Town	4-1
Arsenal v Tottenham Hotspur	3-0
Oldham Athletic v Cardiff City	2-3
Aston Villa v Bolton Wanderers	1-1, 0-0, 2-1

Fourth Round

Manchester United v Bradford	1-1, 1-1, 5-0
Yeovil Town v Sunderland	2-1
Grimsby Town v Hull City	2-3
Stoke City v Blackpool	1-1, 1-0
Sheffield United v Wolverhampton Wanderers	0-3
Liverpool v Notts City	1-0
Gateshead v West Bromwich Albion	1-3
Chelsea v Everton	2-0
Leicester City v Preston North End	2-0
Luton Town v Walsall	4-0
Brentford v Torquay United	1-0
Rotherham United v Burnley	0-1
Portsmouth v Sheffield Wednesday	2-1
Newport County v Huddersfield Town	3-3, 3-1
Derby County v Arsenal	1-0
Aston Villa v Cardiff City	1-2

Fifth Round

Manchester United v Yeovil Town	8-0
Stoke City v Hull City	0-2
Wolverhampton Wanderers v Liverpool	3-1
West Bromwich Albion v Chelsea	3-0
Luton Town v Leicester City	5-5, 3-5
Brentford v Burnley	4-2
Portsmouth v Newport County	3-2
Derby County v Cardiff City	2-1

Sixth Round

Hull City v Manchester United	0-1
Wolverhampton Wanderers v West Bromwich Albion	1-0
Brentford v Leicester City	0-2
Portsmouth v Derby County	2-1

Semi-final

Manchester United v Wolverhampton Wanderers	1-1, 0-1
played at Hillsborough, replay at Goodison Park	
Leicester City v Portsmouth	3-1
played at Highbury	

Final

Wolverhampton Wanderers v Leicester City	3-1
played at Wembley	

Wolverhampton Wanderers: Williams; Pritchard, Springthorpe, Crook, Shorthouse, Wright, Hancocks, Smyth, Pye, Dunn, Mullen.
Leicester City: Bradley; Jelly, Scott, W.Harrison, Plummer, King, Griffiths, Lee, J.Harrison, Chisholm, Adam.
Scorers: Wolverhampton Wanderers — Pye (2), Smyth.
Leicester City — Griffiths.
Referee: R.A.Mortimer (Huddersfield)   Attendance: 99,500

1949-50
First Round

Accrington Stanley v Hartlepools United	0-1
Bradford City v Fleetwood	9-0
Bromley v Watford	1-2
Carlisle United v Lincoln City	1-0
Chester v Goole Town	4-1
Crystal Palace v Newport County	0-3
Darlington v Crewe Alexandra	2-2, 0-1
Doncaster Rovers v New Brighton	5-1
Gateshead v York City	3-1
Gloucester City v Norwich City	2-3
Gravesend & Northfleet United v Torquay United	1-3
Hastings United v Gillingham	1-3
Hereford United v Bromsgrove Rovers	3-0
Ipswich Town v Brighton & Hove Albion	2-1
Leyton Orient v Southend United	0-2
Leytonstone v Chelmsford City	1-2
Mansfield Town v Walsall	4-1
Millwall v Exeter City	3-5
Netherfield v North Shields	4-3
Northampton Town v Walthamstow Avenue	4-1
Notts County v Tilbury	4-0
Nottingham Forest v Bristol City	1-0
Nuneaton Borough v King's Lynn	2-1
Oldham Athletic v Stockton	4-0
Port Vale v Wealdstone	1-0
Rhyl v Rochdale	0-3
Southport v Barrow	1-1, 1-0
Stockport County v Billingham Synthonia Recreation	3-0
Swindon Town v Bristol Rovers	1-0
Tranmere Rovers v Halifax Town	2-1
Weymouth v Aldershot	2-2, 3-2
Witton Albion v Mossley	0-1
Wrexham v Grantham	4-1
Yeovil Town v Romford	4-1

Second Round

Carlisle United v Swindon Town	2-0
Chelmsford City v Ipswich Town	1-1, 0-1
Crewe Alexandra v Oldham Athletic	1-1, 0-0, 0-3
Doncaster Rovers v Mansfield Town	1-0
Exeter City v Chester	2-0
Hartlepools United v Norwich City	1-1, 1-5
Newport County v Gateshead	1-1, 2-1
Northampton Town v Torquay United	4-2
Nottingham Forest v Stockport County	0-2
Nuneaton Borough v Mossley	0-0, 3-0
Port Vale v Tranmere Rovers	1-0
Rochdale v Notts County	1-2
Southport v Bradford City	2-1
Watford v Netherfield	6-0
Weymouth v Hereford United	2-1
Wrexham v Southend United	2-2, 0-2
Yeovil Town v Gillingham	3-1

Third Round

Arsenal v Sheffield Wednesday	1-0
Swansea Town v Birmingham City	3-0
Notts County v Burnley	1-4
Newport County v Port Vale	1-2
Carlisle United v Leeds United	2-5
Coventry City v Bolton Wanderers	1-2
Cardiff City v West Bromwich Albion	2-2, 1-0
Charlton Athletic v Fulham	2-2, 2-1
Brentford v Chelsea	0-1
Oldham Athletic v Newcastle United	2-7
Chesterfield v Yeovil Town	3-1
Aston Villa v Middlesbrough	2-2, 0-0, 2-3
Manchester United v Weymouth	4-0
Watford v Preston North End	2-2, 1-0

Portsmouth v Norwich City	1-1, 2-0
Luton Town v Grimsby Town	3-4
Blackburn Rovers v Liverpool	0-0, 1-2
Exeter City v Nuneaton Borough	3-0
Stockport County v Barnsley	4-2
Southport v Hull City	0-0, 0-5
Blackpool v Southend United	4-0
Reading v Doncaster Rovers	2-3
Plymouth Argyle v Wolverhampton Wanderers	1-1, 0-3
Sheffield United v Leicester City	3-1
Queen's Park Rangers v Everton	0-2
West Ham United v Ipswich Town	5-1
Stoke City v Tottenham Hotspur	0-1
Sunderland v Huddersfield Town	6-0
Manchester City v Derby County	3-5
Bury v Rotherham United	5-4
Northampton Town v Southampton	1-1, 3-2
Bradford v Bournemouth & Boscombe Athletic	0-1

Fourth Round

Arsenal v Swansea Town	2-1
Burnley v Port Vale	2-1
Leeds United v Bolton Wanderers	1-1, 3-2
Charlton Athletic v Cardiff City	1-1, 0-2
Chelsea v Newcastle United	3-0
Chesterfield v Middlesbrough	3-2
Watford v Manchester United	0-1
Portsmouth v Grimsby Town	5-0
Liverpool v Exeter City	3-1
Stockport County v Hull City	0-0, 2-0
Blackpool v Doncaster Rovers	2-1
Wolverhampton Wanderers v Sheffield United	0-0, 4-3
West Ham United v Everton	1-2
Tottenham Hotspur v Sunderland	5-1
Bury v Derby County	2-2, 2-5
Bournemouth & Boscombe Athletic v Northampton Town	1-1, 1-2

Fifth Round

Arsenal v Burnley	2-0
Leeds United v Cardiff City	3-1
Chesterfield v Chelsea	1-1, 0-3
Manchester United v Portsmouth	3-3, 3-1
Stockport County v Liverpool	1-2
Wolverhampton Wanderers v Blackpool	0-0, 0-1
Everton v Tottenham Hotspur	1-0
Derby County v Northampton Town	4-2

Sixth Round

Arsenal v Leeds United	1-0
Chelsea v Manchester United	2-0
Liverpool v Blackpool	2-1
Derby County v Everton	1-2

Semi-Final

Arsenal v Chelsea	2-2, 1-0
played at White Hart Lane	
Liverpool v Everton	2-0
played at Maine Road	

Final

Arsenal v Liverpool	2-0
played at Wembley	

Arsenal: Swindin; Scott, Barnes, Forbes, L.Compton, Mercer, Cox, Logie, Goring, Lewis, D.Compton.
Liverpool: Sidlow; Lambert, Spicer, Taylor, Hughes, Jones, Payne, Barron, Stubbins, Fagan, Liddell.

Scorers: Arsenal — Lewis (2).
Referee: H.Pearce (Luton)
Attendance: 100,000

1950-51
First Round

Aldershot v Bromley	2-2, 1-0
Bishop Auckland v York City	2-2, 1-2

Bournemouth & Boscombe Athletic v Colchester United	1-0
Bradford City v Oldham Athletic	2-2, 1-2
Bristol City v Gloucester City	4-0
Bristol Rovers v Llanelly	1-1, 1-1, 3-1
Bromsgrove Rovers v Hereford United	1-3
Carlisle United v Barrow	2-1
Chelmsford City v Tonbridge	2-2, 1-0
Chester v Bradford	1-2
Cleator Moor Celtic v Tranmere Rovers	0-5
Crewe Alexandra v North Shields	4-0
Crystal Palace v Millwall	1-4
Darlington v Rotherham United	2-7
Gainsborough Trinity v Plymouth Argyle	0-3
Glastonbury v Exeter City	1-2
Guildford City v Dartford	1-5
Halifax Town v Ashington	2-3
Leyton Orient v Ipswich Town	1-2
Linby Colliery v Gillingham	1-4
Lincoln City v Southport	1-1, 2-3
Mansfield Town v Walthamstow Avenue	1-0
Newport County v Walsall	4-2
Norwich City v Watford	2-0
Nottingham Forest v Torquay United	6-1
Port Vale v New Brighton	3-2
Reading v Cheltenham Town	3-1
Rochdale v Willington	3-1
Scarborough v Rhyl	1-2
Tooting & Mitcham v Brighton & Hove Albion	2-3
Witton Albion v Nelson	1-2
Southend United v Swindon Town	0-3
Worcester City v Hartlepools United	1-4
Wrexham v Accrington Stanley	1-0

Second Round

Aldershot v Bournemouth & Boscombe Athletic	3-0
Ashington v Rochdale	1-2
Brighton & Hove Albion v Ipswich Town	2-0
Bristol City v Wrexham	2-1
Bristol Rovers v Gillingham	2-2, 1-1, 2-1
Chelmsford City v Mansfield Town	1-4
Crewe Alexandra v Plymouth Argyle	2-2, 0-3
Exeter City v Swindon Town	3-0
Hartlepools United v Oldham Athletic	1-2
Hereford United v Newport County	0-3
Millwall v Bradford	1-1, 1-0
Port Vale v Nelson	3-2
Reading v Dartford	4-0
Rhyl v Norwich City	0-1
Rotherham United v Nottingham Forest	3-1
Southport v Carlisle United	1-3
York City v Tranmere Rovers	2-1

Third Round

Newcastle United v Bury	4-1
Bolton Wanderers v York City	2-0
Stoke City v Port Vale	2-2, 1-0
West Ham United v Cardiff City	2-1
Luton Town v Portsmouth	2-0
Bristol Rovers v Aldershot	5-1
Hull City v Everton	2-0
Rotherham United v Doncaster Rovers	2-1
Plymouth Argyle v Wolverhampton Wanderers	1-2
Aston Villa v Burnley	2-0
Leicester City v Preston North End	0-3
Huddersfield Town v Tottenham Hotspur	2-0
Sunderland v Coventry City	2-0
Notts County v Southampton	3-4
Newport County v Reading	3-2
Norwich City v Liverpool	3-1
Charlton Athletic v Blackpool	2-2, 0-3
Stockport County v Brentford	2-1

Mansfield Town v Swansea Town	2-0
Sheffield United v Gateshead	1-0
Grimsby Town v Exeter City	3-3, 2-4
Rochdale v Chelsea	2-3
Queen's Park Rangers v Millwall	3-4
Fulham v Sheffield Wednesday	2-1
Derby County v West Bromwich Albion	2-2, 1-0
Birmingham City v Manchester City	2-0
Bristol City v Blackburn Rovers	2-1
Brighton & Hove Albion v Chesterfield	2-1
Manchester United v Oldham Athletic	4-1
Leeds United v Middlesbrough	1-0
Arsenal v Carlisle United	0-0, 4-1
Northampton Town v Barnsley	3-1

Fourth Round

Newcastle United v Bolton Wanderers	3-2
Stoke City v West Ham United	1-0
Luton Town v Bristol Rovers	1-2
Hull City v Rotherham United	2-0
Wolverhampton Wanderers v Aston Villa	3-1
Preston North End v Huddersfield Town	0-2
Sunderland v Southampton	2-0
Newport County v Norwich City	0-2
Blackpool v Stockport County	2-1
Sheffield United v Mansfield Town	0-0, 1-2
Exeter City v Chelsea	1-1, 0-2
Millwall v Fulham	0-1
Derby County v Birmingham City	1-3
Bristol City v Brighton & Hove Albion	1-0
Manchester United v Leeds United	4-0
Arsenal v Northampton Town	3-2

Fifth Round

Stoke City v Newcastle United	2-4
Bristol Rovers v Hull City	3-0
Wolverhampton Wanderers v Huddersfield Town	2-0
Sunderland v Norwich City	3-1
Blackpool v Mansfield Town	2-0
Chelsea v Fulham	1-1, 0-3
Birmingham City v Bristol City	2-0
Manchester United v Arsenal	1-0

Sixth Round

Newcastle United v Bristol Rovers	0-0, 3-1
Sunderland v Wolverhampton Wanderers	1-1, 1-3
Blackpool v Fulham	1-0
Birmingham City v Manchester United	1-0

Semi-final

Newcastle United v Wolverhampton Wanderers	0-0, 2-1
played at Hillsborough, replay at Leeds Road	
Blackpool v Birmingham City	0-0, 2-1
played at Maine Road, replay at Goodison Park	

Final

Newcastle United v Blackpool	2-0
played at Wembley	

Newcastle United: Fairbrother; Cowell, Corbett, Harvey, Brennan, Crowe, Walker, Taylor, Milburn, G.Robledo, Mitchell.

Blackpool: Farm; Shimwell, Garrett, Johnston, Hayward, Kelly, Matthews, Mudie, Mortensen, Slater, Perry.

Scorers: Newcastle United — Milburn (2).
Referee: W.Ling (Cambridge)   *Attendance: 100,000*

1951-52

First Round

Accrington Stanley v Chester	1-2
Aylesbury United v Watford	0-5
Bangor City v Southport	2-2, 0-3
Barnstaple Town v Folkestone Town	2-2, 2-5
Barrow v Chesterfield	0-2
Blackhall Colliery Welfare v Workington	2-5
Blyth Spartans v Bishop Auckland	2-1

Bradford City v Carlisle United	6-1
Brighton & Hove Albion v Bristol City	1-2
Bristol Rovers v Kettering Town	3-0
Brush Sports v Weymouth	2-3
Colchester United v Port Vale	3-1
Crewe Alexandra v Lincoln City	2-4
Crystal Palace v Gillingham	0-1
Grimsby Town v Darlington	4-0
Guildford City v Hereford United	4-1
Hartlepools United v Rhyl	2-0
Ilkeston Town v Rochdale	0-2
King's Lynn v Exeter City	1-3
Leyton v Chippenham Town	3-0
Leyton Orient v Gorleston Town	2-2, 0-0, 5-4
Leytonstone v Shrewsbury Town	2-0
Merthyr Tydfil v Ipswich Town	2-2, 0-1
Millwall v Plymouth Argyle	1-0
Nelson v Oldham Athletic	0-4
Newport County v Barry Town	4-0
Norwich City v Northamapton Town	3-2
Rawmarsh Welfare v Buxton Town	1-4
Reading v Walsall	1-0
Scunthorpe United v Billingham Synthonia	5-0
Southend United v Bournemouth & Boscombe Athletic	6-1
Stockport County v Gateshead	2-2, 1-1, 1-2
Stockton v Mansfield Town	1-1, 2-0
Swindon Town v Bedford Town	2-0
Tonbridge v Aldershot	0-0, 2-3
Torquay United v Bromley	3-2
Tranmere Rovers v Goole Town	4-2
Witton Albion v Gainsborough Trinity	2-1
Wrexham v Halifax Town	3-0
York City v Bradford	1-1, 1-1, 0-4
Second Round	
Bradford v Bradford City	3-2
Bristol Rovers v Weymouth	2-0
Buxton v Aldershot	4-3
Chester v Leyton	5-2
Colchester United v Bristol City	2-1
Gateshead v Guildford City	2-0
Gillingham v Rochdale	0-3
Ipswich Town v Exeter City	4-0
Leytonstone v Newport County	2-2, 0-3
Lincoln City v Grimsby Town	3-1
Millwall v Scunthorpe United	0-0, 0-3
Norwich City v Chesterfield	3-1
Reading v Southport	1-1, 1-1, 2-0
Southend United v Oldham Athletic	5-0
Stockton v Folkestone Town	2-1
Swindon Town v Torquay United	3-3, 1-1, 3-1
Tranmere Rovers v Blyth Spartans	1-1, 2-2, 5-1
Watford v Hartlepools United	1-2
Witton Albion v Workington	3-3, 0-1
Wrexham v Leyton Orient	1-1, 2-3
Third Round	
Newcastle United v Aston Villa	4-2
Scunthorpe United v Tottenham Hotspur	0-3
Reading v Swansea Town	0-3
Rotherham United v Bury	2-1
Portsmouth v Lincoln City	4-0
Notts County v Stockton	4-0
Doncaster Rovers v Buxton Town	2-0
Middlesbrough v Derby County	2-2, 2-0
Nottingham Forest v Blackburn Rovers	2-2, 0-2
Manchester United v Hull City	0-2
West Bromwich Albion v Bolton Wanderers	4-0
Ipswich Town v Gateshead	2-2, 3-3, 1-2
Burnley v Hartlepools United	1-0
Leicester City v Coventry City	1-1, 1-4

Liverpool v Workington	1-0
Manchester City v Wolverhampton Wanderers	2-2, 1-4
Norwich City v Arsenal	0-5
Barnsley v Colchester United	3-0
Leyton Orient v Everton	0-0, 3-1
Fulham v Birmingham City	0-1
Luton Town v Charlton Athletic	1-0
Brentford v Queen's Park Rangers	3-1
Cardiff City v Swindon Town	1-1, 0-1
Sunderland v Stoke City	0-0, 1-3
Chelsea v Chester	2-2, 3-2
Huddersfield Town v Tranmere Rovers	1-2
Rochdale v Leeds United	0-2
Bradford v Sheffield Wednesday	2-1
Sheffield United v Newport County	2-0
West Ham United v Blackpool	2-1
Southend United v Southampton	3-0
Bristol Rovers v Preston North End	2-0
Fourth Round	
Tottenham Hotspur v Newcastle United	0-3
Swansea Town v Rotherham United	3-0
Notts County v Portsmouth	1-3
Middlesbrough v Doncaster Rovers	1-4
Blackburn Rovers v Hull City	2-0
Gateshead v West Bromwich Albion	0-2
Burnley v Coventry City	2-0
Liverpool v Wolverhampton Wanderers	2-1
Arsenal v Barnsley	4-0
Birmingham City v Leyton Orient	0-1
Luton Town v Brentford	2-2, 0-0, 3-2
Swindon Town v Stoke City	1-1, 1-0
Chelsea v Tranmere Rovers	4-0
Leeds United v Bradford	2-0
West Ham United v Sheffield United	0-0, 2-4
Southend United v Bristol Rovers	2-1
Fifth Round	
Swansea Town v Newcastle United	0-1
Portsmouth v Doncaster Rovers	4-0
Blackburn Rovers v West Bromwich Albion	1-0
Burnley v Liverpool	2-0
Leyton Orient v Arsenal	0-3
Luton Town v Swindon Town	3-1
Leeds United v Chelsea	1-1, 1-1, 1-5
Southend United v Sheffield United	1-2
Sixth Round	
Portsmouth v Newcastle United	2-4
Blackburn Rovers v Burnley	3-1
Luton Town v Arsenal	2-3
Sheffield United v Chelsea	0-1
Semi-Final	
Newcastle United v Blackburn	0-0, 2-1
played at Hillsborough, replay at Elland Road	
Arsenal v Chelsea	1-1, 3-0
played at White Hart Lane	
Final	
Newcastle United v Arsenal	1-0
played at Wembley	

Newcastle United: Simpson; Cowell, McMichael, Harvey, Brennan, E.Robledo, Walker, Foulkes, Milburn, G.Robledo, Mitchell.

Arsenal: Swindin; Barnes, L.Smith, Forbes, Daniel, Mercer, Cox, Logie, Holton, Lishman, Roper.

Scorers: Newcastle United — G.Robledo.

Referee: A.Ellis (Halifax)   Attendance: 100,000

1952-53
First Round

Aldershot v Millwall	0-0, 1-7
Bath City v Southend United	3-1

Beighton Miners' Welfare v Wrexham	0-3
Boston United v Oldham Athletic	1-2
Bradford v Rochdale	2-1
Bradford City v Rhyl	4-0
Chester v Hartlepools United	0-1
Chesterfield v Workington	1-0
Coventry City v Bristol City	2-0
Crystal Palace v Reading	1-1, 3-1
Darlington v Grimsby Town	2-3
Gainsborough Trinity v Netherfield	1-1, 3-0
Gateshead v Crewe Alexandra	2-0
Grays' Athletic v Llanelly	0-5
Guildford City v Great Yarmouth	2-2, 0-1
Halifax Town v Ashton United	1-1, 2-1
Hendon v Northampton Town	0-0, 0-2
Horden Colliery Welfare v Accrington Stanley	1-2
Ipswich Town v Bournemouth & Boscombe Athletic	2-2, 2-2, 3-2
Kidderminster Harriers v Finchley	0-1
Leyton v Hereford United	0-0, 2-3
Leyton Orient v Bristol Rovers	1-1, 0-1
Leytonstone v Watford	0-2
Newport County v Walsall	2-1
North Shields v Stockport County	3-6
Peterborough United v Torquay United	2-1
Port Vale v Exeter City	2-1
Queen's Park Rangers v Shrewsbury Town	2-2, 2-2, 1-4
Scarborough v Mansfield Town	0-8
Scunthorpe United v Carlisle United	1-0
Selby Town v Bishop Auckland	1-5
Southport v Bangor City	3-1
Swindon Town v Newport (IoW)	5-0
Tonbridge v Norwich City	2-2, 0-1
Tranmere Rovers v Ashington	8-1
Walthamstow Avenue v Wimbledon	2-2, 3-0
Wellington v Gillingham	1-1, 0-3
Weymouth v Colchester United	1-1, 0-4
Yeovil v Brighton & Hove Albion	1-4
York City v Barrow	1-2
Second Round	
Accrington Stanley v Mansfield Town	0-2
Barrow v Millwall	2-2, 1-4
Bishop Auckland v Coventry City	1-4
Bradford v Gateshead	1-2
Bradford City v Ipswich Town	1-1, 1-5
Brighton & Hove Albion v Norwich City	2-0
Colchester United v Llanelly	3-2
Finchley v Crystal Palace	3-1
Great Yarmouth v Wrexham	1-2
Grimsby Town v Bath City	1-0
Halifax Town v Southport	4-2
Hereford United v Scunthorpe United	0-0, 1-2
Newport County v Gainsborough Trinity	2-1
Peterborough United v Bristol Rovers	0-1
Port Vale v Oldham Athletic	0-3
Shrewsbury Town v Chesterfield	0-0, 4-2
Stockport County v Gillingham	3-1
Swindon Town v Northampton Town	2-0
Tranmere Rovers v Hartlepools United	2-1
Walthamstow Avenue v Watford	1-1, 2-1
Third Round	
Sheffield Wednesday v Blackpool	1-2
Huddersfield Town v Bristol Rovers	2-0
Lincoln City v Southampton	1-1, 1-2
Shrewsbury Town v Finchley	2-0
Arsenal v Doncaster Rovers	4-0
Grimsby Town v Bury	1-3
Portsmouth v Burnley	1-1, 1-3
Sunderland v Scunthorpe United	1-1, 2-1
Tranmere Rovers v Tottenham Hotspur	1-1, 1-9

Preston North End v Wolves	5-2
Halifax Town v Cardiff City	3-1
Stoke City v Wrexham	2-1
Oldham Athletic v Birmingham City	1-3
Newport County v Sheffield United	1-4
Derby County v Chelsea	4-4, 0-1
West Ham United v West Bromwich Albion	1-4
Bolton Wanderers v Fulham	3-1
Leicester City v Notts County	2-4
Luton Town v Blackburn Rovers	6-1
Manchester City v Swindon Town	7-0
Gateshead v Liverpool	1-0
Hull City v Charlton Athletic	3-1
Plymouth Argyle v Coventry City	4-1
Barnsley v Brighton & Hove Albion	4-3
Everton v Ipswich Town	3-2
Mansfield Town v Nottingham Forest	0-1
Millwall v Manchester United	0-1
Walthamstow Avenue v Stockport County	2-1
Aston Villa v Middlesbrough	3-1
Brentford v Leeds United	2-1
Rotherham United v Colchester United	2-2, 2-0
Newcastle United v Swansea Town	3-0
Fourth Round	
Blackpool v Huddersfield Town	1-0
Shrewsbury Town v Southampton	1-4
Arsenal v Bury	6-2
Burnley v Sunderland	2-0
Preston North End v Tottenham Hotspur	2-2, 0-1
Halifax Town v Stoke City	1-0
Sheffield United v Birmingham City	1-1, 1-3
Chelsea v West Bromwich Albion	1-1, 0-0, 1-1, 4-0
Bolton Wanderers v Notts County	1-1, 2-2, 1-0
Manchester City v Luton Town	1-1, 1-5
Hull City v Gateshead	1-2
Plymouth Argyle v Barnsley	1-0
Everton v Nottingham Forest	4-1
Manchester United v Walthamstow Avenue	1-1, 5-2
Aston Villa v Brentford	0-0, 2-1
Newcastle United v Rotherham United	1-3
Fifth Round	
Blackpool v Southampton	1-1, 2-1
Burnley v Arsenal	0-2
Halifax Town v Tottenham Hotspur	0-3
Chelsea v Birmingham City	0-4
Luton Town v Bolton Wanderers	0-1
Plymouth Argyle v Gateshead	0-1
Everton v Manchester United	2-1
Rotherham United v Aston Villa	1-3
Sixth Round	
Arsenal v Blackpool	1-2
Birmingham City v Tottenham Hotspur	1-1, 2-2, 0-1
Gateshead v Bolton Wanderers	0-1
Aston Villa v Everton	0-1
Semi-final	
Blackpool v Tottenham Hotspur	2-1
played at Villa Park	
Bolton Wanderers v Everton	4-3
played at Maine Road	
Final	
Blackpool v Bolton Wanderers	4-3
played at Wembley	

Blackpool: Farm; Shimwell, Garrett, Fenton, Johnston, Robinson, Matthews, Taylor, Mortensen, Mudie, Perry.

Bolton Wanderers: Hanson; Ball, R.Banks, Wheeler, Barrass, Bell, Holden, Moir, Lofthouse, Hassall, Langton.

Scorers: Blackpool - Mortensen (3), Perry. Bolton Wanderers — Lofthouse, Moir, Bell.

Referee: M.Griffiths (Newport) Attendance: 100,000

Leading Average Attendances

1946-47

Division One	*Division Two*	*Division Three North*	*Division Three South*
Liverpool 45,300	Newcastle U 49,400	Hull C 19,800	Cardff C 30,000
Chelsea 44,600	Manchester C 39,300	Doncaster R 15,300	Bristol C 18,700
Manchester U 43,900	Tottenham H 34,700	Rotherham U 13,100	Norwich C 17,100
Arsenal 43,300	Birmingham C 34,500	Oldham A 10,900	Queen's Park R . . . 16,500
Wolves 43,300	West Brom A 26,900	Carlisle U 9,800	Swindon T 16,000

1947-48

Division One	*Division Two*	*Division Three North*	*Division Three South*
Arsenal 54,982	Newcastle U 56,283	Hull C 24,010	Notts C 25,380
Manchester U 54,890	Birmingham C 38,360	Rotherham U 14,330	Queen's Park R . . . 22,273
Chelsea 47,354	Cardiff C 37,871	Lincoln C 13,187	Norwich C 21,444
Liverpool 44,299	Tottenham H 37,679	Carlisle U 13,128	Swansea T 17,856
Everton 44,205	Sheffield W 35,858	Oldham A 12,950	Bournemouth 16,854

1948-49

Division One	*Division Two*	*Division Three North*	*Division Three South*
Newcastle U 53,992	Tottenham H 47,991	Hull C 36,763	Notts C 30,002
Arsenal 51,478	Cardiff C 35,091	Oldham A 16,404	Millwall 24,631
Manchester U 48,933	Sheffield W 33,797	Doncaster R 13,842	Norwich C 24,325
Aston Villa 47,319	West Brom A 33,395	Mansfield T 11,312	Swansea T 22,535
Chelsea 46,363	Leicester C 30,384	Carlisle U 11,129	Bristol R 17,539

1949-50

Division One	*Division Two*	*Division Three North*	*Division Three South*
Arsenal 49,001	Tottenham H 54,111	Doncaster R 19,053	Notts C 35,176
Sunderland 47,785	Sheffield W 40,692	Oldham A 15,185	Norwich C 23,264
Newcastle U 46,468	Hull C 37,318	Bradford C 13,149	Nottingham F 22,148
Liverpool 45,783	Leicester C 30,266	Lincoln C 12,478	Millwall 20,753
Wolves 45,466	Leeds U 30,203	Mansfield T 12,128	Bristol C 19,584

1950-51

Division One	*Division Two*	*Division Three North*	*Division Three South*
Tottenham H 55,509	Manchester C 35,016	Oldham A 13,579	Norwich C 24,503
Arsenal 50,474	Hull C 31,877	Rotherham U 12,958	Nottingham F 22,636
Newcastle U 46,651	Preston NE 31,256	Bradford C 12,516	Millwall 20,164
Everton 42,924	Notts C 30,115	Bradford 12,253	Bristol R 18,919
Sheffield W 41,222	Cardiff C 28,412	Carlisle U 11,696	Bristol C 18,457

1951-52

Division One	*Division Two*	*Division Three North*	*Division Three South*
Tottenham H 51,124	Sheffield W 41,336	Oldham A 16,153	Norwich C 21,866
Arsenal 51,001	Everton 37,391	Grimsby T 14,909	Millwall 19,366
Newcastle U 50,476	Sheffield U 31,185	Lincoln C 13,811	Plymouth A 19,236
Manchester U 42,916	Hull C 29,210	Bradford 12,101	Brighton & HA 17,831
Chelsea 39,932	Cardiff C 28,954	Stockport C 12,030	Bristol C 17,780

1952-53

Division One	Division Two	Division Three North	Division Three South
Arsenal 49,191	Everton 32,629	Oldham A. 17,298	Bristol R 23,411
Newcastle U 44,521	Sheffield U 31,027	Port Vale 14,504	Norwich C 21,121
Tottenham H 44,106	Huddersfield T 27,764	Grimsby T 14,298	Millwall 19,291
Chelsea 43,937	Leicester C 26,250	Bradford 12,123	Bristol C. 18,764
Sheffield W 42,634	Hull C 25,918	Bradford C 10,892	Brighton & HA 16,161

Attendances at Football League Matches
1946-53

Season	Matches Played	Total (Millions)	Division One	Division Two	Division Three South	Division Three North
1946-47	1,848	35.6	15.0	11.1	5.7	3.9
1947-48	1,848	40.3	16.7	12.3	6.7	4.6
1948-49	1,848	41.3	17.9	11.4	7.0	5.0
1949-50	1,848	40.5	17.3	11.7	7.1	4.4
1950.51	2,028	39.6	16.7	10.8	7.4	4.8
1951.52	2,028	39.0	16.1	11.1	7.0	4.9
1852-53	2,028	37.1	16.1	9.7	6.7	4.7

Footballer of the Year

1947-48 Stanley Matthews (Blackpool)   **1948-49** Johnny Carey (Manchester U)   **1949-50** Joe Mercer (Arsenal)
1950-51 Harry Johnston (Blackpool)   **1951-52** Billy Wright (Wolves)   **1952-53** Nat Lofthouse (Bolton W)

Leading Goalscorers

	Division One		Division Two		Division Three North		Division Three South	
1946-47	Dennis Westcott (Wolves)	37	Charlie Wayman (Newcastle U)	30	Clarrie Jordan (Doncaster R)	41	Don Clark (Bristol C)	36
1947-48	Ronnie Rooke (Arsenal)	33	Eddie Quigley (Sheffield W)	23	Jim Hutchinson (Lincoln C)	32	Len Townsend (Bristol C)	29
1948-49	Willie Moir (Bolton W)	25	Charlie Wayman (Southampton)	32	Wally Ardron (Rotherham U)	29	Don McGibbon (Bournemouth & BA)	30
1949-50	Dickie Davis (Sunderland)	25	Tommy Briggs (Grimsby T)	35	Reg Phillips (Crewe A)	26	Tommy Lawton (Notts Co)	31
					Peter Doherty (Doncaster R)	26		
1950-51	Stan Mortensen (Blackpool)	30	Cecil McCormack (Barnsley)	33	Jack Shaw (Rotherham U)	37	Wally Ardron (Nottingham F)	36
1951-52	George Robledo (Newcastle U)	33	Derek Dooley (Sheffield W)	46	Andy Graver (Lincoln C)	37	Ronnie Blackman (Reading)	39
1952-53	Charlie Wayman (Preston NE)	24	Arthur Rowley (Leicester C)	39	Jack Whitehouse (Carlisle U)	29	Geoff Bradford (Bristol R)	33

Bibliography

Captain of Wales (Stanley Paul) Wally Barnes.
Soccer — A History (B.T.Batsford Ltd) Denzil Batchelor.
Football — My Life (Souvenir Press) Ron Burgess.
My Story (Souvenir Press) Matt Busby.
All for the Wolves (Rupert Hart-Davis) Stan Cullis.
Blackpool Football (Robert Hale) Robin Daniels.
Football Round the World (Museum Press) Tom Finney.
The Newcastle United Story (Arthur Baker) John Gibson.
We are the Champions (Pelham) Maurice Golesworthy.
Soccer the World Game (Phoenix) Geoffrey Green.
Soccer in the Fifties (Ian Allen) Geoffrey Green.
Football is my Business (Sporting Handbooks) Tommy Lawton.
Stanley Matthews — The Authorised Biography (Pavilion) David Miller.
Soccer Syndrome (MacGibbon and Kee) John Moynihan.
The Jimmy Seed Story (Phoenix) Jimmy Seed.
Clown Prince of Soccer (Nicholas Kaye) Len Shackleton.
Winners and Champions — Manchester United (Arthur Barker) Alec Shorrocks.
The People's Game (Allen Lane) James Walvin.
Arsenal Story (Sporting Handbooks) Tom Whittaker.
Football is my Passport (Stanley Paul) Billy Wright.
One Hundred Caps and all that (Robert Hale) Billy Wright.